Purchasing Guidebook

Third Edition

Steven M. Bragg

For more information about AccountingTools® products, visit our Web site at www.accountingtools.com.

ISBN-13: 978-1-64221-065-1

Printed in the United States of America

Table of Contents

Preface

The purchasing department performs one of the most vital functions within a business – acquiring goods and services on behalf of the organization. Performing the related tasks correctly can be surprisingly difficult, which is where the *Purchasing Guidebook* can be of use. The book describes every aspect of purchasing, including purchasing processes, supplier selection, contract negotiations, spend management, financial analysis, and a great deal more.

The contents of the book are divided into four general topics. Chapters 1 through 3 present an overview of purchasing, noting the role of the department and its employees, how each purchasing procedure works, and the use of procurement cards. Chapters 4 through 8 are concerned with supplier relations. These chapters address the selection and subsequent management of suppliers, including competitive bidding, negotiations, and contract management. Chapters 9 through 13 are primarily concerned with the management of costs, with a particular emphasis on spend management, logistics, quality concerns, and the handling of inventory. Chapters 14 through 17 address a cluster of additional topics related to purchasing, including financial analysis, supply chain financing, measurements, and information technology.

You can find the answers to many questions about the purchasing function in the following chapters, including:

- Should purchasing be centralized or kept at the local level?
- What is the procedure for manual reorder point notifications?
- What are the criteria to consider when choosing new suppliers?
- What risk management techniques can be applied to suppliers?
- What tactics are used in negotiations with suppliers?
- What pricing alternatives are used in contracts?
- How is a spend management database constructed?
- What is the roll of purchasing in a target costing system?
- How do I calculate the effects of a lease or buy decision?
- Which measurements should be applied to suppliers?

The *Purchasing Guidebook* is designed for someone interested in setting up a purchasing department or learning how to improve its performance. Thus, it can be used by buyers, managers, systems auditors, and consultants.

Centennial, Colorado
March 2021

About the Author

Steven Bragg, CPA, has been the chief financial officer or controller of four companies, as well as a consulting manager at Ernst & Young. He received a master's degree in finance from Bentley College, an MBA from Babson College, and a Bachelor's degree in Economics from the University of Maine. He has been a two-time president of the Colorado Mountain Club, and is an avid alpine skier, mountain biker, and certified master diver. Mr. Bragg resides in Centennial, Colorado. He has written more than 250 books and courses, including *New Controller Guidebook*, *GAAP Guidebook*, and *Payroll Management*.

Steven maintains the accountingtools.com web site, which contains continuing professional education courses, the Accounting Best Practices podcast, and thousands of articles on accounting subjects.

Buy Additional AccountingTools Courses

AccountingTools offers more than 1,200 hours of CPE courses, with concentrations in accounting, auditing, finance, taxation, and ethics. Related courses that you might like include:

- How to Audit Procurement
- Inventory Management
- Operations Management
- Payables Management
- Working Capital Management

Go to accountingtools.com/cpe to view these additional courses.

Chapter 1
Overview of Purchasing

Introduction

Purchasing is the process of obtaining goods and services for an organization. This is much more than a transactional activity. Instead, purchasing can bring tremendous value to a business. The most common view of value creation by purchasing is that it can drive down costs, which is certainly true. In addition, the department can locate the best suppliers that are most capable of delivering high quality goods and services, and in a timely manner. Suppliers of this caliber can make it much easier to run a production line, since few hitches will be associated with the incoming flow of goods. Also, an experienced purchasing staff can advise product development teams on whether certain components should be used, or which raw materials are difficult to obtain. Thus, the impact of using a qualified purchasing team can be felt throughout an organization.

In the following sections, we describe the activities for which the purchasing department is responsible, where it fits into different types of organizations, the types of planning in which the department can be involved, and several ethical considerations.

The Purchasing Function

The title of the purchasing function does not adequately explain the broad array of services that this department brings to a company. The following list of services indicates that purchasing employees are much more than paper-pushers who place orders for goods and services.

Sourcing

- Locate suppliers that can fulfill the company's needs within a designated time frame
- Review and initially qualify suppliers as being capable of dealing with the company's requirements
- Issue and monitor the status of bid packages sent to suppliers
- Evaluate bid responses and determine winners
- Disposition excess or obsolete goods and other assets

Contracts

- Negotiate with suppliers to develop sourcing contracts
- Monitor ongoing contracts for compliance by both parties
- Plan for contract terminations, and replace or extend the contracts as needed

Risk Management

- Assess the risk associated with various materials and suppliers
- Formulate risk mitigation plans
- Locate and contract with alternate sources of supply

Supplier Management

- Create supplier scorecards and discuss results with suppliers
- Coach suppliers on how to improve their performance
- Coordinate with the engineering department to provide support to suppliers
- Negotiate with suppliers to mutually reduce costs
- Minimize the supplier base to concentrate purchase volumes

Transactional Activities

- Issue purchase order authorizations
- Determine the status of existing orders
- Accelerate shipments as needed

Purchasing within the Organization

Within the typical manufacturing company, the purchasing department is under the control of the materials manager. This individual needs to have complete control over the entire flow of goods from the supply chain, through the manufacturing process, and into a finished goods warehouse. Given the need for comprehensive control over this process flow, it makes sense to have the purchasing manager report to the materials manager. This relationship appears within the following sample organizational structure.

Organization Structure in a Manufacturing Business

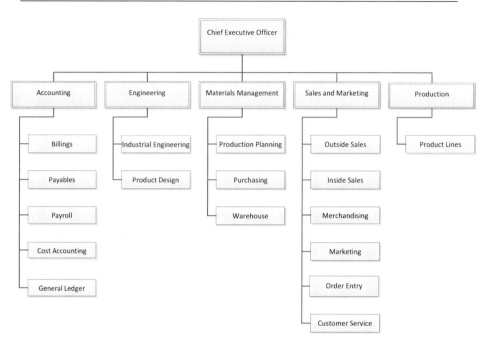

When the percentage of total corporate expenditures devoted to supplier purchases increases, the relative importance of the purchasing function increases along with it. Thus, a business that outsources a large part of its activities may find it necessary to elevate the purchasing function to a separate group whose manager reports directly to senior management.

The organizational structure is simplified in a non-manufacturing business. There is no need for a materials manager in this situation, so the purchasing manager position instead reports directly to senior management, as noted in the following sample organizational structure. In the sample structure, we assume that the entity provides services of some kind, such as a consultancy.

Organization Structure in a Services Business

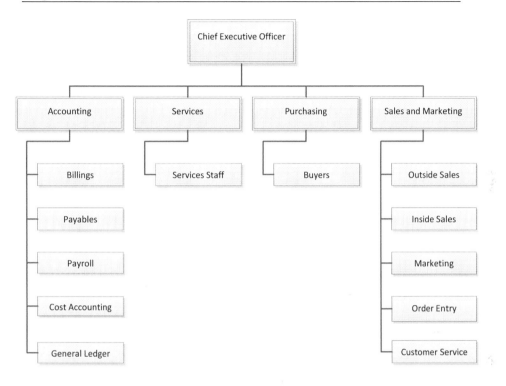

The level of organizational complexity changes when there are several company divisions. In this case, it can make sense to have a corporate-level purchasing group that focuses on company-wide spend and locating those suppliers best able to service the needs of the entire business. Once these decisions have been made and contracts finalized, day-to-day relations with the suppliers is shifted down to the division level. The amount of corporate-level involvement in purchasing is usually best left at the level just indicated. If a more centralized purchasing function is installed, the usual outcome is a reduction in the responsiveness of purchasing to local needs.

When there is a centralized purchasing function, it is typically led by a chief purchasing officer (CPO). This individual has direct control over any centralized spend analysis and supplier contracting tasks. At the individual division level, the CPO is able to enforce the use of the suppliers that her group has identified as key suppliers. However, local purchasing managers still report to their local senior management teams, and only accept direction from the CPO in a "dotted line" relationship. This basic approach to managing a central organizational structure is the most common, since it allows local managers to enforce a high level of responsiveness from their purchasing departments. Some organizations may find that giving the CPO more authority over local purchasing operations makes more sense – it all depends on the situation. The following table notes the circumstances in which differing levels of central control over the purchasing function might be warranted.

Drivers of Purchasing Control Levels

Strategy or Condition	Impact on Decentralized Purchasing	Impact on Centralized Purchasing
Compete based on lowest price	More suppliers will be used in aggregate across all divisions, so volume discounts will be reduced, resulting in higher costs and therefore higher prices.	Makes the best use of volume discounts by ensuring that the number of suppliers is minimized. Full centralization will result in the largest cost reductions.
Disparate product lines	When there are few similarities in the purchasing needs of the various divisions, the ability to reduce the number of suppliers declines, so local purchasing is more cost-effective.	As just noted for the decentralization scenario, centralized purchasing is not cost-effective where there is little parts commonality across the divisions.
High level of responsiveness to customers	This is the ideal situation, since local buyers can work with customers to immediately address their issues.	When the purchasing staff is located elsewhere, it is difficult to convince them of the urgency of attending to the needs of a key customer on short notice.
Large dollar volumes	A decentralized group could still be used to deal with smaller-volume commodity categories, but would need to hand off large-dollar spend categories to a central group to gain the full effect of cross-divisional cost savings.	When the purchasing dollars involved are quite large, a centralized approach can squeeze small percentage price reductions out of suppliers that still equate to significant savings.

While the overall tenor of this discussion has been to leave the bulk of purchasing activities at the local level (other than for volume purchasing activities), there are some advantages to centralizing the purchasing function, which are as follows:

- *Coordinated planning.* All long-range and short-range planning decisions can be easily disseminated throughout the purchasing team, since they are centrally located and are less likely to ignore the mandates of a management team that is probably located just down the hall.
- *Service improvements.* There may be differing service levels being provided by suppliers across the organization for the same commodities. Centralization allows for the enforcement of uniform (and possibly enhanced) service levels from suppliers.

- *Specialists.* It is much easier to assemble a group of highly-trained specialists within the department, since there is so much more purchasing volume to justify their cost. For example, a company could now employ specialists in the spend related to transportation, telecommunications, and travel.
- *Spend management.* A central group reviews spending patterns across the entire enterprise, and consolidates purchases with a select few suppliers in order to improve volume discounts.
- *Standard policies and procedures.* It is much easier to enforce a single set of standard operating procedures when there is just a single purchasing group to oversee.
- *Standard software.* A single purchasing group requires just one purchasing software package. This makes it much easier to create a spend management system (see the Spend Management chapter), since all of the required spend data is located in one place. Having a single software package also reduces the amount of systems maintenance fees charged by the software provider.

Despite these advantages, few organizations fully centralize their purchasing functions. Instead, a large part of the total purchasing activity is still located within local subsidiaries. This is done because management perceives that the combination of the following issues makes it more advantageous to buy at the local level:

- *Local knowledge.* An on-site purchasing group is likely to have an excellent hands-on knowledge of a company's products and sourcing requirements, as well as any unique aspects of its processes that would not be so apparent to a purchasing person located far away in a central purchasing group. In addition, an on-site group has probably met with and built up relations with local suppliers, and so has more power to obtain rush deliveries from them on short notice.
- *New product design.* When a company maintains separate divisions, it usually keeps their product design teams at the local level, to take advantage of division-specific expertise. A local purchasing group can participate in these teams, providing advice regarding the best types of materials to use and the applicability of possible substitute materials.
- *Responsiveness.* A major advantage of using a local purchasing group is that it can respond to requests for purchases immediately, which can be a major advantage in dealing with customers and in ensuring that production is completed as scheduled. A centralized purchasing group does not feel the pressure from local managers to perform, and so tends to be less responsive.

The Supply Chain

In this book, we regularly mention the interactions of the purchasing department with the supply chain. A supply chain is a group of businesses that work together to bring completed products to a customer. This may include several layers (or *tiers*) of suppliers, each one passing along their output to suppliers working more directly with the buying entity. For example, an iron ore mine sells to a smelter, which sends its cast iron products to an engine manufacturer, which sells its engines to a truck company which then sells completed trucks to the final end customer. All of the organizations involved in this process flow are part of a supply chain.

The supply chain concept is important from several perspectives, which include the following points:

- *Cost reduction.* The suppliers in the chain can work together to strip out costs, such as reducing the cost of the packaging used to transport goods from one supplier to another.
- *Responsiveness.* Suppliers can jointly determine the best way to accelerate the delivery of goods to customers, such as by sharing customer order information through several tiers of suppliers.
- *Quality.* The use of error reduction techniques can be applied throughout the supply chain, which greatly reduces the likelihood that a customer will receive nonconforming goods.
- *Traceability.* When there is a clear flow of information up and down the supply chain, it is easier to establish where a bad batch of products originated. A higher level of traceability is important in some industries, such as food products and pharmaceuticals, to ensure that potentially injurious conditions can be resolved at the source.

In many organizations, the specific group of suppliers used and the processes that interlink them can be considered a core competitive advantage. This is especially the case when the supply chain is so tightly interwoven that the outcome is not readily repeatable by other businesses.

It requires a massive amount of coordination by the purchasing department to ensure that the flow of information back through the supply chain is as thorough as possible, while the return flow of goods exactly matches the company's requirements. These coordinating activities include the following:

- *Logistics.* Only designated items should arrive at a company facility, in the correct quantities and at the correct times. When there are many suppliers located over broad regions, this can be a difficult goal to achieve. Coordinating the transportation of the different suppliers can lead to the use of combined loads, which reduces costs.
- *Quality control.* The purchasing staff (or other departments or consultants) can review the quality-related processes and methods of suppliers, and certify their systems as being capable of creating quality goods. If so, costs can be reduced by having supplier deliveries bypass a company's inspection process.
- *Requirements planning.* The purchasing staff works with the materials management staff to determine when certain goods will be needed from suppliers, and in what quantities. Negotiating for these items well in advance makes it easier to obtain supplier discounts.
- *Expediting.* Suppliers must correspond with the purchasing staff regularly to inform them of any deliveries that will be late. This information is needed to

arrange for alternative deliveries. The better the amount of information-sharing in this area, the more time the purchasing staff will have to expedite replacements, which lowers costs.

Purchasing Planning

The purchasing department is involved in three types of planning, which are outlined in this section. Each one involves a different reaction time, and results in differing amounts of value being added to transactions by the department.

Reactive Purchasing

The purchasing department operates least effectively when it is reacting to purchasing requests from other parts of the business. In this case, there is an immediate need for goods or services, so the purchasing staff simply has to find a supplier – fast – at the best possible terms. Reactive purchasing usually comprises a relatively small part of the total spend of a business, but can involve an inordinate amount of purchasing effort, since this work is usually assigned a high priority, and so may interrupt other work.

When a business is poorly-run, the department is much more likely to be inundated with requests of this type. A poorly managed organization engages in so little planning and operates with so few systems that there is little warning of any procurement needs, so every purchasing situation is a surprise.

Lower-value reactive purchasing activities can be sidestepped by authorizing a small number of employees outside of the department to make purchases with procurement cards. The use of these cards is described in the Procurement Cards chapter.

System-Generated Purchasing

In a well-planned organization with excellent systems, customer orders trigger a computerized check of on-hand inventory balances, which in turn generates an automatic purchasing request, with items requiring long lead times scheduled for more immediate action. In this environment, the purchasing department is presented with a well-organized flow of purchasing needs. In addition, a preferred supplier has already been designated in the computer system for all recurring inventory purchases, so the system can generate a complete purchase order with no staff intervention. The bulk of all purchases should be handled in this manner.

In this environment, the purchasing staff simply monitors system-generated purchase orders for anomalies, and lets all other orders be passed through to suppliers.

Proactive Purchasing

When it is possible to plan for new types of purchases properly, the purchasing staff can engage in a number of activities to achieve significant value improvements, including the following:

- Review new-product specifications before they are finalized, in order to give advice on the use of alternative raw materials and components.
- Engage in detailed reviews of potential suppliers, to determine the best possible fit.
- Identify existing preferred suppliers who may be able to take on the work, and determine whether they have sufficient available capacity.
- Complete a financial and operational analysis to see if the work should be completed in-house or outsourced (make-or-buy analysis).

In addition, the department meets at intervals to go over an analysis of the company's historical spending patterns. The outcome of this review is decisions to concentrate the department's attention on certain types of commodities, usually with the intent of concentrating purchases with a smaller number of suppliers in exchange for volume discounts. The details of this process are described in the Spend Management chapter.

Yet another proactive purchasing activity is working with the sales department to estimate the amount of orders to be expected from customers during the next year. This information is then translated into estimates of the unit volume to be placed with suppliers, which in turn is used to engage in negotiations regarding the unit prices to be paid to suppliers. This advance planning is mostly limited to higher-volume purchasing, where detailed negotiations can produce cost savings that offset the cost of planning.

Finally, a key area in which to involve purchasing is management of the company's bottleneck operation. For example, there may be a work center in the production area that is completely overwhelmed with work, and which is impeding the company from growing its sales. If so, the purchasing staff can work with a financial analyst to determine which products are impeding the bottleneck the most, and then outsource the manufacture of these products. See the Purchasing Financial Analysis chapter for more information.

These types of planning require the talents of an experienced group of purchasing specialists, much more so than is needed for reactive purchasing.

Summary of Purchasing Planning

No matter how well-run a business may be, there is always a certain amount of reactive purchasing. However, a well-run business will experience only a trickle of these purchases, while a disorganized one will be dominated by them. When operations are well organized, with integrated computer systems, purchase orders can be generated by the system, so that the purchasing staff is placed in a watchdog role, overseeing the stream of orders. At the most advanced level, the purchasing staff is actively engaged in the development of new products, assisting in the creation of goods for which parts can be easily sourced at reasonable prices.

Purchasing Positions

The buyer position is the dominant one in the purchasing department. There are several types of buyer positions, though they share a core set of responsibilities. Experienced buyers could be more heavily involved with contract negotiations, while other buyers may be focused on particular areas of expertise, such as telecommunications services. In this section, we describe the buyer and other purchasing positions, with the understanding that these roles can be modified to fit the mix of employees within the department.

Purchasing Manager

This position oversees the purchasing department. Depending on the size of the department, the purchasing manager may be strictly confined to the purest management tasks, or could also participate in some buyer-level activities for the larger contracts. The main requirements of the position are:

- Set a high ethical standard for all purchasing employees
- Monitor the daily activities of the purchasing staff
- Develop an expense budget for the department and monitor variances from it
- Develop a plan of prospective purchases over the designated planning horizon
- Develop a training plan for the purchasing staff and ensure that it is being followed
- Review and approve purchases that fall within the manager's dollar approval limit
- Develop a system of policies and procedures
- Ensure that an adequate system of purchasing controls is in place
- Ensure that the document retention system operates properly
- Visit with major suppliers on a regular basis
- Monitor and resolve supplier grievances as applicable
- Decide which suppliers will be dropped
- Visit with the managers of other departments that use purchasing services
- Monitor the performance metrics for the department and investigate negative variances
- Report to management periodically regarding the status of the department

Buyer

There may be a large number of buyers within the purchasing department, since they deal with the highest-volume activity of the department, which is sourcing goods and services. While the requirements of this position will vary somewhat based on experience and expertise, the basic tasks are:

- Locate and investigate new suppliers
- Prepare and issue bid packages
- Evaluate bid responses and select winners
- Negotiate contracts with suppliers
- Process purchase orders
- Monitor the status of current contracts
- Visit or communicate with assigned suppliers on a regular basis

Supply Chain Inventory Planner

This position oversees the flow of inventory-related information between the company and its suppliers, and onward to its customers. This person is responsible for the following activities:

- Monitor the flow of inventory through the supply chain
- Advise on the creation of production schedules that will work with supply chain capabilities
- Advise on the placement of inventory in regional and local warehouses
- Evaluate safety stock levels
- Advise the sales department on the company's ability to meet customer orders

Purchasing Department Relations

The purchasing department has some of the most wide-ranging responsibilities of any department in a company. It must interact with nearly everyone, since most departments have some need to engage in the purchasing of goods or services at some point. Also, purchasing requires cooperation from other departments in order to complete its own tasks. Here are some of the departments requiring more frequent interactions:

- *Legal.* The one department that purchasing depends on for support is the legal staff. The purchasing staff is constantly dealing with contracts, and so must rely on the advice of the legal department regarding the clauses that can or cannot be included in contracts. The legal staff may even take a direct role in the negotiation of contracts.
- *Accounting.* The accounting department pays for the obligations that the purchasing staff incurs. This means that the accounting staff relies on the purchase orders issued by the purchasing department as evidence of authorization, before paying bills. This will likely result in ongoing interaction between the departments to discuss missing purchase orders or supplier variances from the authorized purchase amounts.
- *Engineering.* If the engineering department uses multi-functional teams to design products, it is likely that the purchasing staff will be permanently involved in these teams, giving feedback on likely raw material costs and alternative components and raw materials.
- *Materials management.* The department that purchasing is most likely to be involved with on a continual basis is materials management. The materials

management group is responsible for planning production, and so has detailed plans for when raw materials and components must arrive on the shop floor. These activities may require continual support from the purchasing staff, either to track down incoming deliveries or to locate alternate supply sources.

Given the broad level of interaction with other departments, the purchasing manager cannot treat the department as a high-walled castle, where requisitions are cautiously proffered by outsiders for consideration. Instead, the purchasing staff should be constantly encouraged to meet with employees from all parts of the business, to gain an understanding of what they need. Doing so gives the purchasing staff a better idea of the requests that it must deal with in the future, and also gives the rest of the company the impression that the department is easy to work with.

Purchasing Ethics

The purchasing department handles a large part of the expenditures of a business. Given the inherent level of power that goes along with authorizing the expenditure of so much money, the purchasing staff person can be tempted to favor one supplier over another, accept bribes to direct purchases in a certain direction, or even to set himself up as a supplier and direct purchases to his own corporation. These actions can cause a business to incur much higher costs than should normally be the case.

The purchasing manager needs to set a high ethical standard for the department, not only through his own personal behavior, but also by publicizing and enforcing a set of standards of ethical conduct. The following list includes several standards that could be applied to the department.

Personal Ethics

- *Avoid conflicts of interest.* The purchasing employee should not let his personal affairs impinge in any way on his role as a purchasing agent representing the company. This means that any personal ownership interest in another business should prevent him from directing company purchases toward that entity.
- *Do not solicit or accept assets or preferences.* Suppliers may tempt the purchasing employee with offers of cash, gifts, free entertainment, preferential discounts, and so forth, in hopes of thereby influencing the placement of purchase orders with them. These situations are to be actively avoided, and any payments made by suppliers should be returned promptly.
- *Return samples.* Suppliers may issue samples of their goods, for the ostensible reason that they are review copies. Once reviewed, the purchasing staff should return or pay for them, so there is no impression of having personally accepted the samples.

Business Ethics

- *Avoid reciprocity arrangements.* The federal government does not allow reciprocity arrangements, where a company buys from a supplier in exchange for the supplier making purchases from the company. The objection is that reciprocity eliminates competition, since no other bids from competitors are being considered.
- *Ensure that credited goods are returned.* When goods are considered not usable, the purchasing staff takes the lead on obtaining supplier credits for them. In addition, there is a further responsibility to ensure that the goods are returned to the supplier. Otherwise, the supplier has issued a credit and lost its inventory.
- *Handle confidential information with due care.* Suppliers may include references to their intellectual property in submissions to the department, which could be used by competitors or even by other departments if they were to gain access to it. Examples are designs, plans, and formulas. Similarly, closed bids submitted by suppliers are not to be distributed to other suppliers in order to obtain a lower bid.
- *Maintain supplier relationships in an impartial manner.* The purchasing staff should treat all suppliers in the same way, using the same basis of measurement for all of them. This means that a third party could review suppliers using the same measurement information as a purchasing employee, and arrive at the same conclusions regarding which suppliers should be awarded purchasing contracts.
- *Obtaining free services.* A buyer could pressure a supplier into providing a meaningful amount of free work in advance of a contract award, such as advice regarding a new product design. If the award then goes to a different supplier, the buyer has just taken unfair advantage of the supplier. Instead, the company should pay for this type of work.
- *Ordering in reduced volumes.* A buyer should not obtain pricing from a supplier based on a purportedly large order volume, and then proceed to use this unit pricing to place smaller-quantity orders. Doing so takes advantage of a supplier, and especially of smaller suppliers that need the business.
- *Shopping a bid.* A supplier may proffer a bid, which a buyer then shops to other suppliers to see if a lower bid can be obtained. The original bidder is unlikely to win the related contract, despite having spent the time to prepare a bid. This practice circumvents the much more fair approach of competitive bidding, where bids are solicited from several suppliers at the same time.

Tip: Using a team approach to evaluating suppliers makes it more difficult for a single individual to solicit payments from suppliers, since the influence of one person on a team's final decision is not that large. Consequently, the use of team-based analysis tends to reduce the incidence of unethical behavior.

A reasonable case can be made that a purchasing department needs to conduct itself at a higher ethical standard than any other department, given its close involvement with spending. This means that the proper ethical behavior of the purchasing staff should be considered one of the key responsibilities of the purchasing manager. This responsibility is of particular concern when considering that supplier salespeople may be under such pressure to complete a sale that they routinely tempt buyers with monetary inducements – in essence, the nature of the buyer position greatly increases the probability of encountering ethical conundrums on a regular basis.

Tip: The purchasing manager could periodically run training classes for the purchasing staff, going over sample situations involving ethical problems, and how to resolve them. The direct involvement of the manager in this training emphasizes to employees the importance of proper conduct.

There are several actions that a purchasing manager can take to mitigate the likelihood of having ethical lapses within the department. They are:

- *Schedule an internal audit.* The company's internal audit team can be asked to conduct any number of investigations. For example, an audit might compare purchase prices to published market rates for certain commodities, or examine why a supplier was picked in a competitive bidding situation, despite not having the lowest price. Since these investigations are usually fairly public, the purchasing staff will be aware of them, and so will know it needs to be on its best behavior.
- *Rotate employees.* Periodically shift employees to work on different types of commodities. Doing so interferes with relationships they may have with certain suppliers, who might have been giving them kickbacks in exchange for favorable treatment. Rotation should not be used too frequently, since employees tend to develop commodity-specific expertise over time, and will lose that knowledge when they are shifted elsewhere.
- *Use approval thresholds.* There should be a schedule of required approval levels, where increasing levels of management are needed to approve contracts based on their dollar volume. The use of thresholds tends to reduce the impact of an unethical employee on the placement of favorable contracts.

The risk of having a buyer give in to an ethical lapse is critical for an entire business, since the publicity surrounding a bribery or kickback scandal can tarnish an organization's public image for a long time, and may make it liable for penalties or lawsuit awards.

Summary

A key aspect of the purchasing department is the role it plays in supporting the activities of other departments. In effect, purchasing is a "background" function that, if performed well, makes an entire business function more smoothly. To this end, the purchasing manager needs to reinforce with her staff the need for continual interaction with other departments, assisting them in any way possible. The worst scenario is for the department to be viewed as a hidebound institution governed by rigid procedures, where purchase requisitions take an interminable amount of time to be fulfilled.

The organizational structure into which the purchasing department is inserted will impact the performance of the department. If the senior management team favors strong central control, then the likely purchasing outcome will be better spend management, but at the cost of a lack of responsiveness to local needs. Conversely, allowing a strong local purchasing presence will probably increase the total administrative cost of the business, but provides the offsetting benefit of being able to support the local management team, especially in regard to the development of new products and maintaining a smoothly flowing production operation.

Ethical behavior is more important in the purchasing department than in any other part of a business, given the potential impact on company costs. Accordingly, it is especially important to impose written ethical standards on this department, and to follow up with training at regular intervals.

Chapter 2
Purchasing Processes

Introduction

The purchasing department routinely deals with a large number of transactions on a daily basis. To handle them in an organized manner, it is necessary to have procedures and forms in place that are closely followed at all times. Otherwise, the department's staff is constantly wasting time dealing with incomplete information about requested items, or is using a number of disparate methods to acquire goods and services.

In this chapter, we cover the multiple methods used to notify the department of purchasing needs, as well as the standard approaches to the creation of purchase orders and blanket purchase orders, and the general process flow for a bidding process. We begin with the purchasing objectives upon which a system of purchasing processes is based.

Related Podcast Episode: Episode 262 of the Accounting Best Practices Podcast discusses purchase order clearing. It is available at: **accountingtools.com/podcasts** or **iTunes**

Purchasing Objectives

Any functional area of a business should guard against the excessive use of procedures and forms, since this can lead to a high degree of bureaucracy that can slow down the responsiveness and initiative of the staff. And yet, formal processes are needed in those areas in which there is a high volume of transactions, since a department can only function efficiently if there is a regimented process flow. Consequently, it is useful to create a small number of purchasing objectives that focus attention on the core business of the department; procedures should be developed in these areas. It is much less necessary to adopt standardized systems that *do not* impact the department's objectives.

The objectives selected for a purchasing department will vary, depending on the overall strategic direction of a business and the unique operating characteristics present in an industry. Nonetheless, some objectives are likely to be present in most companies, including the following:

- *Support corporate strategy*. At the highest level of objective setting, the purchasing department must support the overall corporate strategy. For example, if part of the corporate strategy is to be the low-cost producer in the industry, the purchasing department should focus on obtaining volume discounts on long-term purchase orders. Conversely, if the strategy is to service the needs of a select group of well-heeled customers with high-priced service, it may instead be necessary to develop a network of local suppliers that can deliver goods on extremely short notice and in small quantities.

- *Support the purchasing needs of other departments.* The purchasing staff must be responsive in locating items and services requested by other departments. This is more of a tactical issue than the support of corporate strategy just noted. For example, this can involve materials for the production department and supplies for the maintenance department. Further, the requested items must arrive on time, within the desired specifications, and at a reasonable price. A detailed objective related to this topic might be to engage in spend analysis for a certain proportion of the total spend of the organization, which focuses attention on pricing.
- *Operate in a cost-effective manner.* The purchasing department can find itself overwhelmed by the multitude of activities related to purchasing, including certifying suppliers, engaging in competitive bidding, evaluating pricing, and following up on late deliveries. The purchasing manager must use all possible best practices to ensure that other departments are serviced, while still keeping the department's costs at a reasonable level.
- *Develop the optimal set of suppliers.* Having an excellent group of suppliers can make life much easier for an organization, because orders placed arrive exactly as expected. It is also much easier for the purchasing staff to deal with highly-reliable suppliers. Developing the ideal set of suppliers is an ongoing challenge, since the purchasing requirements of a business will change over time, requiring the purchasing staff to drop some suppliers and search for replacements. In addition, there is an ongoing need to measure the performance of existing suppliers, and work with them to enhance their performance. This can be a particularly difficult task if the purchasing staff is also tasked with finding suppliers that can bring new product development skills to the company, or other forms of technological or process advice.

Of the four purchasing objectives noted here, the first two in particular need to be supported by a small number of robust procedures. Specifically, there needs to be a procedure for funneling requests for purchases into the purchasing department, another to research prospective orders and issue authorizing purchase orders, and (for larger orders) a bidding procedure. These procedures are discussed in the following sections. An overview of the general process flow appears in the next exhibit.

Overview of Purchasing Processes

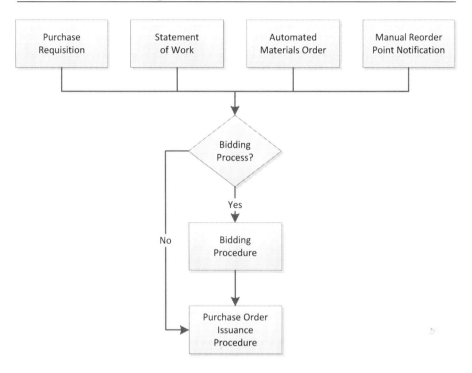

Purchase Notification Alternatives

There should be a formal process governing requests from the different parts of a company for materials and services. Otherwise, there is no control over the amounts spent, and the purchasing department will be buried with requests. There are a number of ways in which the department can be notified, for which procedures are described in the following sub-sections.

The Purchase Requisition

The purchase requisition is used by all company departments to request that the purchasing department acquire goods and services. The form is designed to give the purchasing staff extremely specific information about what is being ordered, including the suggested supplier, the catalog number used by the supplier for the item being ordered, and the price offered by that supplier. The form also includes space for a due date for each line item, which allows the requesting department to set different due dates for different items in the form. There is also space for a charge code for each line item, which keeps the purchasing staff from having to guess at where each purchase should be charged. Finally, the form contains a number of spaces for approval signatures, depending on the expense level of the item(s) being ordered. The budget approval signature is designed to ensure that there are sufficient funds in the budget to pay for the items being ordered.

Sample Purchase Requisition

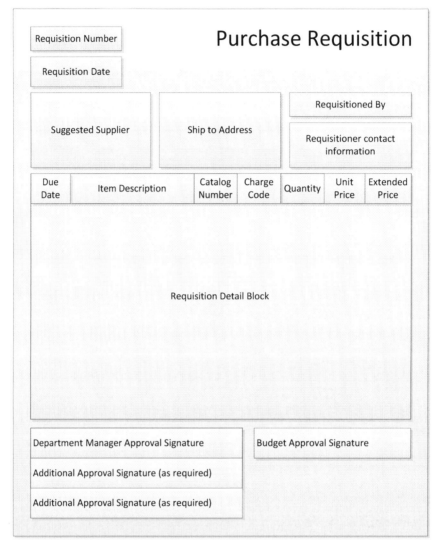

A variation on this form is to eliminate the budget approval signature and replace it with a budget approval initials block for each line item. This alternative approach may be useful when the items being ordered are to be charged to different accounts, each of which has a separate budget. This approach is not necessary as long as the department manager is only verifying purchases against the grand total amount of the department budget, rather than for individual expense line items.

Another variation on the requisition form is to require the requesting person to supply bidder information for at least three bidders. This information is usually contained within a series of blocks near the top or bottom of the form, and reduces the work load of the purchasing staff when bidding is required. However, this format assumes that all of the items listed on the requisition can be obtained from the three bidders, which may not be the case. Also, the requesting party is not necessarily the most knowledgeable person for selecting prospective bidders.

The procedure for processing purchase requisitions is outlined below, along with comments regarding possible control issues:

1. **Complete requisition form.** The person requesting that an item be purchased obtains a two-part purchase requisition form and fills in the following information:

   - Item to obtain
   - Required delivery date
   - Shipping address
   - Account number to be charged
   - Recommended supplier and supplier part number

   Control issue: It may be useful to use prenumbered purchase requisitions, so that the purchasing department can keep track of which requisitions are still open. This control is not needed in a computerized system, where the software assigns a unique number to each requisition.

2. **Obtain approval.** At a minimum, the requesting person obtains the approval of the department manager, who signs the requisition. If the request is for a more expensive item, the individual obtains additional approval signatures as per the company authorization table (for which a sample appears later within the purchasing procedure).

   Control issue: It may be useful for the purchasing department to periodically route back to the department managers a listing of the requisitions that they have purportedly signed, which can be used to detect fraudulent requisitions. However, this can be a time-consuming control activity.

Tip: Include a field in the requisition form where the requesting person verifies that there is sufficient funding left in the budget for the requested item. Otherwise, there is a risk (especially towards the end of the budget year) that items will be inadvertently purchased for which there are no funds available.

---

3. **Forward to purchasing.** The requesting person retains one copy of the requisition and forwards the other copy to the purchasing department.

    Control issue: The purchasing department could send an acknowledging e-mail back to the requester, stating that they have received the requisition. However, given the extra work involved, this extra control is rarely used.

4. **Match to purchase order** (optional). If the purchasing department sends back a copy of the purchase order that was created from the requisition, the requesting person compares it to the requisition to ensure that the correct items have been ordered. If not, the individual contacts the purchasing staff to have the purchase order revised or replaced.

The following exhibit shows a streamlined view of the purchase requisition procedure, including the optional matching step.

Purchase Requisition Process Flow

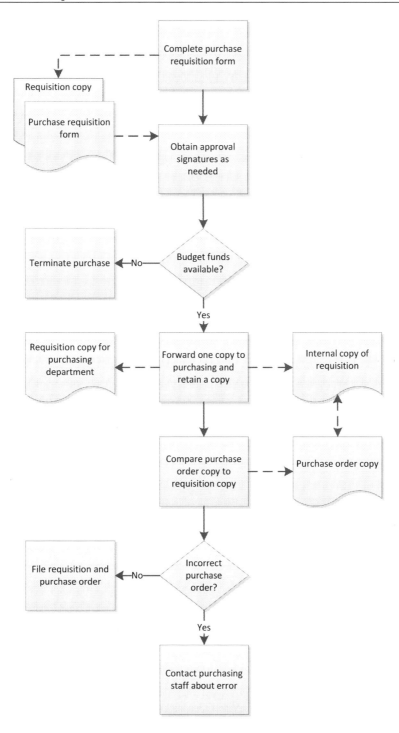

The Statement of Work

Not all purchases are for goods. Instead, someone may need to have a third party provide services to the company, such as a consulting project, equipment servicing, or a research project. If so, the standard purchase requisition form is not of much use. Instead, a statement of work form is filled out, which specifies the following information:

- The type of work needed (such as to develop the optimum layout of the purchasing department to enhance work flows)
- How frequently the work should be provided
- The date by which the work should be completed, which may include specific milestone review dates
- The performance parameters (such as providing a list of the review steps taken, alternatives discarded, the final layout proposed, and the resulting changes in department workflows)
- The type of service provider needed

The procedural steps for a statement of work are the same as for a purchase requisition. A possible addition is to meet with the purchasing staff to go over the proposed requirements of a statement of work. This added step may be necessary, to ensure that the more detailed requirements of the statement are sufficiently clear.

Control issue: There is a risk that a supplier may have helped the submitting individual create a statement of work. If so, it is possible (if not likely) that the requirements were structured so that there is only one possible supplier that fits all of the stated requirements. The purchasing staff can watch for the excessive levels of specification that can indicate undue supplier influence.

Automated Materials Orders

Many manufacturing businesses control their production processes using a computerized material requirements planning system (MRP). There is a production schedule that runs on MRP software. The software explodes the planned production into its constituent raw materials to determine which items are needed as input to the planned production run. The system then compares these requirements to on-hand inventory to determine which items need to be ordered. Finally, the system incorporates estimates of supplier lead times to determine when required items should be ordered. The system can even issue electronic purchase orders straight to suppliers, or the purchasing staff can act as an intermediary, printing and reviewing proposed purchase orders and forwarding them to suppliers. If the purchasing staff acts as an intermediary, the process flow (a simple one) is as follows:

1. **Examine proposed purchase orders**. At a regular time interval (such as early each morning), the responsible person in the purchasing department accesses the

preliminary purchase orders screen in the MRP software and scans through the orders to see if any proposed purchases look unusual.

Control issue: There is a risk that the responsible person will not review the proposed purchase orders in a timely manner. If the software has a workflow management feature, set it to automatically issue a warning if the review is not conducted within a certain period of time, after which a notification is sent to a backup person to conduct the review.

2. **Approve/reject proposed purchase orders**. Click the flag next to each proposed purchase order to accept or reject the order. Once this review is complete, the system processes the approved purchase orders.

3. **Investigate rejected purchase orders.** If any of the purchase orders were rejected, investigate the reasons why they were created by the MRP software. It is quite possible that some underlying data is incorrect, and needs to be fixed. Otherwise, the system will continue to produce proposed purchase orders that are still incorrect.

Manual Reorder Point Notifications

When there is a database of inventory records, all low-stock conditions are examined by the MRP system, which automatically creates materials orders to order replacement stock. However, what if there is no inventory database? Management may have decided that it is too labor-intensive to maintain a perpetual inventory system, where all inventory receipts and drawdowns are logged into an inventory database. Instead, it may be more cost-effective to allow users to take items from stock as needed, and to periodically conduct a visual check of the remaining inventory to see if additional inventory should be ordered. This situation commonly arises for floor stock, where fittings and fasteners are stored close to the production area in bulk, for easy access by the manufacturing staff.

In a manual reorder point system, inventory is typically stored in a bin, which has a line marked on it that denotes the inventory level at which a reorder point has been reached. If a warehouse staff person can see this line, he forwards a reorder point notification card to the purchasing department. The card may be stored next to the bin, and identifies the item to be reordered, the amount to be reordered, and which supplier to use. A variation on the concept is to use a two-bin system; when one bin is emptied, it is time to forward the notification card to the purchasing department. Thus, the process flow is as follows:

1. **Review storage bins**. Examine each storage bin on a regular basis, perhaps daily.

Control issue: If no one is reviewing the storage bins, there is an excellent chance that there will be a stockout condition, which will require a scramble to bring in parts on short notice. Consequently, a system must be in place to ensure that someone on the warehouse staff always conducts a manual review.

2. **Pull notification cards.** When a reorder point has been reached, remove a notification card from next to the relevant bin. Rip away the bottom part of the notification card and store it in the warehouse files. Send the top part of the card to the purchasing department.

   Control issue: The reason for retaining a portion of the notification card in the warehouse is to maintain a record that the notification was sent to the purchasing department. If no replacement items arrive within a reasonable period of time, the retained portion of the card can be used to follow up with the purchasing staff.

3. **Match to retained notification.** If the purchasing department sends a copy of the resulting purchase order to the warehouse, physically match this copy to the retained part of the notification card. This indicates that the original notification was acted upon, and that replacement items are in transit.

   Control issue: By including this step, all unmatched notification cards are more likely to indicate that a purchase order was *not* placed. This can lead to more prompt action by the warehouse staff to verify that purchase orders were issued.

Purchase Order Issuance Procedure

The classic approach to ordered goods and services is the purchase order. It is a formal approach to buying that involves the issuance of a legal document, the purchase order, to a supplier. The purchase order identifies the items being ordered, as well as the price and other conditions under which a company is willing to make a purchase. Though the issuance of purchase orders is usually well-controlled, it also requires a considerable amount of time to complete. For this reason, it is generally restricted to more expensive purchases.

The purchase order is the primary document used by the purchasing department to order goods and services. A sample purchase order is shown next. It should specify a detailed set of information in order to avoid confusion with the supplier. In addition to the usual itemization of items to be purchased and their price, the following sample purchase order also states the due date, both freight and payment terms, and a phone number to call to confirm receipt of the order.

Sample Purchase Order

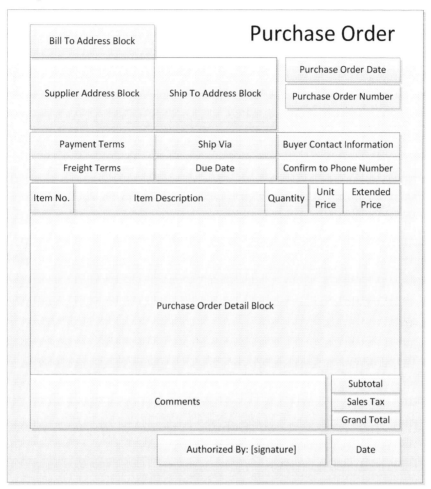

Several other variations on the purchase order form are possible. For example, if a company routinely issues adjustments to its purchase orders, it can include a revision number field below the purchase order number. Another possibility is to include a page number, for those situations where a purchase order spans multiple pages. Yet another option is to include a cumulative total dollar amount for the purchase order that includes all revisions; this may be used to see if the revised purchase order total has increased to the point where an additional authorization is required.

The purchasing procedure is outlined below:

1. **Obtain pricing**. When the purchasing staff receives a purchase requisition or other form of notification, it needs to ascertain pricing in order to determine the level of authorization needed by the requesting party.

Control issue: It is very time-consuming to obtain multiple prices for the items listed on every purchase requisition, so the purchasing manager should set rules for allowing purchases from a small number of designated suppliers, with multiple bids only needed for larger purchases.

2. **Match against authorization table.** Once the purchasing staff has obtained preliminary pricing estimates, compare the amounts requested to the company's authorization table. If the requesting person represents sufficient authorization to approve the purchase, proceed with the ordering process. If not, retain a copy of the purchase requisition and send the original to the person whose approval is required. An example of an authorization table follows.

Sample Purchase Authorization Table

	Department Manager	Division Manager	Chief Operating Officer	Chief Executive Officer	Board of Directors
<$25,000	✓				
$25,000-100,000	✓	✓			
$100,001-250,000	✓	✓	✓		
$250,001-1,000,000	✓	✓	✓	✓	
$1,000,000+	✓	✓	✓	✓	✓

Control issue: The purchasing staff should routinely review its copies of unapproved purchase requisitions, and follow up with approvers regarding their status.

> **Tip:** It may be more efficient for the purchasing department to shift this task onto the requesting person, so that all purchase requisitions contain the required approvals. However, this approach may not work if the requesting person is not sure of the prices of items being requested.

3. **Obtain additional documentation** (optional). If the item being requested exceeds the company's capitalization limit, send the purchase requisition back to the requesting person with a request to complete a capital request form. This is a separate process usually managed by the accounting department or a financial analyst, to decide whether to buy a fixed asset.

Control issue: This step essentially terminates the purchasing process, so there is no need to retain a copy of the purchase requisition.

4. **Prepare purchase order.** Complete a purchase order, based on the information in the purchase requisition or bid results (see the following procedure). Depending on the size of the order, it may be necessary for the purchasing manager to approve and sign the purchase order. Retain a copy of the purchase order in a pending file, stapled to the department's copy of the purchase requisition, and send the original to the supplier. Additional copies go to the receiving department (to match against

received goods) and accounts payable staff (to match against supplier invoices). Though not necessary, another copy could be sent to the person who submitted the requisition, as evidence that the order was placed. If the purchasing system is computerized, only a single copy is printed and sent to the supplier.

Control issue: If purchase orders are prepared manually, have them prenumbered, track all numbers used, and store unused purchase orders in a secure location. This is needed to keep someone from removing a purchase order and using it to order goods or services that have not been authorized.

5. **Obtain legal review** (optional). If the purchase order contains terms and conditions that are not the standard ones normally used in purchase orders, route the document to the legal staff for review.

   Control issue: It can be difficult to determine what constitutes a reasonable exception from the normal terms and conditions, which would require legal review. Also, a legal review slows down the purchasing process. For both reasons, the purchasing staff may be reluctant to obtain a review. This issue can be detected after-the-fact with a periodic investigation by the internal audit team.

   > **Tip:** A legal review can be avoided for recurring contracts whose terms were approved by corporate counsel in an earlier version, but only if the terms and conditions have not subsequently changed.

6. **Monitor change orders** (optional). If change orders are issued, keep track of the resulting change in the cumulative total authorized to be spent. If the cumulative total exceeds the original authorization level noted in the authorization table, obtain the higher authorization level needed for the new expenditure level.

   Control issue: This step requires significant monitoring, which the purchasing staff will be reluctant to do. It can be made easier by modifying the purchase order form to include a field for the cumulative dollar total, which the purchasing staff updates for each successive change order.

7. **Monitor purchase acknowledgments** (optional). For the more important items being purchased, it may make sense to ensure that purchase orders have been received by suppliers and acknowledged. This can be a simple phone call to the supplier, or it may be a formal written acknowledgment. Another option is to include a "confirm to phone number" field in the purchase order, as was shown earlier in the sample purchase order template. If the company is issuing purchase orders by electronic means, the supplier's computer system may automatically send back an acknowledgment message.

Control issue: This step is probably of least use when dealing with long-term business partners, but could be important when ordering from new suppliers where the purchasing department has no idea of supplier performance levels.

8. **Monitor subsequent activity**. Following the due date of the purchase order, remove the department's copy from the pending file and verify with the receiving department that the related goods were received. If not, contact the supplier to determine the status of the order. If complete, file the purchase order by supplier name. If the purchasing system is computerized, the receiving department will flag purchase orders on-line as having been fulfilled, which effectively eliminates this step.

   Control issue: For more important items, the purchasing staff might consider contacting suppliers *in advance of* the due date to ensure that items were shipped on time.

Tip: If the purchasing staff finds that small residual balances were not fulfilled on a purchase order, and the company no longer requires the residual amount, issue a notification to the supplier that the order for the remaining amount has been cancelled.

---

9. **File documents**. When all activity associated with a purchase order has been completed, file the purchasing documents by supplier name for the current year. This will certainly include the purchase order and purchase requisition or similar document, and may also include a cancellation notice that terminates any residual unfulfilled balances on a purchase order, as well as any purchase order acknowledgments received from suppliers.

The following exhibit shows a streamlined view of the purchasing procedure, not including the optional steps to obtain additional documentation, conduct a legal review, or monitor change orders. It also does not include the bidding process, which is addressed later in the Bidding Procedure section.

Purchasing Process Flow

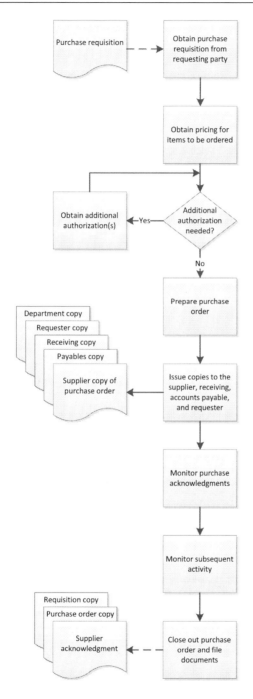

Variations on the Purchasing Procedure

A more advanced purchasing department is likely to use blanket purchase orders, where a single funding commitment is issued to cover recurring purchases for a long period of time, such as a year. Doing so eliminates the work that would otherwise be required to issue a series of purchase orders for incremental purchases. This approach is commonly applied to the acquisition of materials used in the production process, as well as for supplies.

When blanket purchase orders are used, a purchase order release is issued for individual purchases, rather than a standard purchase order. This document references the governing blanket purchase order, the release number, the release date, and the details of what is being ordered.

In the following sample release form, we see that it is quite similar to a standard purchase order form. However, standard contract terms (such as payment terms) are removed, with a reference back to the blanket purchase order, where the contract terms are located. Also, the release references the blanket order upon which it is based.

Sample Blanket Purchase Order Release

	Blanket Order Release			
Bill To Address Block				
Supplier Address Block	Ship To Address Block		Blanket Order Number	
			Release Number	
			Release Date	
Ship Via	Due Date	Buyer Contact Information	Confirm to Phone Number	
Item No.	Item Description	Quantity	Unit Price	Extended Price
	Blanket Order Release Detail Block			
			Subtotal	
			Sales Tax	
Blanket order terms and conditions apply to this release			Grand Total	
	Authorized By: [signature]		Date	

31

Only items included in the blanket purchase order should be ordered in a subsequent release. The internal audit staff can review this issue for compliance. Alternatively, if the purchasing system is computerized, the system can restrict purchases to authorized items, as well as track the total dollar amount of cumulative purchases under the blanket purchase order.

The Bidding Procedure

If a purchase is for a very expensive item and there are multiple qualified suppliers in the marketplace, it may be prudent to obtain bids from several of the suppliers. If so, the purchasing department typically compiles a request for proposals (RFP) document and issues it to an approved list of suppliers. It then holds a bidder conference to clarify any uncertainties in the RFP, and then evaluates supplier bids to determine which vendor is offering the best mix of price, product, delivery, and so forth. The bidding procedure is outlined below:

1. **Prepare bidding documents.** The purchasing staff prepares a request for proposals document, which contains the required specifications for the item(s) to be purchased.

   > **Tip:** Use a template to construct bidding documents, thereby improving the efficiency of the process.

2. **Issue bidding documents.** Determine the appropriate list of recipients, and issue the bidding packet to them.

   Control issue: It may be useful to have a list of approved suppliers with whom the company does business; this is useful for eliminating from consideration any suppliers with whom the company has had problems in the past. At a minimum, there should be a list of banned suppliers that are not to receive bidding documents.

3. **Host a bidder conference** (optional). If a prospective purchase involves an extremely large expenditure, it may be necessary to host a bidder conference in which bidders can obtain clarification of such issues as the company's expectations, timeline, and budget.

   Control issue: Someone should take notes at the bidder conference and distribute the results to all bidders, including those who could not attend the conference. Doing so ensures that everyone bids based on the same information.

4. **Evaluate bids.** All bids received shall be evaluated based on the following criteria (samples are shown; actual criteria may vary):

   - Total cost to acquire (including price, freight, site preparation, setup, and training)
   - Ongoing maintenance and warranty fees
   - Disposal costs
   - Prior history with supplier

   Control issue: It is useful to develop the evaluation criteria before the requests for proposal have been issued, which makes it more difficult for someone to later derive their own criteria to use as the basis for selecting a favorite supplier. It may also be useful to document the reasons why the winning bid was selected, in case questions are raised at a later date.

   > **Tip:** For larger purchases, it may make sense to form a bid evaluation committee, including members from all impacted departments. They may have a better idea than the purchasing staff of which bid will best meet the company's needs.

5. **Issue purchase order.** This step was dealt with in detail in the preceding procedure. Note that purchases sufficiently large to require a bidding process will probably also involve unique terms and conditions, which will require a review by legal counsel.

6. **Monitor supplier performance** (optional). The purchasing staff monitors deliveries under the purchase order, including delivery and quality performance, and corresponds with the supplier regarding any issues encountered.

   Control issue: There should be an ongoing system in place for tracking supplier performance, which is used by the purchasing staff to determine which suppliers it will do business with in the future. Results should also be distributed to the suppliers, who can use the information to improve their performance.

The following exhibit shows a streamlined view of the bidding procedure, including both optional steps.

Bidding Process Flow

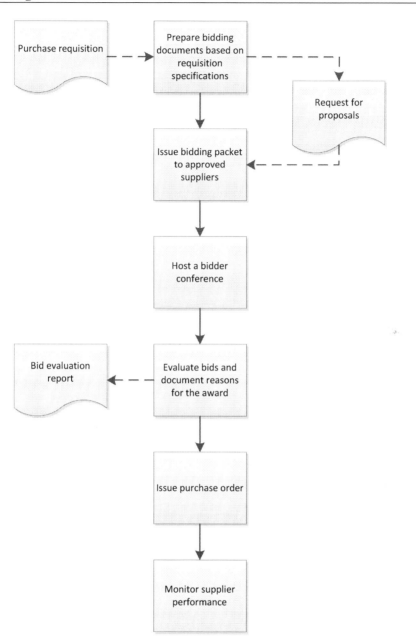

More information about bidding is available in the Competitive Bidding chapter.

E-Procurement

The processes described in the earlier sections were all presented from the perspective of a business that uses a manual, paper-based system. This is likely to be the case in a smaller organization that cannot afford a computerized purchasing system with links to suppliers. However, larger organizations can afford such a computerized system, and would consider the preceding process descriptions to be a step backward; the amount of paperwork they would have to wade through would call for more staff and may result in more purchasing errors.

The electronic alternative to these processes is *e-procurement*. An e-procurement system does not require any printed documents. Instead, the information normally contained within a document is stored in the e-procurement database. The information needed to process a purchase order begins with an on-line requisition to the purchasing department, is then assembled into an electronic transmission, and is sent directly into the order entry database of the relevant supplier. There are a number of benefits to e-procurement, including the following:

- The complete absence of paper, which in turn eliminates filing labor and paper storage costs.
- Queue time is eliminated, since the company's and the relevant supplier's computer systems process all orders without any need for manual intervention.
- Errors related to transferring information between documents are eliminated. However, it is still possible for the initial entry of information into the system to be in error.

The net benefit of e-procurement from the perspective of the purchasing staff is that a large part of their clerical tasks are eliminated. This allows them more time to concentrate on more value-added activities, such as evaluating suppliers and creating spend management plans.

Summary

This chapter has addressed the most formal approach to purchasing, which is the process of documenting a purchase request, converting it into a bid, and using a bidding process for the more expensive purchases. While this is the classic approach to purchasing, it is so paper-intensive that it is not used for the large number of less-expensive and recurring purchases that a company engages in every day. For these other types of purchases, we use procurement cards, which are described in the next chapter.

Chapter 3
Procurement Cards

Introduction

The general rule of purchasing is that 80% of the requisitions comprise 20% of the dollar volume of all requisitions processed (which is an application of the Pareto principle). These smaller orders consume the bulk of the time of the purchasing department, despite their low value. A common outcome is that the cost of the time spent placing orders exceeds the value of the orders. A good way to eliminate this labor is to distribute a procurement card to someone in each department, and let them buy lower-cost items directly. By doing so, a large number of inconsequential purchase transactions can be completed without involving the purchasing department. The use of these cards also eliminates a large number of payments to suppliers in favor of a single large monthly payment to the bank that manages the procurement card program, which is a major benefit for the accounts payable staff.

In this chapter, we describe when and how to use procurement cards, as well as several minor related topics.

When and How to Use Procurement Cards

The purchasing department is usually placed in charge of the procurement card program, since this represents a variation on how goods and services are obtained. When procurement cards are used, most of the paperwork normally processed by the purchasing department vanishes. This can represent a control risk, since inappropriate purchases could be made that would otherwise have been detected if they had been routed through the normal purchasing process. Given this issue, the purchasing manager should approach the rollout of a procurement card program with a certain amount of caution. Consequently, we recommend a multi-step phase-in of procurement cards, using the following steps:

1. *Create a policy.* Develop a procurement card policy that states who can use the cards, and under what circumstances. Possible topics to include in the policy are:

    - *Card user characteristics.* This may include specific job titles within the company that are allowed use of the cards, or perhaps the types of job responsibilities that might warrant being allocated a card.
    - *Usage parameters.* State the circumstances under which a card should and should not be used. For example, all purchases under $250 should be made with a procurement card, with the exception of purchases related to the cost of goods sold. If there are spending limits, either on a per-transaction or per-day basis, state them in the policy. Also

prohibit the use of split purchases, where a card user asks a supplier to split an invoice into multiple smaller invoices in order to go under the procurement card purchasing cap; this behavior clearly circumvents the intent of the spending limit.

- *Preferred suppliers.* The company may have a spend management program, under which it concentrates purchases with a small number of suppliers in order to gain volume discounts. If so, provide a list of these suppliers.
- *Consequences.* State the consequences of card misuse, which may include the termination of employment.

Tip: Have each card user sign the policy before being issued a procurement card. This indicates that they have read the policy and agree to comply with its contents. This document may prove to be of use if an employee misuses a card.

Tip: A good way to locate potential card users is to comb through the purchasing records and see who is making small-dollar purchases now, irrespective of their job titles or formal responsibilities.

---

2. *Develop procedures.* Create procedures that state, in detail, exactly how card users are to activate their cards, keep track of receipts, reconcile card statements to those receipts, report lost cards, and so forth.
3. *Conduct training.* Present the procedures to designated users in training sessions. The intent is to reinforce how the cards are to be used. In addition, write down all questions asked and use them to flesh out the procedures in their next iteration, so that they are more understandable to users.
4. *Monitor usage.* Review the level of card usage at regular intervals, by user. The goal is to spot any instances where cards are being used to buy excessively expensive or inappropriate items, and give robust feedback when this occurs. In addition, if a user is under-utilizing a card, either push for more usage or move the card to a different person who is more willing to use it.
5. *Reinforce behavior.* Whenever a supplier invoice is submitted to the payables department that could have been paid locally by a procurement card holder, route the invoice back to the card holder, with a request for that person to pay for it with a card. Though initially time-consuming, this approach eventually reinforces the fact that the company is serious about using its procurement cards.
6. *Examine parameters.* Periodically review the results of the procurement card program, to see if the number of card users is appropriate, and if the targeted usage levels have been met. It is quite possible that the initial results of the program will indicate that a further expansion of the parameters should be used. For example, the maximum purchase might be shifted from $500 to $1,000. If the parameters are changed, be sure to update the card policy and accompanying procedures.

The preceding phase-in steps can be useful for addressing concerns about the control over procurement cards. The initial rollout phase may reveal some control problems, which can then be addressed before a further expansion of the program is initiated. Thus, the initial rollout could be considered a pilot for a more comprehensive card system at a later date.

Additional Procurement Card Topics

We have thus far discussed the initial rollout and ongoing use of procurement cards, but not the additional tweaking of the system that can improve its financial results and mitigate the risk of loss. The following sub-sections address topics ranging from the use of card rebates to the timing of supplier payments.

Card Issuer Relations

The key point in dealing with the bank that issues procurement cards is to make sure that the card balances are always paid on time. This can be a problem, especially when the corporate treasurer insists upon not paying until as close to the due date as possible. A solution is to arrange with the card provider to extract the funds directly from the company's bank account with an ACH debit. Doing so eliminates the risk of a late payment.

Card Rebates

Given a certain amount of negotiation, procurement card providers may offer monetary rebates when a company spends a large amount through its cards. The discount percentage may increase as the volume of purchases made increases. Given this payback feature, it could be quite valuable to insist on a high level of card usage. This feature may be a good incentive for a business to increase the maximum allowable card purchase, thereby providing an immediate boost to the rebate.

A good way to increase the amount of card usage is to route all card rebates back to the using departments based on their volume of card usage. Once the department managers realize that they have more money to spend, they usually take over from the purchasing manager in demanding the use of procurement cards.

> **Tip:** Cancel all other company credit cards, such as fuel cards, so that these expenditures will instead be paid for with the mandated procurement card. Doing so concentrates expenditures on the cards and increases the potential amount of rebate to be earned.

The card provider may offer longer payment terms in exchange for no rebate. This is generally a bad idea, since the implicit interest rate on the lost rebate tends to be quite high. Instead, it usually pays to pay sooner in exchange for a higher rebate.

Cash Flow Management

If used adroitly, it is possible to use procurement cards to enhance the cash flows of an organization. The technique is to wait until the due date on an invoice, and then call the supplier and ask to pay with a credit card. Doing so then shifts the payable to the card provider, who may not require payment for several additional weeks.

A certain amount of management is required to maximize cash flows with this method, so it may make sense to reduce the work load by only timing payments for the largest invoices. Timing payments for the smallest supplier invoices will have a minimal positive impact on cash flows.

Card User Relations

The ideal card user is one who keeps his or her card information private, only purchases authorized items, and reconciles the month-end statement to receipts as soon as possible. Unfortunately, the typical card user does not necessarily fit this profile. A common scenario is that a few card users perpetually give the purchasing and payables staff ulcers by submitting their month-end reports late. It is quite common for these individuals to display the same behavior every month. If so, the purchasing and payables staff should not be required to backfill for the behavior of these few employees. Instead, pull the card privileges from these individuals and shift the card user responsibility to someone else. Life is too short to continually deal with someone whose work habits are slovenly.

Departure of Card Users

When holders of procurement cards leave the company, be sure to retrieve the cards from them as part of the exit interview, and cancel the card. Otherwise, there is a risk that the card will be used after the person has left the company.

The retrieval of procurement cards requires active involvement by the human resources department. The human resources staff is responsible for the exit interview, and so must remember to ask for the card at that time. To ensure that this is done, make sure that procurement card retrieval is listed as a standard task on the exit interview checklist.

If the human resources staff forgets to retrieve a procurement card, a backup procedure is to review the procurement card statements at the end of each month, and see if the purchasing activity on any cards have changed or fallen off. If so, contact the human resources department to see if these changes correspond to an employee departure. A variation on this concept is to send the current list of card users to the human resources staff each month, with a request to flag any users who have left the company.

International Purchases

Procurement cards are less commonly used for international payments, because the payer is also charged a fee for any conversions of foreign currencies back into the credit card processor's home currency. There are a small number of cards that do not charge this fee.

Summary

The managers of the purchasing and payables departments usually want to shift as much purchasing activity as possible to procurement cards, thereby reducing the purchasing workload of their departments. This emphasis on procurement cards can mean that quite a large proportion of all expenditures are made with the cards. If so, it is critical to install a card reconciliation procedure that incorporates an approval process, along with a set of controls over every aspect of card usage. Otherwise, it will be much too easy for employees to make a significant number of purchases that are not in the best interests of the company.

Chapter 4
Supplier Selection

Introduction

When a company operates a closely-coordinated production or fulfillment process, it depends on its suppliers to deliver goods and services exactly as needed. Otherwise, the company's reputation with its own customers suffers. This means that a business cannot afford to have low-quality suppliers – which it likely has if the historical approach to purchasing has been to award contracts to the lowest bidder. Instead, the purchasing department needs to evaluate suppliers based on many other criteria than just price. This evaluation may involve a lengthy process of supplier location, evaluation, and scoring before the best group of suppliers has been located. Once this selection process has been completed, a company can work on building long-term relations with its supplier base. Eventually, the core group of suppliers will be so closely associated with a business that there will be little chance of their being replaced by other suppliers. Thus, the supplier selection process should be viewed as the start of a long-term marriage.

In this chapter, we describe the general considerations that can drive the selection of suppliers, how to locate prospective suppliers, which selection criteria to use, and how to aggregate the resulting scores.

Overview of Supplier Selection

One of the key roles of the purchasing department is the identification and evaluation of potential suppliers. It is critical to locate suppliers that are financially stable and which are capable of providing goods and services that are of high quality and which can be delivered in a reliable manner.

In this section, we address a number of considerations regarding the types of suppliers wanted, and when a supplier selection process is warranted.

General Considerations

There are a number of issues to consider before even beginning a search for suppliers. These issues provide structure to the search for a supplier. The issues are:

- *Communications*. If the company is planning to buy industry-standard materials for which the specifications are well known, it can make sense to source the goods with a foreign supplier that is many time zones away, since there should be little need for ongoing communications regarding orders. However, this can be more of a concern when there are likely to be ongoing specification changes. In the latter case, management should consider the inconvenience of contacting distant suppliers during non-working hours, and possibly the cost of having to routinely travel to supplier locations in other countries to coordinate work.

- *Distributor or manufacturer*. The usual assumption is that a supplier is the original manufacturer of goods. However, it can make more sense to work with a distributor, which can advise the company on the relative merits of the offerings from several different manufacturers, and which may be more willing to make large numbers of frequent deliveries. Distributors may charge somewhat higher prices than manufacturers in order to cover their inventory holding costs. Consequently, it is more common to use distributors just for spot purchases, and manufacturers for longer-term, higher-volume purchasing arrangements.

- *Diversity*. A company may be subject to government minority purchasing rules. If so, the purchasing department must source a certain amount of the entity's purchasing requirements with minority and women-owned businesses.

- *Geographic distribution*. If a company needs to receive goods and services at multiple locations, this may call for the use of suppliers that have facilities over a broad area, each of which can service a separate company facility. Alternatively, this may call for the use of suppliers that have excellent distribution networks, with warehouses positioned in many key locations.

- *Hedging*. When using an international supplier, the supplier may require that it be paid in its local currency. If so, the company will be at risk of an adverse change in the exchange rate by the time the payment is due. This may call for hedging activities to mitigate the risk of loss, which might be an undue burden for a smaller enterprise.

- *Innovation*. When the company needs to incorporate the most technically advanced and innovative components into its products, it will likely find that this requirement substantially reduces the number of available suppliers. It is also quite likely that costs will increase, since these suppliers are in a position to charge more for their components.

- *Lifespan of purchased goods*. Some goods have quite a short lifespan, and so will not survive a lengthy routing in pristine condition unless expensive air freight is used. This issue can drive the maximum range over which a company may be willing to obtain certain goods.

- *Local sourcing requirements*. If a company wants to expand into a new country, the local government may mandate that it can only do so if local suppliers are used for a certain percentage of sales. This can be a difficult problem if the quality of the local supplier base is not adequate, and could limit the ability of a company to enter certain markets at all.

- *Logistics*. The time, effort, and cost associated with transporting inbound goods over international borders can be substantial. For example, there may be taxes, customs duties, and additional fees charged by the shipper. If the company is highly price-sensitive, this could drive a sourcing decision in favor of a domestic supplier.

- *Payment methods.* When a supplier is located in another country, it may require that payment be made using a letter of credit. A letter of credit involves a modest amount of paperwork, and the sponsoring bank can require the company to set aside funds for the payment well in advance. A smaller business that is not used to this type of arrangement might only consider domestic suppliers in order to avoid the payment hassle.
- *Presence in foreign market.* If the company wants to sell products in a foreign market, it is possible that the local government's laws require that some proportion of the products sold be sourced locally. If so, the company must find local suppliers. It may make sense to source locally even when there are no laws mandating such activity, since the company gains local contacts and builds goodwill through its sourcing activities, which may carry over into the success of its product sales.
- *Proximity to the company.* If the company needs to have goods delivered on short notice and in small quantities, it may be necessary to limit the supplier search to the immediate vicinity of the supplier. Local proximity can also reduce freight costs. Conversely, this may not be an issue if obtaining the lowest possible price is the main goal, in which case the search could expand to encompass other countries. Expanding the search area can also give the company access to a much larger range of potential suppliers from which to choose.
- *Quality.* Some customers demand the highest possible levels of quality in what they buy, which forces the company to buy goods only from those suppliers that can meet the quality standards of its customers.
- *Single or multiple-supplier sourcing.* Should a company commit to buying from a single supplier, or spread its purchases among several suppliers? It is easier to manage a single supplier, but having several available suppliers mitigates risk by allowing for orders to be shifted to a backup supplier if the primary supplier is unable to accept an order.
- *Supplier management of inventory.* The intent of management may be to have certain suppliers both own and manage their inventory at the company's location. Doing so results in a lower investment in inventory by the company, which reduces its need for funds. However, suppliers may need to charge more in exchange for taking on the increased inventory monitoring and ownership burden.
- *Supplier size.* A larger supplier may have better processes and possibly lower prices. However, if the company is a small one, its orders may not have much impact on such a supplier, so that special treatment will not happen. If so, it could make sense to look for a smaller supplier, for which the company's orders will be more meaningful.

Of the many considerations just noted when deciding to add suppliers, the overriding issue is typically the risk associated with a new supplier. The purchasing department cannot afford to have a key supplier fail, so there is a strong (and well-justified) tendency to select the larger and more established suppliers.

When to Conduct a Supplier Selection

The supplier selection process is not a one-time event. There may be an initial focus on researching suppliers when the decision is initially made to upgrade the quality of the supply chain. However, there are other events that will occur at regular intervals that will also call for periodic supplier analyses. Examples of these periodic events are:

- *New product introduction.* When an extension of an existing product is being planned, the design team is more likely to use existing suppliers, since they are already familiar with the product components. This is not necessarily the case for entirely new products, since these products may require entirely new components for which the existing suppliers do not have any expertise.
- *New geographic sales.* When a company moves into an entirely new sales region (especially within a different country), it may be more cost-effective to produce goods within the new region, which will call for the use of a new group of suppliers.
- *Supplier replacement.* An existing supplier may exhibit such poor performance that the purchasing manager decides to replace it with a new supplier; otherwise the company's own performance with its customers will be negatively affected. This situation may also arise when an existing supplier's performance has been adequate, but its finances or capacity are constrained. If so, the company has essentially outgrown the supplier, and needs to find a larger one.
- *Outsourcing.* The senior management team may make the strategic decision to outsource entire segments of the company, such as production or information technology. This calls for a detailed examination of supplier candidates, since the company will likely be entering into quite a long-term outsourcing arrangement.

In short, there will be an ongoing need to evaluate new suppliers, even in companies that already have a relatively settled core group of suppliers.

Locating Suppliers

There are many ways to locate suitable suppliers. The following list addresses the more common methods:

- *Technical staff.* The staff of the design team that has created a new product may have quite strong opinions about which suppliers to use, since these people have likely already had hands-on experience with the offerings of certain suppliers.
- *Trade listings.* Most industries have a trade group that publishes a supplier directory. These directories are structured to present a consistent set of contact information and services provided. There is no indication of supplier quality, but these guides are reasonable starting points for a search.

- *Internet search.* The search engines do a reasonable job of matching up possible suppliers with the geographic region input by a company. These listings may also contain reviews posted by customers of the listed suppliers. There are also many directories of minority-owned businesses listed on the Internet.
- *Trade shows.* Those suppliers willing to invest additional funds in marketing may attend their industry trade shows. If the purchasing staff does not have time to attend these shows, it can at least review the web sites of the trade shows, which usually list the names and contact information of attending suppliers. If the purchasing staff does have time to attend a trade show, it can be a good way to establish contacts with a large number of suppliers within a short period of time, as well as to review their offerings.
- *Buyers.* Those members of the purchasing staff that have been buying for a long time have likely built up a deep knowledge of which suppliers are available for certain commodities, and so can provide contact information for a number of supplier candidates. A variation on the concept is to request information from the purchasing departments of fellow subsidiaries. These other departments have detailed knowledge of many different suppliers.
- *Sales representatives.* The more aggressive suppliers will send their own sales representatives to the company, asking for introductory meetings. Though time-consuming, accepting a selection of these requests for meetings can at least result in a database of potential contacts.
- *Consultants.* When the purchasing staff is conducting a supplier search in a new area of goods or services with which it has limited expertise, it can make sense to hire a consultant. The ideal consultant is one with years of hands-on experience in the targeted field, who can provide advice regarding potential suppliers. This is an especially attractive option when there is a short timeline for locating a supplier, and when the goods or services to be sourced are of particular importance.

If the purchasing department conducts a detailed supplier search every time it wants to select a new supplier, it may be duplicating work that was already completed as part of a prior search. To avoid duplication, consider creating a database of information about suppliers, which contains the information gleaned from prior searches. This database can be especially useful from a negative perspective, to keep the purchasing staff from wasting time researching suppliers that have already been considered to be inadequate supplier prospects.

Supplier Selection Criteria

It may not be especially difficult to locate several possible suppliers that can provide a needed item. However, it is not so easy to reliably extract from this group the specific supplier that can provide reliable *service*. Instead, it is all too common to select a supplier that ships late, overcharges, sends low-quality goods – or all three. There are a number of methods available for improving the odds of selecting a quality supplier on the first attempt, as we will discuss in the following sub-sections. However, we will begin with the reverse situation – where the purchasing staff is told which supplier to use.

Mandated Suppliers

The sales staff of suppliers may attempt to work around the purchasing department by insinuating themselves with decision makers high in the corporate hierarchy. If they are successful, then the purchasing manager will be told which supplier to use. A possible outcome is that the purchasing staff is then forced to work with a supplier whose performance may be sub-par. And, given its support by senior management, such a supplier may have little reason to improve its performance. The end result can be continuing inadequate supplier performance.

In this case, the purchasing manager can only forward reports of inadequate supplier performance to the management team, and hope that they rescind their mandate to use that specific supplier.

Selection Rigor

It is not sufficient to select a supplier because the purchasing manager has developed an excellent rapport with the sales representative of a supplier, or because the company president knows the president of the supplier and so can "get things done." Instead, it is necessary to engage in a rigorous and quantitative analysis of the benefits and disadvantages of working with each supplier.

Once this analysis has been completed, there is still room for the introduction of opinions into the final decision. For example, a detailed supplier analysis may result in a table of scores assigned to each supplier, which may be weighted to emphasize those characteristics deemed most important to the company. These weightings are a matter of opinion, so someone determined to route business to a particular supplier can campaign in favor of a weighting scheme that favors their candidate. Nonetheless, even such a skewing of the results is at least based on an underlying analysis of the characteristics of each supplier. If a supplier's performance later turns out to be inadequate, the weightings can be changed to alter the emphasis being placed on the final decision.

Tip: Include several people in the review process who are based in different departments, such as the engineering and purchasing departments. This tends to reduce the amount of bias that just one reviewer may introduce into the analysis of prospective suppliers.

Selection Criteria

What criteria are used when deciding whether to accept the services of a new supplier? There are many possibilities, some of which are specific to a particular industry. However, the following three general classifications of criteria will apply to most situations:

- *Finances*. A supplier must be not only solvent, but also have sufficient funding to pay for its own ongoing research programs and the capital spending needed to expand its production capacity as needed.
- *Capability*. A supplier must be able to service the company's needs after an order has been placed.
- *Responsiveness*. A supplier must be able to perform the tasks required by the company. This is the most difficult of the criteria to evaluate, since the related information is the most difficult to collect.
- *Global issues*. One must be cognizant of the risks associated with sourcing goods from a supplier in a different country, especially since pandemics and other crises can potential cut off access to these suppliers.

We discuss each of these selection criteria in the following sub-sections.

Supplier Financial Analysis

The accounting department or a financial analyst can be asked to conduct a financial review of a prospective supplier. The intent of this review is to gain an understanding of the profitability and liquidity of a supplier. In particular, the company does not want to tie itself to a supplier whose financial basis is so shaky that it could drop into bankruptcy proceedings at any moment. The primary tool for this financial review is ratio analysis, where different line items in the financial statements are compared to each other. Some of the more useful ratios to use are as follows:

- *Quick ratio*. This ratio compares the current assets of a supplier to its current liabilities, not including inventory. The intent of the quick ratio is to estimate the ability of a supplier to pay its bills. There should be a larger amount of current assets than current liabilities, so that the assets can be sold off to pay for the liabilities. A 2:1 ratio is ideal. The inventory asset is not included in this ratio, since it can be difficult to sell off.
- *Receivables turnover*. This ratio compares net annual credit sales to average accounts receivable. The intent of this ratio is to estimate the amount of time it takes for a supplier to collect on the bills it has issued to customers. If the time period is excessively long, it indicates that a supplier may have a number of uncollectible invoices, or that its customers have forced it to accept long payment terms.
- *Inventory turnover*. This ratio compares the annual cost of goods sold to average inventory. The intent of this ratio is to estimate the amount of time it takes for a supplier to sell off its inventory. If the ratio indicates a long holding period, this implies that the supplier may have a large amount of obsolete inventory, or that its internal processes are inadequate, which results in all types of excess inventory.
- *Payables turnover*. This ratio compares the annual cost of goods sold to average accounts payable. The intent of this ratio is to see if a supplier is taking a long time to pay its own suppliers. This is particularly relevant if the supplier has a minimal cash balance, and especially if it is also carrying a significant

amount of debt. When combined, this information indicates a business that is operating on the edge of insolvency.

- *Debt to equity ratio*. This ratio compares the total debt of a supplier to its equity. If the ratio is too high, it implies that the supplier will be at risk of being unable to pay its debts in the event of a downturn, since interest and principal payments will then comprise a large part of its cash outflows.
- *Times interest earned*. This ratio compares the interest expense to earnings before interest and taxes. A low ratio implies that most of a company's cash flow is going toward the payment of interest on its loans, which leaves little money for any other purposes.
- *Net profit margin*. This ratio compares the reported net profit of a supplier to its sales. An adequate percentage indicates that a supplier is able to enforce adequate product price points on its customers, while also managing its expenses judiciously.

All of the preceding ratios should be tracked on a trend line for the past few years, to see if there is a trend in the condition or performance of a supplier. A downward trend should trigger additional inquiries to determine the nature of the decline.

The ratios described here are only an introduction to the full range of analyses that can be conducted on a supplier's financial statements. For a comprehensive investigation of this topic, see the author's *Interpretation of Financial Statements* course.

It is also useful to obtain a credit report on finalist suppliers. These reports provide additional details regarding the payment histories of suppliers, and should be checked at regular intervals to see if the financial circumstances of a supplier have changed. Credit reports are available from Dun & Bradstreet.

Supplier Capability Analysis

The evaluation team needs to estimate the ability of a prospective supplier to fulfill the company's orders in a timely manner. This may be a relatively minor issue if the unit quantity of orders expected to be issued comprises a minor percentage of a supplier's total capacity. However, this may be the most important selection issue of all if the prospective orders could overwhelm a supplier.

If there is a suspicion that a supplier may not be able to handle the company's order volume, inquire about the following:

- *The company's historical capacity levels*. Ask for a historical comparison of the supplier's order backlog to its sales. If the backlog figure has been increasing while sales have been flat or increasing at a slower rate, this indicates that the supplier is probably already operating at maximum capacity.
- *Plans for additions to capacity*. It is useful to understand exactly when additional capacity is expected to be available, which would make it easier to process the company's orders. If the equipment to be installed usually requires a lengthy testing period, this can imply that the new capacity may not be ready by the estimated date.

- *Rush order capacity*. A useful capability is when a supplier routinely reserves a portion of its capacity for rush orders. The supplier has likely found that it can charge more for rush orders, which is fine – the main point is that capacity has been set aside to deal with these orders, and that the supplier knows how to handle them.
- *The nature of the company's bottleneck*. The supplier may have a production bottleneck, or a bottleneck located somewhere else in its facilities. Inquire about the nature of this bottleneck, and discuss how the supplier intends to process the company's orders through this bottleneck.
- *Subcontracting*. If the supplier intends to subcontract a significant part or all of an order, this triggers several concerns. The act of subcontracting implies that the supplier does not have the internal capacity to deal with the company's orders. Also, the review team has no idea what the capabilities of the subcontractor may be in regard to quality or delivery performance. The use of subcontractors does not automatically disqualify a supplier, but it raises warning flags for the review team, which will need to investigate further.
- *Technological capabilities*. A characteristic of an ideal supplier is one with a reputation for continually developing new processes and products. These suppliers are likely to be somewhat more expensive, since they need to fund their research activities from profits, but there is a payoff in gaining access to the best products. Conversely, a supplier that offers rock-bottom pricing has probably gutted its general and administrative expenses budget, and allocated the minimum amount of funding to improvements of any kind. The latter approach may still be acceptable in industries where there is a major focus on low prices.
- *Raw material issues*. Does the supplier suffer from any of its own raw materials supply issues? If one of its suppliers is allocating certain materials, this issue could cause production delays for the company's orders placed with the supplier.

When the acquisition of a new supplier involves a major sourcing contract, it can be worthwhile to send some of the company's industrial engineers or a consultant to the supplier location, to observe its operations and discuss the preceding capacity issues with their counterparts.

The supplier capacity topic also includes the issue of whether a supplier has the production systems needed to properly monitor the status of the company's orders. An ideal monitoring system is an enterprise resources planning system, where orders are monitored through the same database from the order entry point through to final shipment, including the status of any jobs that are in production. An adequate alternative is when these systems are present but not linked together, which presents the risk of orders being lost as they progress through a company. The worst case is when the tracking systems are entirely manual or informal, which greatly increases the risk that orders will be incorrectly fulfilled or delivered late.

Supplier Responsiveness Analysis

As noted earlier, responsiveness is the ability to perform the tasks required by the company. The most common of the methods used to review responsiveness is to request a set of references, and to contact these references to discuss their experiences with the supplier. Prior to doing so, develop a standard set of questions to ask each person contacted, and follow the questions list during each discussion. If an additional question arises partway through these discussions, then go back to those references already contacted, and ask them the same question. By following this regimented approach, the review team will arrive at a consistent set of information about each supplier.

A concern with contacting a supplier's references is that these contacts are undoubtedly the supplier's best possible references, and so are likely to provide little more than the most glowing commentary about the supplier. It is entirely possible that there are other customers that have had less enthralling experiences – the trick is to locate them. One option is to ask for a longer list of references, such as ten instead of the usual three references. A supplier will need to dig deeper into its prior sales to find excellent references, so there may be at least a slightly disgruntled person somewhere in this longer list. Another option is to check with the references to see if they are aware of any additional customers of the supplier. Or, conduct an Internet search to see if any additional names crop up.

The level of detailed investigation needed to examine responsiveness is most necessary when the items being sourced are especially critical to a company, or the amount of money to be spent is significant. When it is considered very important to have a high level of supplier responsiveness, consider spending the additional time to visit the reference customers, or other customers that additional investigation has uncovered. An in-person visit gives the reviewer a hands-on experience with the final results of a supplier's efforts. It also allows for a more broad-ranging discussion with the customer regarding the characteristics of the supplier in question, which could result in additional insights that could impact the final selection decision.

Another area in which to investigate responsiveness is the level of detail that a supplier has provided in responding to the company's questions. If there are certain questions that were clearly sidestepped or not answered at all, return to these questions for more information. It is quite likely that these particular questions provide the best clues regarding the weak points in a prospective supplier's case for working with the company. For example, it may be trying to gloss over the fact that it has a short operating history, weak finances, or few customers.

Global Sourcing Issues

It can be quite tempting to source goods from another country, especially when they are being offered at a low price point and the quality is acceptable. As long as shipping costs are low and goods can be delivered in a reliable manner, it might initially appear like an excellent idea to source goods internationally, thereby improving profits. Another factor encouraging the spread of global sourcing is that a company can outsource the construction of complex components to other parties, thereby reducing its investment in production capacity. Both of these factors can make global sourcing an obvious choice.

However, before automatically shifting to overseas suppliers, it is worth considering the risks associated with doing so. One is that a pandemic can trigger the closing of national borders, making it impossible to obtain scheduled deliveries. Another possibility is a major natural disaster severely impacting a supplier facility, of which there have been many examples in the past few years – earthquakes in Japan, wildfires in Australia, and so forth. Yet another problem – this one man made – is trade wars. A trade war can result in hefty tariffs being imposed on imports, which suddenly makes inexpensive imported goods far more expensive. These problems make it clear that there are significant concerns linked to any goods being delivered over a national border.

Given the issues just noted, the supplier selection process needs to move beyond a simple analysis of cost and quality, to evaluate whether a supplier is located in a high-risk area, and what the probabilities are that identified risks will actually occur. A likely outcome of this analysis is that the more critical raw materials and components will need to be sourced as close to home as possible. Furthermore, one should determine where *their* suppliers are located, to see if there are hidden risks somewhere further down in the supply chain that could halt deliveries in the event of an international problem.

Which goods can be sourced internationally? A good choice is any component that can be re-sourced quickly, and for which there is a hefty global supply. When these criteria are met, it makes more sense to source from the lowest-cost and most reliable suppliers, no matter where they are located in the world, because any sudden crises can be mitigated by switching elsewhere within a few days.

What about cases in which an international supplier is the only valid solution? In this case, consider redesigning products to use less of the components coming from this supplier. Also, build up a reserve of components in inventory, to guard against shorter-term shortages. And finally, discuss the matter with local suppliers, to see if any of them are interested in investing in production facilities that may eventually result in the required goods being produced locally.

In short, the events of the past few years have made it clear that, despite the cost advantages of global sourcing, it is time to start shifting supply chains closer to home. Doing so increases the reliability of the supply chain, which in turn makes it much easier to produce goods in a timely manner for customers.

Other Analysis Issues

There are a number of other issues that do not fall within the preceding three main classifications of selection criteria, but which might still be considered significant when making the final selection decision. Here are several topics to consider:

- *Competitors as customers.* Ask if any of the company's competitors are customers of a prospective supplier. If so, this could pose a problem if the company plans to share proprietary information with the supplier, such as the designs for upcoming products. In this case, there is a risk that the information could be leaked to a competitor. However, this should be an issue in a small minority of cases, since most purchases are for parts having industry-standard specifications.

- *Credit policy*. If the company is having issues locating sufficient funding, a key issue would be the willingness of a supplier to offer generous payment terms. Conversely, if a supplier requires exceedingly short payment terms, this could persuade the selection team to go with their second choice.
- *Regulatory violations*. Review the public records of the government's regulatory agencies to see if warnings or fines have been issued to a prospective supplier. An ongoing history of significant violations could indicate that a supplier's management team is cutting costs to an excessive degree, and may also have less concern for the health of its employees. This is unlikely to be the type of supplier that will have a robust research group, or innovations to share with its customers.
- *Terms and conditions*. Ask for a prospective supplier's standard set of terms and conditions. These items may be especially onerous, such as not including any standard warranty period, or not allowing equipment to be resold to a third party. If this is the case, it can be so difficult to renegotiate the standard terms that it is not worthwhile to engage the services of the supplier. The terms renegotiation task is made even more difficult if the company is significantly smaller than the supplier, since the company will have little leverage to alter the terms. An additional point is that unusually onerous terms and conditions provide a clue to what it would be like to deal with a supplier, since it indicates a pervasive attitude of not being willing to work with customers.

The purchasing department may find that the full review requirements for a prospective supplier are too time-consuming. If so, consider using a two-stage review, where a group of supplier candidates are eliminated from consideration if they do not pass a small number of threshold criteria. For example, a supplier might not be reviewed further if it has reported a loss in the past two years, has no product quality program, and does not offer product design services. The exact types of threshold criteria will be based on a company's specific needs.

Site Visits

When it is especially important to pick the right supplier, the selection team may decide to engage in site visits. These visits are both expensive and time-consuming, so they should only be used when a supplier is to provide a critical part, or the amount of spend targeted at them is substantial. This means that site visits are only needed for a minority of supplier selections.

When conducting site visits, the entire selection team should visit each of the finalist suppliers, so that the group has complete information about each one. To ensure that their time is not wasted, there should be a large amount of preparation work before the visits begin. The intent of this preparation is to develop a checklist of topics to address during each visit. The team may split up during a site visit, where each person follows up on his or her area of specialization, so each person must be clear about the information to be collected.

The types of information to be collected will vary somewhat, depending on the type of supplier, but will probably encompass most of the following topics:

Order Fulfillment Process

The order fulfillment area covers the process flow from the receipt of customer orders, logging them into the supplier's order management system, scheduling them for production or fulfillment, and shipping them out to customers. The investigation in this area should address the following issues:

- What software is being used to process orders?
- Does the system seamlessly monitor orders from the point of order receipt to shipment, or is there a manual transfer of information at some point from one system to another?
- How does the supplier initially and subsequently prioritize submitted orders?
- Is expediting used to force orders through the system?
- How does the supplier monitor delayed orders, and what actions does it take to accelerate delayed orders? Does this include backordered items?

Operational Capabilities

An investigation into the operational capabilities of a supplier should encompass all activity areas that impact customer orders. The core of this investigation will address the supplier's manufacturing and materials management functions, but may also extend to the engineering department, if product customization is a key part of their services. Investigative topics could include the following:

- Is the production area configured into production lines or cells?
- Is the production system based on a forecast-driven "push" model, or a just-in-time "pull" model? Is there a production scheduling and control system in place?
- At what level of full capacity do the manufacturing operations usually operate? Are there periodic spikes in demand that use up the remaining capacity?
- How do the production and fulfillment operations change their capacity levels to deal with sudden spikes in customer demand? Is the work kept in-house, or is it shunted off to subcontractors?
- What is the nature of the company's bottleneck operation? How is the supplier managing it? Is there an inventory buffer in front of the bottleneck, and is the buffer of sufficient size to protect the bottleneck from variations in the incoming flow of materials?
- What is the level of automation that the supplier uses? Does the automation appear to assist the production flow, or do maintenance records indicate that automated operations have an unusually high degree of downtime?

- Is there a program of preventive maintenance? Do the maintenance records indicate that there are unusual amounts of machine downtime for unexpected maintenance?
- Does the production system monitor the progress of each job as it progresses through the shop floor?
- Does the production system have a lot tracking capability, and is it used?
- What is the level of housekeeping on the shop floor and in the warehouse?
- Is there a sourcing system in place for evaluating the supplier's own suppliers? Are there designated preferred suppliers?

Quality Management

When the goods to be acquired from a supplier are of the non-standard variety, it is especially important that the supplier be able to match the company's quality standards. This calls for some on-site investigation to answer the following questions:

- What quality-specific processes, review steps, and measurements does the supplier use?
- How does the management team respond to identified instances of low quality?
- How does the supplier monitor its level of quality? At what points in the production process are quality reviews completed?
- Does the organization follow the quality guidelines established for the ISO 9000 certification or the Malcolm Baldrige National Quality Award?

Cost Management

When a company partners with its suppliers to reduce costs, this means that the suppliers acknowledge the need to continually reduce costs, and have systems in place for doing so. Otherwise, a company will be in danger of tying itself to a supplier whose cost structure is inflexible, and which may therefore lead to company products having uncompetitive price points. To examine these issues, investigate the following questions:

- What system is used to compile costs for each production job? What costs are assigned to each job? What method is used to allocate overhead to jobs?
- How well does the cost variance feedback loop work? Does management investigate the indicated unfavorable variances?
- Which sub-systems feed labor and materials costs into the job accounting system? How well do these sub-systems accumulate costs?
- Is there a target costing system in place (see the Cost Management chapter)? How thoroughly is target costing incorporated into the new product development process?
- What systems are in place to incentivize employees to reduce costs?

Some suppliers consider their cost data to be proprietary, on the grounds that it is a competitive advantage. If so, the review team may have to estimate the costs incurred by a supplier candidate, which will be subject to some inaccuracy.

Finances

Even if all other topics described in this section result in a glowing score for a supplier candidate, a company cannot realistically select it if the supplier suffers from inadequate financial results and/or poor financial condition. A review in this area should address the following concerns:

- What is the supplier's ability to pay its bills in a timely manner (see the quick ratio noted earlier)?
- Does the supplier have enough positive cash flow to engage in ongoing investments in its operations?
- Is the supplier comfortably able to make scheduled payments on its debt?
- What is the breakeven point of the business?

The information needed to answer these questions comes from the income statement, balance sheet, and statement of cash flows of a supplier. The income statement reveals the sales, offsetting expenses, and resulting profit or loss for a reporting period. The balance sheet shows the assets, liabilities, and equity of a business. The statement of cash flows lays out the sources of cash inflows and reasons for cash outflows for a reporting period. Additional information can be found in the footnotes that accompany a comprehensive set of financial statements.

Management Compatibility

A key issue is the ability of the company's management team to work with its counterparts at a supplier. If there are differences in how the two parties like to manage their businesses, this can cause significant rifts that may cause a partnership to fail. Key questions to investigate are:

- Does the management team enforce a top-down pyramid management system, or does the supplier's organizational structure force decision making down into the organization?
- Does the supplier's bonus plan focus most payouts on just the senior management team, or does it spread around payments lower in the organization?
- What is the level of turnover among managers?
- Is there an ethical code of conduct, as well as evidence that the supplier's management team enforces it?
- How does the supplier treat its customers? Is there any evidence of short shipments, overbilling, or low quality?
- How long have the relationships of third parties with the supplier lasted?
- Is there a planning system in place for the future competitive positioning of the business? Does the plan include an adequate amount of capital and training investment in the business?

- Does the management team appear to be willing to discuss the supplier's internal processes?

Relationship Commitment

When the review team wants to award a significant amount of work to a supplier over a long period of time, an issue to explore is whether the supplier wants to commit to the relationship. The following questions could be pursued to find an answer:

- Will the supplier commit resources to the relationship? Will there be a designated relationship manager? Will capacity be reserved for the company?
- Will the supplier send designers to product design meetings?
- Is the supplier willing to share its technical expertise with the company?
- Has the supplier indicated that it will guard any confidential information imparted to it? If so, what are its policies and procedures for doing so?
- Is the supplier willing to share information about its product costs and general cost structure?

Human Resources

- What is the rate of employee turnover? If the turnover level is unusually high, is there a reason for it?
- Are any employees represented by unions? If so, what are the relations with the unions? When is the union contract scheduled for renegotiation? Is there a history of strikes or work slowdowns?
- What is the nature of the employee training program? What topics are covered? How much money is budgeted per employee for training? What is the level of management commitment to training the staff?

Metrics

Many financial metrics can be derived from the financial statements, but what about operational metrics? A site visit is a good time to collect information about the following measurements:

- How long does it take for a typical order to cycle through the company's processes, from order receipt to final shipment?
- What is the supplier's on-time delivery performance?
- How has the order backlog varied recently? Is it being maintained at a steady level, or is there a noticeable increase or decline?
- What is the unscheduled downtime percentage for production equipment? This yields insights into the level of preventive maintenance being conducted.
- What percentage of shipments is returned? An upward trend or spike indicates a quality or design problem with the supplier's products.

> **Tip:** Create a master list of site visit questions that contains every conceivable topic, and use it as the basis for a somewhat narrower and more focused list that will be used for each set of site visits. This saves time in constructing the list every time a new supplier investigation is conducted.

All of the information accumulated in a site visit should be documented into a standard format and archived. This information can be quite useful as a baseline, if a supplier candidate is eventually selected and the company wants to review its performance again at a later date.

Besides the detailed analysis topics that cover the bulk of the time spent in a site visit, this also represents a good opportunity to meet the employees of each supplier. When contracts are eventually awarded to the winning supplier, this means that some face-to-face relationships will have been established, which can be useful for creating processes and clearing up difficulties at a later date.

Supplier Scoring

As the review team collects information about the criteria in the preceding section, it fills out a supplier scoring form, on which they assign a rank to each supplier for each item listed.

The evaluation of suppliers should not just include employees of the purchasing department. In addition, those people in other departments who will be directly impacted by the supplier chosen should also have a vote in the selection. For example, the production manager might want to pick a supplier that has a reputation for manufacturing within tight tolerances, because a particular machine will otherwise jam open if a slightly out-of-specification part is loaded into it.

A simplified version of a supplier scorecard appears in the following table, where there is a single cumulative score for each of the main classification areas; in reality, there could be scores for dozens of more detailed topics. In this first sample, no weighting is given to any particular category; that is, all classifications are assumed to have equal importance.

Simplified Sample Supplier Scoring Table

	Supplier A	Supplier B	Supplier C
Finances	70	43	90
Capability	19	15	28
Responsiveness	35	40	20
Totals	124	98	138

The summary-level scoring table just noted could reflect a roll-up of a number of subcategories. For example, the "capability" line item might contain a number of additional ratings that only appear on a backup page. An example follows.

Sample Detail for One Classification of a Scoring Table

	Supplier A	Supplier B	Supplier C
Capability			
Available capacity	5	0	5
Bottleneck management	4	2	5
Raw material constraints	1	5	4
Rush order capacity	2	2	5
Subcontracting	4	3	4
Technology	3	3	5
Totals	19	15	28

The scoring method used in the preceding detailed scoring model assigns anywhere from zero points to five points to each sub-category. Points in the sample tables are assigned based on the following logic:

Point Scoring Logic

Points	Scoring Logic
0	Does not meet any aspect of the requirement
1	Significant issues with meeting the requirement
2	Minor nonconformities in meeting the requirement
3	Adequate ability to meet the requirement
4	Exceeds expectations set by the requirement
5	Best-in-class ability to meet the requirement

Some of the scoring mixes appearing in the preceding sample scoring table reflect certain types of suppliers. For example, Supplier B is probably rather small, with questionable finances, and so is desperate for the business (which explains the high responsiveness score). Supplier C is likely to be much larger, with excellent finances and capabilities; however, because it has many customers, the company is unlikely to be considered a valuable customer, which explains the low responsiveness score.

The assumption in the first sample table was that all scoring categories had the same weighting, which may not be the case. For example, what if a company expects to grow rapidly, and so needs a supplier with a strong capability score? Or a company specializes in custom orders, and so needs a quick response time from its suppliers? In these cases, a weighting can be introduced into the scoring table. In the following sample scoring table, we have assumed that a business places a high emphasis on supplier responsiveness, and so introduces a higher weighting to this classification.

Sample Supplier Weighted Scoring Table

	Weighting	Supplier A (Weighted)	Supplier B (Weighted)	Supplier C (Weighted)
Finances	1.0	70	43	90
Capability	1.0	19	15	28
Responsiveness	1.5	53	60	30
Totals		142	118	148

In the revised sample table, Supplier C still retains the leading score, but the introduction of the weighting has allowed the competing suppliers to edge closer. The reason for the difference is the weighting given to supplier responsiveness, which is Supplier C's weakest area.

The supplier scoring system described here might appear to be highly quantitative, but it is based on the subjective opinions of the team members who originally designated scores for each supplier. Consequently, a supplier score that is only slightly higher than the scores of other suppliers is hardly a mandate to award business to that specific supplier – instead, it indicates that there is no clear winner. Conversely, if there is a large scoring gap between one supplier and the others in a group, it indicates that the evaluation team has settled upon a clear winner.

Preferred Suppliers

The purchasing department could consider maintaining a separate list of preferred suppliers, which is that group of suppliers that always scores the highest on the company's rating scorecards for excellent supplier performance. When a new sourcing situation arises, it may be more efficient to avoid the cost of the preceding supplier selection process, and simply contact a preferred supplier to see if they want to take on the work.

The use of a preferred supplier list to shortcut the selection process should be a major incentive for existing suppliers to improve their performance so that they can be added to the preferred list.

Summary

The correct group of suppliers is needed for a company to achieve its goals. This group can be immensely helpful in forwarding new ideas for component parts, offering advice regarding material choices, and assisting with cost reductions. Conversely, the wrong group will treat the company with indifference. Further, it is extremely difficult to change the operating characteristics of a bad supplier – chances are, poor performance will continue into the future. Thus, it is essential to select the right suppliers to work with an organization. This does not mean that an exhaustive analysis needs to be conducted for the supplier of every conceivable raw material or service. Instead, a deep analysis should be conducted for the most critical supply contracts. This analysis can continue through progressively less-critical contracts, until it is apparent that the bulk of all spend has been allocated to a group of preferred suppliers; reviews of the remaining suppliers can be conducted if it is cost-effective to do so.

Chapter 5
Supplier Management

Introduction

Suppliers form a key part of the products and services that a company provides to its own customers. For example, if a supplier's goods are of low quality, the company may have to initiate a product recall in order to fix the issue, which in turn will damage its relations with customers. Thus, if suppliers cannot perform up to expectations, the company's fortunes can also suffer. To keep these issues from arising, the purchasing department must engage in an ongoing system of supplier management.

As noted in the following sections, supplier management involves measuring supplier performance, consistently engaging in detailed communications with them, upgrading their performance, and mitigating any risks associated with certain suppliers.

Commodity Strategy

When dealing with suppliers, it makes sense to first develop a strategy for how the company plans to deal with its key commodity areas. For example, a manufacturer may decide that it needs to lock down its sources of rare earth minerals for the next ten years, and to engage the services of a consumer goods final assembly operation in a low-wage area. These two commodity strategies are designed to (in the first case) secure a key component, and (in the second case) ensure that the company drives down the labor content of its products. Once these commodity strategies have been settled, the purchasing staff has a good idea of how to deal with the suppliers located in each commodity area.

The commodity strategy defines the range of alternatives available for managing a supplier. To continue with the rare earth minerals scenario, the main point of supplier management could involve either a long-term supply contract or even buying a stake in a mine that extracts rare earth minerals. In the latter example, supplier management would be more likely to revolve around obtaining the lowest possible price, as well as the use of shorter-term contracts so that the company can shift to a lower-wage area if the initial supplier's costs begin to increase too much. In short, keep the applicable strategy in mind when engaging in supplier relations.

Supplier Relations

In a business that does not have a plan for dealing with suppliers, relations with them may simply consist of the issuance of bid packages and purchase orders, with no attempt to develop a working relationship at all. A more visionary company will understand the need to develop strong ties with the most important suppliers, which involves a great deal of ongoing communication. These ties may include the following:

- *Supplier reviews.* There may be periodic reviews during which the purchasing team goes over its measurements of a supplier's performance. If the results are poor, the intent of these reviews is not to be accusatory, but rather to mutually find ways to improve supplier performance.
- *Process analyses.* Whichever organization has installed best practices in its processes can send its experts to the other entity, to conduct a similar review. The outcome is enhanced profitability, reduced processing time, and/or an error rate reduction for the target of this review, which creates an obligation to help the other party.
- *Project development teams.* The company can invite suppliers to participate in its new product development teams. Suppliers can contribute their expertise to this work, and receive orders for the related components in return.
- *Regular visits.* Take every opportunity to visit suppliers, and vice versa. The intent of these visits is to build relations with each party's key players, as well as to see how a supplier produces the goods used by the company, and how these goods are incorporated into the company's products. These visits can also be used to share plans. For example, a supplier may need to know that the company is planning to enter a new sales region, since this will impact the order rates for goods sold by the supplier.
- *Salesperson relations.* The purchasing staff may request that a supplier send a salesperson to discuss supplier offerings. If so, the salesperson should be treated with a proper level of respect. This means meeting with the person promptly, and working with the salesperson's schedule to find a convenient time to meet. Also, if the staff elects to purchase elsewhere, it should contact the salesperson to explain the reason why his or her employer is not being given the business.

Attending to Supplier Needs

A company does not simply make demands of its suppliers and then judge their subsequent performance. The situation is quite likely to be reversed for the most valuable suppliers. These suppliers can choose which customers to work with, and will only deal with those that conduct themselves in the most professional manner. Attending to supplier needs can include the following activities:

- *Pay all supplier invoices on time.* Rather than merely paying on the invoice due date, this can even involve paying a few days early, so that payments arrive at the supplier on the invoice due date.
- *Do not hold up invoices.* The accounts payable staff may have a habit of holding up payments when there are issues concerning proper authorizations, pricing, or delivered quantities. It can be useful to reinforce with the accounts payable manager that these are internal issues that should not impinge on the cash flow needs of suppliers. In other words, if there is a procedural issue to be investigated, the payables staff should resolve it as expeditiously as possible, without annoying suppliers.

- *Consistently apply ratings.* If a scorecard system has been created (see the next section), apply it consistently to all suppliers. There can be no suspicion among suppliers that the company is unfairly favoring certain suppliers. This can be a particular concern if a few suppliers are owned by the families of the owners or management, so consider imposing a policy that prevents purchasing from such suppliers.

In brief, the best suppliers only work with those companies displaying high levels of integrity, so be sure to structure company operations to fulfill their expectations.

The Supplier Scorecard

When a company enters into a formal relationship with a supplier, it may demand that the supplier agree to a service-level agreement (SLA). An SLA usually states the performance criteria that the company expects of the supplier, such as timely deliveries and specific quality levels. These performance criteria are stated as measurements, which are included in a supplier scorecard.

This scorecard is continually compiled by the company's internal systems, tracking such measurements as a supplier's fulfillment rate, defect rate, billed price variance, and perfect order percentage. These measurements are described at length in the Purchasing Measurements chapter. Other quantitative measurements may also apply, or replace the ones noted here – it all depends on the priorities of the company.

It is also possible that the purchasing staff may apply qualitative scores to suppliers, though these measurements are inherently more difficult to compile, and are subject to widely-ranging outcomes, depending on who is conducting the scoring. Possible qualitative measures are:

- *Cost management support.* Does a supplier proactively point out ways in which the company can reduce its costs? For example, it might point out that less-expensive raw materials could replace the ones being used.
- *General compatibility.* How well do the supplier and the company work together? Is this a generally collegial relationship, or is it more adversarial?
- *Problem resolution support.* How quickly does the supplier act to resolve problems as they arise? Is there finger pointing, or does the supplier simply fix whatever issue is brought up?
- *Product development support.* How well does a supplier assist the company in its efforts to create new products? Do their engineers attend review sessions? Do they offer the use of their latest intellectual property?

The final scorecard version might present a lengthy list of items on which suppliers are being reviewed. A key issue from the supplier's perspective is figuring out which of these ratings are the most important from the perspective of the company. The issue can be resolved by including a weighting for each line item. Those line items assigned a large weighting are more important to the company. In the following sample scorecard, the issuing company has decided that on-time delivery is the most important line item to bring to the attention of suppliers, so that criterion has been assigned the largest weighting. The sample scorecard employs a five-point scoring system.

Sample Weighted Scorecard

Performance	Weighting	Score	Weighted Score
Billed price variance	0.5	3	1.5
Cost management support	1.0	1	1.0
Fulfillment rate	1.2	2	2.4
On-time delivery	2.0	4	8.0
Problem resolution support	1.5	5	7.5
Product development support	0.5	1	0.5
Total			20.9

Supplier scorecards may be posted on a secure company website for suppliers to peruse, or they could be transmitted to supplier representatives at regular intervals by e-mail. In cases where the scorecard results are in serious need of improvement, it may be necessary to have a formal meeting to discuss the findings, and how to improve them. From an internal perspective, unusual scorecard results should be sent to the purchasing staff at once, so that indicated issues can be acted upon immediately.

The scorecard should be considered a two-way street – that is, suppliers also need to be able to comment on the company's treatment of them. In particular, they may have a valid point that the company's actions are causing their performance measurements to look sub-standard. For example, if the company is constantly altering its short-term production schedule, this makes it much more difficult for suppliers to meet their on-time performance targets. In order to hear these comments, it is useful to have in-person meetings, to dig into the underlying reasons for problems.

The scorecard system is not just a feedback loop for suppliers. It can also be used to support more long-term efforts regarding the rationalization of the supply chain. Those suppliers with persistently low scores can be dropped, while those with high scores can be designated as preferred suppliers. The business that had been routed to the low-scoring suppliers can be shifted to the preferred suppliers. The result is a gradual concentration of purchases with only the best suppliers.

Supplier Performance Index

A different way to evaluate suppliers is to base the analysis entirely on cost. Doing so removes any subjectivity from an evaluation. Under this approach, called the supplier performance index (SPI), the cost of the purchases from a supplier is combined with all costs of supplier nonconformance, and then divided by the cost of the purchases. The formula is:

$$\frac{\text{Total purchases cost} + \text{Cost of nonconformance}}{\text{Total purchases cost}}$$

The ideal score is 1.0, which only occurs when there are zero nonconforming incidents. Clearly, the entire point of this index is to focus on the cost of nonconformance, which can include many items, including the following:

- Customer returns traced back to the supplier
- Deliveries outside the required delivery window
- Nonconforming goods
- Subsequent rework costs
- Subsequently scrapped materials

This index can be difficult to implement, because the accounting system does not track costs in accordance with the nonconformance events just described. Quite a major overhaul of the accounting system would be required to come anywhere near the requirements of a nonconformance cost tracking system. Instead, it is much simpler to conduct a one-time cost accounting project to develop a standard cost for each of these nonconforming events, and then assign this cost to each identified event. By doing so, the SPI database can be kept largely separate from the accounting system.

EXAMPLE

The purchasing department of Luminescence Corporation is developing a system to track the supplier performance index of its suppliers. All exception conditions are noted in a database, which automatically creates a cost of nonconformance based on a standard cost per type of event. The system also pulls in the total purchases cost from the purchase orders file maintained by the department. The nonconformance calculation for one of its suppliers is:

Nonconformance Event	Number of Events	Standard Event Cost	Extended Cost of Nonconformance
Customer returns caused by supplier	4	$3,000	$12,000
Deliveries outside delivery window	12	500	6,000
Nonconforming goods	9	425	3,825
Rework	2	175	350
Scrapped materials	--	--	1,700
Total			$23,875

The scrapped materials line item does not show a standard cost, because Luminescence has a separate cost tracking system for scrap. The system nets the cost of scrapped materials against the revenue gained from selling the items for metal scrap. The scrap figure traced to the supplier is included in the table.

During the measurement period, Luminescence purchased $500,000 of goods from the supplier. The resulting SPI is calculated as follows:

$$\frac{\$500,000 \text{ Total purchases cost} + \$23,875 \text{ Cost of nonconformance}}{\$500,000 \text{ Total purchases cost}}$$

$$= 1.048$$

The amount of the index was strongly influenced by the total purchases cost. If the amount purchased had been twice as large, the index would have declined to 1.024. Conversely, if the amount purchased had been half the amount, the index would have increased to 1.096.

Some of the standard event costs noted in the example might appear to be unusually high. This is not the case, for a nonconformance event can have broad (and expensive) ramifications for a business. For example, a late delivery may trigger a production line stoppage or the use of air freight to bring in alternative goods from a different supplier. Even worse, a customer return can trigger the scrapping of the returned product, as well as a damaged relationship with the customer.

> **Tip:** Share with suppliers the standard cost of nonconformance. This gives them a better idea of the costs incurred by the company, and can drive them to further improve their performance.

The SPI is particularly useful when a company is already doing business with several suppliers, and wants to determine which one actually costs the least. It is entirely possible that a comparison of their SPIs will reveal that the supplier charging the lowest cost per unit is actually more expensive than another supplier, because it has shaved its costs so much that it is unable to meet the company's performance criteria, and so continually experiences nonconforming events.

An issue with the SPI is its sole orientation toward cost. As noted in the preceding supplier scorecard section, there are also qualitative factors to consider that may be quite important. To keep the SPI from being too one-dimensional, an option is to attach to an SPI analysis a summary of the qualitative scores that have been assigned to a supplier. The result is a comprehensive view of all aspects of a supplier relationship.

Other Supplier Monitoring Systems

It is possible to rely too much on the supplier scorecard, because both parties tend to concentrate exclusively on improving the information in the scorecard. The trouble is that the scorecard measurements may not address all of the issues that can arise. Scorecard items tend to be comprised of mainstream measurements for the most common issues, such as late deliveries – they do not address less-common issues that may be precursors of major problems. To spot issues that lie further out on the bell curve, it is necessary to rely on less-formal systems. These systems must be able to efficiently present anomalies to the purchasing staff, since they cannot be expected to pore through the information pertaining to thousands of suppliers. Here are several options:

- *Exception reports.* Program the purchasing, receiving, and accounting systems to report on any exception conditions. Examples of exceptions are purchase orders that have not been fulfilled, received goods with unusually large rejections, and instances of supplier overbillings.
- *Audits.* The purchasing manager can ask the internal audit manager to schedule occasional reviews in areas where there appears to be a higher risk of problems. For example, the audit team could examine the usage of procurement cards in different departments, to see if suppliers are asking the card holders to make several smaller payments, rather than submitting an invoice for payment through the company's accounts payable system.
- *Inventory exceptions.* Review the exception transactions related to inventory. For example, there may be an unusual number of scrap items returned to the warehouse, which could indicate sub-standard raw materials. Or, there may be an unusually large number of inventory items being tagged as spoiled, perhaps because they were not fresh when first received.
- *Customer returns.* If customers return an inordinate amount of products, the reason could be that component parts were flawed. When closely examined, returns information can reveal consistent evidence that certain raw materials or components were included in returned goods.
- *Suggestions box.* The management team can be persistent in asking employees if they have made any observations regarding supplier goods or services. This information can involve the use of a formal suggestion box, but any type of communication system that feeds comments back to the purchasing team would be sufficient.

Supply Chain Improvement

Supplier performance needs to improve continuously. Otherwise, the performance of the supply chains of competitors will eventually outstrip those of the company, placing it in a disadvantageous competitive position. This improvement will need to be a cooperative venture, where the key players meet at regular intervals to decide upon which activities should be conducted, who will pay for it, which party is responsible for improvements, and when the changes should be completed.

A reasonable outcome of the improvement process is a decision by management to only work with the best suppliers. This means that the scorecard system mentioned earlier will be employed to determine which suppliers to drop, based on marginal performance. It is also possible that a number of suppliers are performing fine, but the amount of purchases from them is so small that it would be easier to concentrate purchases with a larger supplier.

An issue with supply chain improvement is the manner in which low-performing suppliers are dropped. If the purchasing manager elects to impose a large number of world-class performance criteria on suppliers, it is entirely possible that *none* of them will meet the criteria. A more reasonable (and longer-term) approach is to first win-now out those suppliers that are obviously not performing, and then put the remaining suppliers through a series of performance requirements. For example, the initial focus may be on meeting delivery times, after which an additional performance requirement is a high level of product quality, followed by price reduction goals. After each new performance requirement is imposed, the remaining suppliers are evaluated again. Those suppliers clearly unwilling or unable to meet the company's requirements are dropped, while assistance is given to those suppliers that cannot quite meet the criteria, but which show promise. Meanwhile, any suppliers that are easily passing each hurdle are awarded more business, so that they have an incentive to continue working with the company. This approach results in the continuing examination of suppliers and coaching of those requiring assistance, and ending with a deeply motivated and high-performing group of the best suppliers.

The supply chain improvement process should not simply concentrate on an on-going reduction in the total number of suppliers. Instead, a closer analysis of the situation will likely reveal that there is an optimum number of suppliers in each spend category. Here are several examples of reasons for keeping the supplier base at a somewhat expanded level:

- *Absolute expertise*. A supplier may be quite small, and yet has by far the great-est level of expertise of all suppliers in a particular commodity area. A com-pany would probably retain this supplier to take advantage of its expertise, even though most of the other purchases in this area are directed toward other suppliers.
- *Risk mitigation*. An excellent supplier may be located in an area that presents a geographic or political risk to the company, such as a risk of seasonal flood-ing or of asset expropriation by the government. There may be excellent rea-sons for using this supplier, but the company must mitigate the associated risk profile by retaining a backup supplier.
- *Sub-assembly*. It can make sense to employ a separate supplier positioned be-tween other suppliers and the company, which assembles parts delivered from next-tier suppliers. The intent is to simplify the final assembly process at the company's facility by pushing work back into the supply chain. This approach calls for the use of an extra supplier.

When the number of suppliers has been sufficiently reduced, the company will be left with a small number of highly capable suppliers. A logical next step is to push addi-tional, higher-complexity work onto these suppliers, which may include product de-sign work. This is only done if the suppliers are more capable of taking on these tasks than the company. A useful side effect of this transition is that the suppliers are now earning more revenue from their relations with the company, and so are more closely tied to the company's success.

When there are fewer suppliers, the purchasing manager will find that the admin-istrative cost of dealing with this smaller group is vastly reduced. Previously, the pur-chasing staff would have been overworked with the responsibilities of negotiating with hundreds (or thousands) of suppliers, administering requests for quotes, negotiating contracts, evaluating suppliers, and dealing with nonconforming conditions. When the number of suppliers declines, the amount of associated administrative labor declines at an accelerating rate. The reason is that more purchases will be sole-sourced, thereby eliminating the need for any bidding situations. In addition, the remaining suppliers are of excellent quality, and so will have fewer nonconforming conditions for the purchasing staff to address.

Improving the supply chain does not just involve winnowing down the number of suppliers. In addition, it may be necessary to offer direct operational assistance to suppliers. This assistance can take a number of forms. For example, the company may offer to interlink its computer systems to a supplier, so that the supplier has direct access to the company's supply schedule. Or, the company may have developed expertise in process analysis, and offers to send its engineers to supplier locations to offer free consulting advice.

The types of involvement in supplier affairs can be one-time events that are targeted at specific problems. For example, the receiving department notes that a specific type of flaw continually occurs in a supplier's products, so a team from both entities is formed to jointly investigate and root out the problem. Or, the involvement could be of a more general variety, where engineers are tasked with finding issues or simply improving upon the current situation. These latter investigations can uncover a myriad of issues that can be profitably resolved over the course of a number of more targeted reviews.

An operational investigation may reveal that a supplier does not have the financial ability to hire the extra staff or invest in the fixed assets that are needed to eliminate a problem or improve efficiencies. If so, there are several alternatives available. One is to provide training to a supplier's existing staff and then monitor their progress, so that the supplier's capabilities can be increased without any additional staff investment. The company can also accelerate payments to a supplier, if doing so will give the supplier enough additional cash flow to lease the required equipment. Yet another option is a modest increase in pricing, under the condition that the supplier uses the profits to invest in its operations.

Tip: Set aside a group of industrial engineers that is permanently tasked with supplier support. They rotate through supplier facilities on a continuing basis, with no responsibilities back at the company's location. This approach results in a permanent resource for suppliers to use, and which cannot be diverted by in-house problems.

A company is unlikely to offer a significant amount of operational assistance to its suppliers unless they give something back in return. This could be a promise to share any cost savings resulting from an investigation, perhaps in the form of a price reduction. Another option that is perhaps less intrusive is an understanding that the company will want to bargain harder for price reductions when the next contract negotiations occur – after all, it knows that the supplier is now more profitable than had previously been the case, and so can afford some amount of price reduction.

These improvements can even extend down to the suppliers of the suppliers. However, there may be so many suppliers in this second tier that the company will have to restrict its offers of assistance to just those suppliers whose products comprise a notable proportion of the purchases of its primary suppliers. An alternative approach to dealing with this extra tranche of suppliers is to require a primary supplier to render them assistance, in exchange for the company providing assistance to the primary supplier. This results in a cost reduction trickle-down effect that will eventually result in lower prices for the company.

Supplier Risk Management

A close examination of the supply chain will likely reveal a number of areas in which a company is at risk of having an issue that will impact its operations. For example, the amount of available capacity to produce a certain component is shrinking, or there is a potential for government regulatory control over a supplier that involves child labor, or perhaps there is a risk that the price of a raw material will increase due to a natural disaster. There are a number of ways to mitigate these risks, as discussed in the following bullet points:

- *Shrinking supplier capacity.* There may be cases in which either strong industry demand or a shrinking amount of available supply is making it more difficult to obtain an adequate amount of raw materials. There are several ways to deal with this. One is to arrange with a supplier for an option to take a larger part of its capacity. In essence, the company pays for the right (but not the obligation) to take an increased amount of a supplier's capacity. If the company's internal demand increases to the point where the additional supplier capacity is needed, it exercises the option. If not, the supplier pockets the amount paid for the option, with no further obligation. Another possibility is a longer-term contract, possibly at an above-market price that makes the contract enticing for the participating supplier. Yet another option is to buy a minority position in a supplier, which may give the company a certain amount of control over the supplier's production schedule. The key point is to address a supplier capacity issue in a proactive manner, so that there is no need to pay spot prices at the last minute in order to obtain goods.
- *Poor delivery performance.* A supplier may not have adequate internal systems and processes to ensure that deliveries are always made within designated delivery windows, or with 100% order fulfillment. If so, a reasonable risk management tactic is to conduct an ongoing search for alternative suppliers with better performance levels. These alternate suppliers can be initially brought on as secondary suppliers, while their performance is evaluated. If their performance proves to be superior to the primary supplier, then their status is elevated to be the primary supplier.
- *Supplier dependency.* A company could so thoroughly outsource some of its functions that it comes to be completely dependent on a particular supplier, which introduces the risk of having to accede to aggressive pricing by the supplier. This issue is dealt with in advance by being especially careful about

selecting suppliers that might place the company in this position. If a supplier begins to impose excessive pricing after it has been selected, then the purchasing manager will need to make a judgment call about whether to accept the pricing or conduct a complete switch to an alternative supplier.

- *Poor supplier finances*. When a supplier is having a difficult time making ends meet, there are several possible solutions. One is to deliberately negotiate to pay higher prices, but only in exchange for concessions, such as being given first priority for rush orders, or in exchange for having a certain amount of capacity reserved for the company, or in exchange for not allowing competitors access to the supplier's intellectual property. Another option is to arrange for supply chain financing, where suppliers can receive immediate payment for their outstanding invoices (see the Supply Chain Financing chapter). Yet another option is to award a modest contract to an alternative supplier; this allows for the ongoing evaluation of the alternate, in case the primary supplier fails and needs to be replaced.

- *Scope creep*. The most complex supplier projects are subject to a number of pressures that can cause their completion dates to extend, or for scope changes to arise that require more funding. It is usually not possible to completely avoid scope creep, but it is possible to see it coming. The purchasing staff can incorporate periodic or milestone reviews into these types of contracts, so that the potential issues can be spotted as early as possible. The result could range from a dogged determination to remain within the original scope to a great deal of additional funding – but at least the management team will be forewarned.

- *Natural disasters*. There are a number of natural disasters that can impact the supply chain, including floods, fires, tornados, earthquakes, and hurricanes. For example, a tornado may completely destroy a supplier's production capabilities, which in turn impacts a company's own production schedule. There are several ways to mitigate the effects of natural disasters, though there are likely to still be some negative operational or financial effects. For example, a secondary supplier could be retained to guard against a natural disaster at the primary supplier, with an agreement to reserve a certain amount of capacity for the company's needs in exchange for periodic payments or unusually high unit costs. A variation is to pick suppliers that have multiple locations, so that a disaster at one facility will just trigger an increase in production at a different facility. Another option is to identify those suppliers located in areas that are subject to an unusually high risk of destruction (such as a facility in a flood plain) and switching these suppliers to backup status, with the bulk of order placements going to new primary suppliers. Yet another option is to obtain business interruption insurance, though this does nothing to ameliorate the negative operational effects of a disaster. A final option when the risk of a natural disaster is seasonal is to place orders for excessive quantities of goods prior to the start of the worst season, and use it as buffer stock in case the supply is subsequently interrupted.

- *Political risk*. There are a few countries in which there is a heightened level of political risk. This can include discontent with the central government, the risk of asset expropriation, an unreliable court system, high levels of corruption, high tariffs, lack of attention to intellectual property rights, and so forth. Political risk can be a factor for adjacent territories, if there is a risk of conflict spilling over the border. When significant, these issues could lead to the complete destruction of a key supplier, or an increase in the unreliability of deliveries from it, or simply in a supplier's cost of doing business. The main risk mitigation activity is the decision to shift to a supplier in a different country. This involves the balancing of risk and reward, with particular attention to continually re-evaluating the situation, since political risk can change markedly within a short period of time.

- *Unfavorable exchange rates*. A company may contract with a foreign supplier for the delivery of goods and services, with payment to be made in the currency of the supplier. There is a risk that the applicable currency exchange rate will become unfavorable as the payment date approaches, resulting in the payment of more funds than expected to pay the supplier at the final exchange rate. This issue can be offset by entering into a forward contract to buy the required foreign funds at a predetermined exchange rate on the payment date. There is a cost associated with this forward contract, but the contract eliminates the risk of incurring a loss on an unfavorable swing in an exchange rate. There are several other ways to deal with this situation, as outlined in the author's *Corporate Cash Management* book. Another possibility is to shift to a domestic supplier, which will want to be paid in the company's home currency.

There are any number of additional risks that might arise over time, many of which no one in the company would reasonably expect. However, it may be possible to anticipate them by conducting additional research. For example, consult with those employees in the company who have been involved with the supply chain for a long time. Their "institutional knowledge" might reveal that certain problems have arisen at regular intervals, but not so frequently that they would be readily apparent to someone who had only been working for the company for a couple of years. Another similar option is to consult with an expert on a supplier's industry or on the geographic region within which a supplier is located, to talk about issues that have arisen in the past or which might be expected to occur in the future.

Once a set of risk scenarios have been developed, the purchasing team and any experts it chooses to bring in should evaluate the probability of occurrence for these scenarios. It is probably not possible to derive a percentage probability, but the team could assign general rankings, such as very high, high, moderate, low, and very low. These rankings can then be combined with an estimate of monetary loss if an event actually occurs. The result will direct the team toward risk management activities for those risks having a reasonable probability of causing a notable negative financial event.

A further consideration is the cost of any proposed risk mitigation activities. If the cost of risk mitigation is excessive in comparison to the associated risk reduction, it may make more sense to accept the underlying risk.

EXAMPLE

The Gecko Island Resort is located on a small island in the Great Barrier Reef, a one hour flight from Cairns on the mainland of Australia. The resort depends on a supplier to fly in a large load of food once every three days. There have been a few instances in which a passing cyclone has interrupted these flights. The resort's purchasing manager is examining supply chain risks, and notes that the best mitigation of this risk would be a combination of a large industrial-grade freezer and an emergency power generator to keep any stored food properly refrigerated if a cyclone knocks out the island's power grid. The cost of this mitigation plan is $150,000, which the resort's owners consider to be too high. Instead, they elect to accept the risk of delayed flights.

Another feature of a system of risk management is to understand the events that can give management advance warning that a problem is about to arise. For example, subscribing to a credit reporting service will result in a company being warned by e-mail when the credit rating of a supplier has been downgraded. Or, a staff person can review the 10-day weather forecasts in an area where it has suppliers, and which is subject to hurricanes. Yet another option is to set up an automated report in the company's computer system that issues a notification when a supplier delivery is late; this elevates the level of watchfulness over that supplier, to see if there is an ongoing series of delivery failures that might be indicative of more serious problems. Watching over these advance indicators of problems can give the purchasing staff a jump on issues that will allow for proactive risk mitigation.

EXAMPLE

Hodgson Industrial Design purchases a key part from a supplier located next to the Mississippi River. Hodgson's purchasing staff has noted that the supplier is located in a flood plain, and that there have been three flooding incidents in the past 50 years. A staff person is assigned to monitor water levels on the Mississippi during the spring months, and notes that heavy rainfall is forecast 500 miles to the north of the supplier's location. Hodgson's purchasing manager contacts the president of the supplier to warn of the situation. In addition, the purchasing manager reviews the delivery schedule and notes that the supplier is scheduled to ship a large number of units to Hodgson in five days. The manager asks to have the order shipped early from the supplier's finished goods stock, and offers to pay a modest early delivery bonus to expedite the delivery, along with an additional order that will cover Hodgson's needs for the next three months.

A final note regarding supplier risk management is that the risk profile of the supply chain is always changing. New suppliers with different risk issues will be added, while product lines involving other supplier risks will be dropped. Political risks will change, as will the impact of climate change on different types of weather-related events. Because of this constant state of flux, the purchasing team should periodically re-evaluate the risk profile of the supply chain, and alter its risk mitigation activities accordingly.

EXAMPLE

The Florida Parka Company, which (strangely enough) produces a wildly popular parka for extremely cold conditions, is concerned about threats it has been receiving from animal rights activists regarding its use of coyote fur to line the hoods of its parkas. The activists have been threatening to firebomb the company's main production facility in Orlando. The management team believes that the coyote fur is a key attraction for the buyers of its parkas, and so will not consider replacing it with a less objectionable material.

The purchasing manager is tasked with finding a risk mitigation strategy to deal with the situation. She arrives at multiple solutions. One is to product test a synthetic fur with customers, to see if it will really cause a reduction in sales. Another option is to move the production facility to a region of Idaho where there is a coyote infestation, and the facility is more likely to receive support from the locals. Yet another possibility is to begin discussions with a less-radical group of animal rights activists, to see if an alternative solution can be found that is agreeable to all parties.

The On-Site Supplier Representative

In a few cases, it can make sense for a larger company to encourage selected suppliers to have a permanent representative on the premises. This individual can provide assistance in managing the materials or services being sold by the supplier to the company. The person can also provide technical support. This service is especially useful to the company when it is critical to maintain adequate inventory levels for certain raw materials and equipment spare parts at all times, as well as when the goods and services being offered are of a highly technical nature, such as computer equipment.

A supplier representative can ensure that orders are correctly placed by the company by inserting himself into the process of creating a purchase order, entering it into the supplier's order entry system, and monitoring its progress through the supplier's processes. The representative can also work with the company's inventory planning staff, to ensure that goods are ordered sufficiently far in advance to be produced and shipped by the supplier with enough time for them to be delivered when needed. Another function is for the representative to work with the company's design staff, to provide advice on how the supplier's products can be integrated into the company's products. In short, this person can be quite beneficial for the company.

Though an on-site representative might at first appear to be an inordinate expense for the supplier, this is not necessarily the case. An on-site representative can be a cost-effective choice, since this individual can act as an on-site sales representative, and so can replace the salesperson who would normally visit the company. Also, the use of a representative implies a high level of integration between the supplier and the company, which makes it unlikely that a competitor will ever take sales away from the supplier. Further, the supplier obtains the earliest possible knowledge of new company products, and so has the best insights into how to develop a winning bid for this business.

The Maverick Supplier

We note elsewhere in this book that maverick spending (which is purchasing from unauthorized suppliers) tends to result in excessively high prices being paid, and so should be avoided. The trouble is that maverick spenders may be engaging in this behavior because they are being actively pursued by suppliers (which we will call maverick suppliers). These maverick suppliers have decided not to work through the purchasing department, and instead have elected to directly contact and sell to end users.

This situation is quite common. For example, a purveyor of production equipment will contact the industrial engineering manager, while a seller of cloud storage will contact the IT manager, and consulting firms will talk directly to the company president. Supplier salespeople are trained to locate decision makers within a business, and to persuade them to buy the supplier's products. By getting preferential treatment from one of these individuals, a supplier can sell at higher prices, and may not have to submit a competitive bid at all.

The solution to maverick suppliers does not include prohibiting them from pursuing their sales targets within a company. In some cases, these suppliers can provide a real service by imparting information about their products and the problems that can be corrected by using those products. Instead, the purchasing department should educate the rest of the company regarding the point in the selling process when a buyer contemplating a purchase needs to hand off the situation to the purchasing staff, and let them follow through. This point is usually when the decision to buy has been made, and there is funding available to do so. If the goods or services provided by a supplier are considered unique, then the purchasing staff can conduct price negotiations with the indicated supplier. If the supplier forcing the issue is not considered unique, then the department can become involved in a more detailed assessment of the situation, possibly resulting in competitive bidding.

In short, maverick suppliers should not necessarily be considered a hindrance to the purchasing department, but rather entities that are actively providing information to the company, and which could eventually result in a purchase – just not necessarily from these suppliers.

Summary

The importance of having a system of supplier management in place cannot be overstated. If the purchasing department inadvertently ignores or mistreats its suppliers, they may respond in kind when the company really needs them to perform. To ensure that the proper level of relations is maintained, it can make sense to formally review the entire scope of supplier relations at regular intervals, as well as to have a third party polling firm conduct an anonymous survey of all suppliers. The purchasing manager can use the results of these surveys to enhance supplier relations as needed.

A key aspect of supplier management is only using the optimum number of suppliers, which is likely to be far fewer than the number currently used. Eliminating a large number of suppliers results in a core group that performs well, and which requires no excess administrative time by the purchasing department. A likely outcome will be that the purchasing staff will have far more time available for value-added activities.

Chapter 6
Competitive Bidding

Introduction

One way in which the purchasing department can achieve low pricing and favorable terms is through the use of competitive bidding. This is the process of contacting multiple suppliers to request them to bid on prospective work, which can range from raw materials for a company's production process to the development of custom software.

In this chapter, we note the circumstances under which competitive bidding should be used, how to construct a bid package and manage the bidding process, and several related topics.

When to Use Competitive Bidding

A great deal of time is required to prepare for, manage, and complete a competitive bid, which limits its use. There are specific circumstances in which initiating such a process makes sense. The following bullet points note the optimum conditions in which to use this approach:

- *There are multiple qualified suppliers.* There are many suppliers that could provide the necessary goods and services, and which are likely to bid.
- *There are clear specifications.* If the purchasing department can develop a clearly-defined set of specifications for what is needed, suppliers will be able to develop well-founded responses and prices.
- *The size of the prospective contract is attractive.* Responding to bid packages is time-consuming and the risk of losing out to a competitor is high, so suppliers will only be attracted to a bidding situation if a large amount of revenue can be gained.
- *There are likely to be offsetting savings.* The bidding process is time-consuming for the purchasing staff, so it should only be used where there is a reasonable prospect that offsetting cost reductions can be achieved.
- *There is enough time to conduct the bidding process.* This is not a quick endeavor, requiring multiple weeks (if not months) to complete. Consequently, a prospective purchase that needs to be completed quickly is not a good candidate for bidding.

Ideally, *all* of the preceding conditions should be present before deciding to initiate competitive bidding.

Types of Bidding Requests

There are several variations on the general concept of putting a prospective purchase out to bid. These variations are based on the amount of information available. A *request for quotation* (RFQ) is issued when there is a complete set of specifications available for what is to be purchased. A *request for proposal* (RFP) is issued when the specifications are vague, or when there are several ways in which the company's needs can be fulfilled. Consulting or design work is usually solicited with an RFP. A *request for information* (RFI) is exactly what the name implies – the buyer is collecting information from suppliers. Once the informational responses to an RFI have been received, a company may elect to then issue an RFQ or RFP. Thus, an RFI is only a transitional document that may or may not lead to a bidding situation. To reduce confusion in the following sections, we will simply refer to the documents issued as the *bid package*, which could be either an RFQ or an RFP.

Third-Party Assistance

A company may need to put a prospective purchase out to bid, but has little in-house expertise to construct the bid documents. This can be an issue, since the more experienced suppliers are used to receiving bid packages that are professional and complete. If they receive an inadequate bid package, they may not respond at all.

One possible source of the requisite expertise is a supplier of whatever is to be put out to bid. A supplier has a deep knowledge of the targeted goods or services, and has likely also responded to a large number of bidding packages in the past, and so has an excellent idea of the requirements that a company needs to insert into the bid documents. This can be a great benefit for the company, since it ensures that comprehensive bid documents will be released. However, the downside risk is that the supplier will deliberately skew the bid requirements to favor its own goods and services. For example:

- A large supplier inserts into the bid package a requirement for a surety bond, for which smaller suppliers may not be able to qualify.
- A software developer inserts a requirement that the software must work with a certain operating system, which happens to be the one which works with the supplier's software.
- A national field service supplier inserts a 24 × 7 response period into the bid package, which is a requirement that only the largest competing suppliers can match.

When working with a supplier to develop a bid package, review the requirements to see if there are any of these roadblocks that will automatically eliminate potential suppliers from contention, and consider whether they are really necessary. In some cases, the contributing supplier has made a valid point regarding their inclusion, but it is possible that some can be eliminated.

It is extremely common for those suppliers offering assistance in bid package preparation to be among the finalists chosen by a company. This is still acceptable, as long as a reasonable evaluation and selection process is used to pick the eventual winner.

A more impartial assistant can be found when a company hires a consultant to assist with the bid package development process. These consultants should have in-depth experience in the subject area, including access to a complete bid package that they can modify to meet the company's requirements. Consultants are expensive, but they are a good choice when the goods and services being acquired are high-cost or of critical importance to the company.

Contents of a Bid Package

The purchasing department should insist on including as comprehensive a set of information as possible in a bid package. By doing so, there will be fewer inquiries from suppliers regarding clarifications (for which the answers are then distributed to all interested suppliers). To ensure that a bid package is complete, it can be worthwhile to hire a consultant to review the preliminary documents and suggest additions or alterations.

A bid package should contain a number of distinct sections, all of which are needed by suppliers to prepare a bid or by the company to control the bidding process. These sections include:

- *The organization.* This is a brief description of the company, which can be used by bidders to gain a better understanding of the entity's operating environment and its general size. Numerical information provided may include the company's sales, headcount, types of products, number of customers, and number of years that it has been in business.
- *Background.* This section states the reason(s) why the company is issuing the bid package, perhaps stating a specific problem that management wants to eliminate. The current situation may also be described.
- *Key dates.* This section states the dates on which there will be a bidder's conference (if any), the dates by which any inquiries must be received, and the date and time by which all responses must be received by the company.
- *Technical specifications/requirements.* This is a detailed listing of the physical characteristics of the goods to be provided, such as their dimensions, physical properties, durability, and so forth.
- *Statement of work.* If services are to be provided, then there is a complete statement of work, noting the type of service to be provided and its frequency. This should include a detailed listing of all required deliverables.
- *Supplemental requirements.* This section states any additional informational requirements to be provided by suppliers, such as the size of the supplier, the number of years it has been in business, references, and contact information. There may also be a requirement to post a surety bond if the supplier is awarded a contract.

- *Standard terms and conditions.* The usual terms and conditions that the company is accustomed to include in its contracts are noted. These terms may be negotiable when the contract between the parties is being written.
- *Qualifications.* If services are to be performed, this section mandates that the supplier provide the resumes of the assigned project team, what they have worked on in the past, and the detailed budget for their hours, with hourly billing rates.
- *Subcontractors.* If services are to be performed, this section states the company's position regarding the use of subcontractors. The company may reserve the right to reject certain subcontractors.
- *Evaluation.* It can be useful to list within the document the criteria and weighting factors that will be used to determine the winning bid. This is useful for self-selection, since some suppliers will realize that their own limitations will not allow them to succeed under the stated criteria, so they will not waste time submitting a bid.

The items presented here are among the more common elements of a bid package, but these documents can go on at much greater length. If so, a likely outcome is massively detailed supplier bid responses. If the team assigned to review supplier responses does not have a great deal of review time available, it should cut back on the level of detail it is requiring in its bid package, so that the responses will be correspondingly smaller.

It is much easier for both the company and bidders if the requirements are stated in a grid format, with a yes/no box next to each requirement line item. Then require bidders to work through the document, marking the applicable box if they can or cannot meet the indicated requirement. It can also be useful to include a notations box next to these answers, so that suppliers can clarify their responses. This yes/no format can be extended to the standard terms and conditions part of the document, to see if bidders have any issues with certain items.

Locating Suppliers

As noted in the When to Use Competitive Bidding section, one of the criteria for bidding is when the size of the contract is large enough to attract suppliers. Given the large amount of money to be awarded under a bid contract, the purchasing department must be particularly careful in vetting the suppliers who will receive a bid package.

One option is to drop from consideration all suppliers who have been awarded work by the company in the past, and received failing-to-average scores for their work. These scores may be based on late project completion dates, cost overruns, poor work quality, and so forth. Whatever the reason may be, it is useful to have a process in place for recording the outcomes of completed projects, along with their associated scores, and referring back to it when compiling a list of prospective suppliers for a new contract.

A reverse outcome from having such a database is that one can extract from it those suppliers having previously received outstanding scores. This information can be used to limit the distribution of bid packages to just those suppliers whose prior scores classify them as top-notch suppliers. An expansion of the concept of using these better suppliers for bidding purposes is several rating classifications in the database, which are as follows:

- *Qualified suppliers.* These are suppliers that meet the company's minimum threshold criteria to be considered as suppliers, but which have not yet been qualified at a higher level. These suppliers can be contacted regarding lower-level bid packages that do not involve tight specifications, narrow delivery windows, or other more advanced performance criteria.
- *Certified suppliers.* These are suppliers whose processes and methods have been examined and certified by the company's quality assurance personnel. Any deliveries from these suppliers can bypass the company's normal receiving and inspection processes, and move directly to the production or warehousing areas. This classification of supplier would receive bids related to raw materials and merchandise.
- *Preferred suppliers.* These are suppliers that have proven over time to have superior characteristics, including high-quality products, excellent support, and near-perfect delivery performance. All preferred suppliers are already classified as certified suppliers. There may be a purchasing policy to direct as much business toward these suppliers as possible.

If there is to be a ratings database for suppliers, consider populating the database with additional information, such as supplier office locations, last known billing rates, contact information, and other comments. These additional data elements can prove useful if employees want to search through the database for suppliers and learn more about them.

Tip: If a ratings database is used, expand it to all parts of the company, including other subsidiaries. By doing so, a supplier that has been identified as inadequate will be classified as such for anyone reviewing the database, anywhere in the company. This prevents a poor performer from working for the company again.

The Bidding Process Flow

Once a bid package has been created, the purchasing department manages a tightly-choreographed bidding process. This process is intended to conclude the bidding process within a reasonable period of time, while also treating all participants in a fair and equitable manner. The process flow may include the following steps:

1. *Pre-bid conference.* A notice is issued to all suppliers likely to be interested, stating a time and place at which a pre-bid conference will be held. This meeting is used to go over the specifications and bidding requirements, as well as to discuss any other issues with the members of the company's bidding team. Attendance may be mandatory – if so, this conference acts as an automatic gate for reducing the number of participating suppliers. A pre-bid conference

is time-consuming for all parties, and so is generally avoided unless the requirements of a bid package are unusually complex.

2. *Bid package issuance.* The bid package is issued to all suppliers that have indicated an interest in receiving the documentation.

3. *Response receipts.* Those suppliers choosing to participate submit their proposals to the purchasing department. Their responses are logged in, so there is an official record of receipt.

4. *Bid opening.* No further bids are allowed after the predetermined bid closing date has passed. Shortly thereafter, all bids are opened, and their key contents are transferred to a summary sheet.

5. *Bid evaluation.* The detailed information from each bid is transferred into a summary comparison sheet, where the answers provided by suppliers are scored and multiplied by a weighting factor for each answer or aggregation of answers given. Based on the weighted results, a winning bidder is chosen.

6. *Contract creation.* The winning bidder is contacted, and the parties mutually craft a contract that is based on the terms stated in the successful bid.

There are many consulting firms that provide companies with bid construction and evaluation services. They have templates of possible requirements, which are then refined during meetings with company employees. The consultants can develop a complete RFQ or RFP package, and provide additional support during the bid evaluation process, including compiling scores for all successful bids. Their job is not to select a supplier for a company, but rather to facilitate the process.

Handling Inquiries

Even the best bid package will include phrases that are unclear, have terms that are not defined, or do not address certain topics at a sufficient level of detail. This means that suppliers actively interested in responding to the package will likely make inquiries on certain points. When the purchasing department receives one of these inquiries, it records the date and nature of the inquiry, as well as the response made to the supplier. The person managing the bid package can then choose to either issue a copy of this correspondence to all of the suppliers whenever such an inquiry is made, or let them pile up for a short time and then issue a consolidated notice. It is important to ensure that all parties receive the responses to all inquiries made – otherwise, those suppliers that have obtained points of clarification can use these clarifications to their advantage in preparing their bids.

Handling Complaints

From time to time, a supplier may protest the outcome of a bidding situation. Perhaps the supplier feels that certain aspects of its proposal were not fully considered, or perhaps there is a suspicion that the outcome was skewed. Whatever the reason for the complaint, the purchasing department should have a procedure in place for dealing with it in a standardized manner. This usually encompasses the following steps:

1. *Provide a written complaint.* Have the supplier write down its complaint, stating the nature of the issue, and attaching any relevant supporting documentation. This is an improvement over a verbal complaint, where the nature of the issue may be subject to interpretation.
2. *Formal log-in.* Each complaint is logged in, so there is a record of receipt. Otherwise, there is a risk of a complaint being "lost" within the organization and not being dealt with.
3. *Review by separate committee.* A group of senior staff and managers meets periodically to review all supplier complaints. This group should not include anyone directly involved with the bid package under review, to keep from skewing the results of the group's findings. This committee is empowered to conduct its own investigation and issue rulings.
4. *Issue response.* Any supplier that has taken the trouble to formally protest an award should certainly be given the dignity of a response. Consequently, the review committee should write a response to the supplier, stating its reasons for or against the original award.

If an award has been made by a government entity, suppliers routinely file complaints regarding contract awards. These complaints are much less frequent when an award has been issued by a company – perhaps because suppliers are aware that a frequent complainer will not be included in future bidding processes. In the latter case, an aggrieved supplier will probably just stop submitting bids if it does not believe it is being dealt with fairly.

Reverse Auctions

When the focus of a purchase is primarily on price, it may be possible to set up a reverse auction with a pre-qualified group of suppliers. This is an on-line bidding situation in which suppliers can repeatedly bid their prices lower on a predefined set of criteria in order to obtain the lowest bid. The identities of the participating suppliers are kept confidential. Because of the nature of the process, it can result in substantial price reductions for the buyer.

Depending on the type of reverse auction system used, the following information will be available to all bidders:

- Actual bid prices that have been submitted; or
- The relative rankings of the bidders, based on their prices submitted

Bids will continue until no one is willing to bid any lower, or until a predetermined expiration time is reached.

Reverse auctions are usually confined to situations in which the items needed are fully commoditized, with no differentiating features by supplier, and with industry-standard specifications.

A reasonable concern posed by suppliers is that reverse auctions excessively focus on price. When a supplier prefers to compete on other factors than price (such as fast order turnaround), it is at a disadvantage in a reverse auction. Also, the use of reverse auctions sends the message that there will be no attempt by a company to build relations with a specific supplier – it just wants the best price.

Unethical Supplier Bidding Practices

There are several ways in which a supplier can improve its odds of submitting a winning bid, while still assuring itself of a reasonable profit over the course of a contract. These methods include the following:

- *Avoid up-front fees.* A canny bidder will not include up-front charges associated with molds or tooling in a bid for large numbers of units. Instead, the supplier depends on subsequent inflationary price increases to absorb these charges. This bidding format makes the initial price of the bidder appear to be quite low, and relies on negotiating pressure to trigger excessive inflationary boosts in later periods.
- *Change orders.* A common ploy is to bid low in order to gain the initial contract, and then use every possible stratagem to bill the company for change orders. Change orders are typically priced to contain above-average profits, so the supplier earns an overall profit that is quite respectable.

While these methods can result in excess profits for a supplier, a canny financial analyst who conducts a post-contract review will probably spot them. If the purchasing department uses a supplier database, then the analyst can enter his findings in the database, along with a negative score for deceptive practices. This will effectively end the supplier's future involvement with the company, since the database scoring system will prevent the supplier from being contacted about any future bids.

Summary

A great deal of work is involved in developing a bid package, distributing it, managing supplier responses, and deciding which supplier wins. Depending on the type of response required, the amount of work by suppliers to respond to a bid package can be even greater. Consequently, competitive bidding is not a purchasing activity that should be followed for very many purchasing situations; it is just not cost-effective. Instead, it is usually better to sole source most purchases through a small number of preferred suppliers that the company can rely on to provide a combination of reasonable pricing and service.

Chapter 7
Supplier Negotiations

Introduction

Negotiation is the process of having two parties formally discuss their differences, with the objective of forming a mutually-beneficial agreement. Each party has something that the other party needs, and so is willing to compromise or give concessions on certain points in order to satisfy its own needs.

No one is born with a complete set of negotiation skills. Instead, they must acquire these skills through reading, observation, and direct experience. In this chapter, we provide a summary of the reading part of that skills acquisition process, noting negotiation tactics, topics, and related considerations.

The Need for Negotiations

Negotiations are time-consuming, and so should be reserved for situations where they are really necessary. Many day-to-day purchasing activities require no contract negotiations at all. For example, terms may be adequately settled through a competitive bidding situation, or when goods and services are readily available in competitive markets.

There are a number of situations in which goods and services are not readily available in a competitive market, or where certain terms and conditions are likely to be an issue for one or both parties. Examples of purchasing situations that may call for negotiations are:

- *Blanket purchase orders*. A company may want to issue a blanket purchase order, which is a general authorization under which a number of purchase orders are issued. It may be necessary to negotiate the terms in a blanket order in some detail, especially when it covers a large amount of funding. There may need to be clarification about the purchasing levels at which volume discounts will take effect, and any penalties if the company does not reach the promised purchase amount.
- *Capacity commitments*. There may be situations in which a company wants to purchase a supplier's capacity, rather than its products. This calls for discussion regarding the amount of capacity to be reserved, the amount of notice that the company must give to the supplier, the supplier's ability to service other customers in the meantime, and the notification process that the company must use to take the reserved capacity.
- *Complexity*. The company has complex component requirements, and especially when these requirements are completely new – there is no experience

with already having procured them. In this situation, the supplier is likely to demand some sort of cost-reimbursement contract.

- *Expanded roll.* There may be a long-standing relationship between a company and a supplier, but the company now wants to expand the supplier's role to take on more complex work (such as producing subassemblies). If so, negotiations are needed to discuss those aspects of the evolving relationship that the parties have not addressed in the past.
- *Long time line.* In some cases, the amount of time required by a supplier to produce requested goods is quite long, perhaps well over a year. If so, the supplier may have difficulty estimating its costs that far in the future, and will want to discuss cost-sharing or cost-reimbursement alternatives that will mitigate its risk.
- *Joint development.* The cost to develop a product may be so large that the parties need to discuss sharing the cost of development. If so, the negotiations can encompass the amounts of payments to be made by both parties, sharing of the resulting intellectual capital, ownership and control interests, and how either party can back out of the arrangement.
- *Payment terms.* Either party may demand special payment terms. Depending on the financial resources of the organizations, this can constitute a serious issue. For example, a larger retailer with a great deal of purchasing volume could demand payment terms of several months (or more), which could cripple a small supplier.
- *Penalties and incentives.* Either party may want to attach penalties and incentives to a contract. If so, this calls for a detailed discussion of the amounts of the penalties and incentives, how each one is triggered, how they are measured, and when the parties are paid.
- *Performance criteria.* When the company is demanding that a supplier meet a number of performance criteria, the supplier will probably demand a face-to-face negotiation. This is needed, so that that the supplier can gain a better understanding of the various criteria.
- *Progress payments.* When custom goods are being manufactured or there is a long-term consulting arrangement, both parties will have great interest in the terms related to progress payments. The supplier will want frequent payments to compensate it for to-date expenditures, while the company will want to withhold some portion of these payments against the proper completion of the work.
- *Special shipping requirements.* The company may want to use a less-common shipping arrangement, such as having a supplier drop ship goods directly to the company's customers, or dropping off small deliveries at the company's locations several times per day. A supplier may find that its existing process flow will not accommodate these requirements, so the parties need to discuss the specifics of how the special shipping will function.
- *Vagueness.* The required specifications are so vague that there is no way for a supplier to develop a price. In this situation, it is likely that the two parties

will have to go through several iterations of the proposed product design before there is even agreement on the final specifications.

When more than one of these purchasing situations arises for a single contract, it is even more necessary for the parties to engage in negotiations.

The Negotiation Team

The size of the negotiation team could range from just a few members to a much larger group, depending on the amount of funding at stake or other factors, such as the importance to the company of the technology that a supplier has. At a minimum, there will be a senior member of the purchasing department, who is usually expected to both lead the group and the negotiations. There will also be a technical expert, who fully understands the technical specifications that the company needs to acquire, and who can address any technical issues that come up during the negotiations. There should also be a user; an individual whose department will be the direct beneficiary of the goods or services being purchased. This person should be aware of the required service levels and have a priority list for which aspects of a purchase are the most important. A financial analyst may also be needed. This person investigates the financial ramifications of each offer and counteroffer, and reports his findings back to the negotiation team. There may also be a junior member of the purchasing department present, who acts as an observer or scribe. The intent behind having this person is to give someone experience in negotiations, with the objective of having her later lead her own team. In addition, having someone write down the details of the negotiations results in a record regarding the flow of the negotiations and positions held that can be useful when the company eventually conducts another contract negotiation with the same supplier.

Initial Positions

Prior to the start of negotiations, the person responsible for negotiations must determine her least acceptable position. This is the worst case scenario that is still acceptable to the company. Any offer from a supplier that is worse than this "bottom line" scenario will force the company to walk away and go with an alternative (usually a different supplier). It may require a fair amount of research to determine the least acceptable position. If there is an alternative to dealing with the supplier in question, then the advantages and costs of using that alternative must be fully quantified and then compared to the bottom line scenario, to ensure that this least acceptable position is correct.

Once the least acceptable position has been established, it must never be revealed to the other party. If this information were imparted, the other party would simply set that position as its negotiating objective, and drive the company back to that point.

Another preparatory issue is to itemize, in ranked order, all of the company's needs. At the top of the list will be the core items that the company must obtain from the negotiations. Further down the list will be a number of less critical items that could be given away as concessions. It is entirely possible that only one or two items are actually necessary, and that the negotiation team makes up a number of additional items that are *all* intended to be concessions. As the negotiations progress, it is useful for a negotiator to refer back to this list, to ensure that the key points are either settled or within reach; if not, then the negotiations have gone beyond the least acceptable position, and it is time to terminate the negotiations.

When the parties state their initial positions at the start of negotiations, these points are likely to be well away from their least acceptable positions. Instead, initial positions are quite optimistic, and are intended to leave a large amount of negotiating room. In some countries, the standard negotiating pattern is to set an initial position that is absurdly far away from the likely outcome, which then requires lengthy negotiations to bring back to a reasonable median point.

To move from the initially stated positions to a point that is reasonable for both parties can require a great deal of probing of the parties' positions by their counterparts. The underlying interests of each party in the negotiations will drive their negotiating positions, so it is the job of each negotiator and her team to understand the other party as fully as possible. For example:

- Does the company need a supplier's intellectual property, which is tied up in a key patent? If so, the supplier can likely negotiate for a high price.
- Is the company actually indifferent to which supplier gets a contract (common for a bulk commodity)? If so, the company can easily walk away and buy elsewhere with little difficulty.
- There is a rumor that a supplier has just lost a major customer. If so, it needs to replace the revenue quickly or it will face massive losses. This means the supplier could be more willing to negotiate on price in order to close a deal.

Understanding the other party fully means that it is more important to understand its interests, rather than focusing too much on its opening or subsequent bargaining positions. With a better grasp of the other party's interests, the negotiator can then develop proposals that take account of the interests of both sides, making it easier to reach an agreement.

Negotiation Tactics

The key to using negotiation tactics is to research the other party and its likely needs well in advance. With this information, the purchasing staff can develop a list of what it wants, what the supplier wants, and the likely negotiation strategies that the supplier will employ. The negotiation team can then select from a basket of possible negotiation tactics to achieve its own objectives. These tactics include:

- *Concessions.* As part of the planning for a negotiation, each party comes up with some throwaway demands that it does not really need. As the negotiations progress, these demands can be used to counterbalance the requirements of the other party – which may be more substantial. Thus, a concession is made in exchange for a concession by the other party. The usual pattern for granting concessions is to start with minor concessions and gradually build up to more significant concessions later in the negotiations.

- *Last-minute changes.* Just before the terms of a contract are declared settled, one party or the other may throw in one last change. The timing is intended to have the other party as invested in the negotiations as possible, so that it is more likely to accept the late change.

- *Signaling.* The negotiation team may decide to use signaling to show its intentions to the other party. For example, setting an initially reasonable position and following it up with one or more major concessions signals to the other party that a deal is quite likely. Conversely, setting an aggressive position and then agreeing to minor concessions at a niggardly rate sends several signals – lack of interest, prolonged negotiations, or perhaps an outcome that will not favor the other party.

- *Trial balloons.* A possible alternative could be presented to the other negotiation team to see if the concept is acceptable to them. If so, the concept can be expanded upon further. If not, there is no damage to the presenter. The use of trial balloons can provide information regarding the interests of the other party.

- *The hold back.* If one party lays out all of its desires at the beginning of negotiations, the other party may elect to hold back on settling one of the key items on the list until late in the negotiations. The intent is to "hold a club" over the other party until the last minute, collecting more concessions than might otherwise have been forthcoming.

- *Wait.* If the other party is in a hurry to finalize a contract, an option is to stall the negotiations for a few days. By doing so, the supplier may make a concession in exchange for accelerating the closing process. In most cases, a delay of a few days or weeks is not a significant issue for a company, if the outcome is a significant concession.

- *Best and final offer.* A negotiator can present what is presented as a final offer on a particular negotiating point. This "line in the sand" approach sends a signal that no further counter-proposals are expected or will be considered. However, this tactic can cause problems if the stated position is still too far away from the other party's minimum acceptable position, or if the negotiator subsequently modifies the offer.

- *Periodic progress summarizations.* During a lengthy negotiation, it may sometimes appear that there has been little progress for a long period of time, which can be discouraging. If so, consider summarizing the progress that has been made to date, and presenting it to both sides in the negotiation. This can be useful for clarifying that there has indeed been movement from both parties toward reaching an agreement.

Negotiation Sessions

When two parties engage in negotiations, these meetings tend to follow a standard pattern, which is as follows:

1. *Information sharing.* Each party presents its current position, after which both parties ask questions to ascertain what they can about the reasons for those positions, as well as to clarify the current position.
2. *Break.* The parties break to discuss with their support staffs the current situation, incorporate any new findings into their positions, assess their relative strengths in comparison to those of the other party, and formulate what to include in the next meeting. It is also possible that members of each negotiating team will meet informally during the break period to explore alternative positions, which are relayed back to the chief negotiators.
3. *Concessions.* Based on the discussions during the break period, altered positions are presented by both parties, which may involve concessions of various kinds.
4. *Conclusion.* Eventually, following what may be a number of meeting iterations, all issues are agreed to, and the parties write a contract (which may require further dickering as the attorneys for both sides agree upon contract language).

If a point is reached at any of these stages where there is no longer any willingness by either party to budge from its current position, it may be better to arrange for another meeting at a later date. Doing so allows the negotiators and their principals to decide whether there are additional concessions to explore, or whether it is not worthwhile to reach a settlement at this time.

Negotiator Characteristics

The most successful negotiators have characteristics that center on flexibility – they are willing to explore options and adjust their targets to achieve a successful outcome, while ensuring that the least acceptable position is still achieved. Characteristics to look for include the following:

- *Alternatives.* The best negotiator is willing to explore every possible alternative to resolve an issue. For example, if a supplier wants shorter payment terms, the company's negotiator could propose the use of supply chain financing to allow the supplier to receive payment sooner (see the Supply Chain Financing chapter). A more narrow-minded negotiator is more likely to plod through a predetermined number of options and then grind to a halt.
- *Buy-in.* The best negotiator is one who spends time in advance to discuss her proposed positions with management, to ensure that they are in agreement regarding minimum acceptable positions and the concessions to be made. The reverse approach is to spring the results of a completed contract negotiation on management, and risk an adverse reaction.

90

- *Compromise.* The successful negotiator can time the correct point in a nego-tiation process to offer an adjusted position, which may lead to a correspond-ing adjustment by the other party. A less experienced or more recalcitrant negotiator will wait too long or offer too small a concession, leading to frus-tration by the other party and possibly the abandonment of the talks.
- *Independent topics.* The more effective negotiators will discuss and negotiate on any topic that their counterparts want to bring up. Both parties have likely presented a number of issues that they want to address, so any topic within that package is acceptable for discussion. By doing so, some parts of a nego-tiation may be successfully concluded, and other parts may not. A more rigid negotiator will attempt to have a complete package of requirements com-pleted, or not at all; this tends to result in a higher failure rate, since some of the company's needs may be anathema to the other party.
- *Interests focus.* A perceptive negotiator will focus primarily on the core inter-ests of the other party, rather than its current negotiating position. The current position may be completely outrageous, and so tends to frustrate or annoy a lesser negotiator.
- *Polish.* A good negotiator has well-polished skills. She never makes dispar-aging comments about the other party, presents an urbane image at all times, dresses appropriately, and appreciates the niceties of cultural differences. This behavior can make a great impression on the other party, especially in situa-tions where the entities are contemplating a long-term partnership, where the impression given is that the entire company behaves in the same manner.
- *Practice.* The best negotiators engage in role-playing in advance of an actual negotiation. Doing so gives them time to polish their presentations, and also bring up alternatives from the other participants that might otherwise not have been considered. Practice is especially important for large-dollar contracts. The reverse approach used by a less-successful negotiator is to rely on his innate negotiating skill. Usually, the better-prepared team will overwhelm the team that has not spent sufficient time working on a negotiation in advance.
- *Tactical changes.* A discerning negotiator has familiarity with a broad range of negotiation tactics, and is willing to switch to different tactics when it is apparent that the existing approach is not working. Such an individual is con-stantly reviewing her actions following a negotiation, and deciding whether other alternatives might have worked better. This constant introspection is needed to achieve a fluid approach to negotiation. Conversely, a poor per-former has a limited set of tactics, and so is flummoxed when they do not yield the expected results.

The perfect negotiator is the result of years of experience and training. Within the purchasing department, a good way to ensure that those involved in negotiations im-prove over time is to assign them to a senior negotiator in an apprenticeship role. The senior person is then responsible for assigning more challenging tasks to trainees, and constantly giving them feedback regarding their performance.

Negotiation Topics

There are a number of subjects over which a company and its suppliers may wish to negotiate, including the following:

- *Capacity commitment.* For higher-volume situations or cases where the supplier has a limited amount of capacity available, the company may want a commitment for a certain number of produced units to be delivered within a specific time period. The supplier will likely counter with a minimum guaranteed order quantity per month or quarter. The exact terms for a capacity commitment may be vigorously debated.

- *Contract duration.* The precise duration of a purchasing contract can be of some interest to both parties. The company may wish to lock in a high-grade supplier for an extended period, while a supplier may want the security of a longer contract term in order to be assured of the cash flow to invest in its capacity levels and processes. Conversely, a shorter contract period might be a better alternative for the company if it is unsure of the financial circumstances of a supplier or does not believe it will need the supplier's services for an extended period of time. Similarly, a supplier may want a shorter contract duration if it wants to keep its options open to obtain higher prices elsewhere. A possible alternative to these opposing choices is to insert an automatic contract extension clause, which will be triggered unless either party provides adequate notice of contract termination.

- *Cost sharing.* The company may be willing to send its industrial engineers and quality review staff to a supplier's facilities, in order to locate problems and assist in improving processes. The outcome is likely to be a reduction in supplier costs. The company may want consideration in exchange for this service, such as outright sharing of any cost reductions, or perhaps a reduction in the per-unit prices being charged by the supplier. The same situation may arise when the volume of purchases from a supplier is massively increased, allowing the supplier to benefit from the reduced labor costs that come from the effects of the learning curve (see the Purchasing Financial Analysis chapter). The company may want to be paid some portion of the gains that the supplier is deriving from the volume increase. Specific points of negotiation may include the following:

  - *Cost sharing percentage.* Clearly define the cost sharing percentage that each party will receive, or the cost sharing formula being used. Also provide an example of how the percentage or formula is derived.
  - *Applicability.* Note the specific cost reduction events that will trigger the cost sharing clause. The supplier will want to limit these events, so that it can retain all cost savings occurring in other parts of its business.
  - *Start and stop dates.* Cost sharing should cover a specific date range. The supplier may want to delay the start date, so that it can retain all profits earned before that date.

- *Early termination*. The company may want to terminate a contract before its scheduled termination date, perhaps due to supplier nonperformance. Suppliers oppose early termination, since they lose revenue and may also still need to amortize tooling costs over the remainder of a contract. Specific points of negotiation may include the following:
  - o *Notification*. The supplier will likely want as long a lead time as possible, if only to continue to issue goods to the company in the meantime.
  - o *Nonperformance*. The supplier will want to have a certain period of time in which to correct any nonperformance issues, after which termination can occur if the supplier has not corrected the situation.
  - o *Termination fee*. The company may have to pay a fee to the supplier, in compensation for tooling and mold costs that have not yet been amortized. This may involve a formula that reduces the amount of the fee for every additional month that the contract runs.
- *Initial pricing*. If there is an inflation clause in a contract, the company must focus intently on ensuring that the initial price at which it is purchasing is as low as possible. By doing so, subsequent inflationary increases have a reduced impact on the prices paid in later periods.
- *Price adjustments*. In a longer-term contract, inflationary pressures can make the initial price points unprofitable for the supplier. If so, the parties may agree to subsequently adjust the initial prices based on an inflation index. When doing so, examine the proposed index to see if the basis for its derivation closely corresponds to the costs being incurred by the supplier. If not, the index may mandate a price increase, while the supplier is not actually incurring an equivalent increase in its costs.
- *Product development*. The company may want access to a supplier's particular expertise in certain areas as it designs a new product. A supplier is more willing to send its staff to the company if it can benefit from subsequent sales of the new product. Specific points of negotiation may include the following:
  - o *Commitment*. The nature of the supplier's commitment to new product development is clarified, such as the use of two senior engineers on a full-time basis for three months per year.
  - o *Subsequent sourcing*. If a supplier actively participates in the new product development process, it wants to be the sole source provider of certain components. The nature of these components may be stated.
- *Service levels*. The company may need a certain response time from a supplier for parts deliveries, on-site service technicians, field service support, weekend support, and so forth. Extremely rapid response times could exceed the abilities of a supplier (such as requiring a service technician to be pre-positioned nearby). If so, there may need to be significant give-and-take on this issue.

- *Specifications*. There is usually an inverse cost relationship between having tight specifications and the price that a supplier will charge. That is, broader tolerances will yield a lower price, and vice versa. This becomes a technical issue, where the technical specialist on the negotiation team examines proposed alterations to the specifications to see if they will work, while the financial analyst reviews the corresponding supplier price change.

The negotiation topics noted here can certainly prolong the time required to conclude contract negotiations. However, attending to these issues up front may sidestep serious issues that might otherwise occur over the term of a contract.

Negotiation Considerations

When engaging in negotiations with a supplier, the purchasing staff may be in a powerful position, especially if it has the ability to pull a large contract away from a supplier. In this case, it can be tempting to squeeze the supplier too much, to the point where the supplier is barely turning a profit. While this approach may make the purchasing staff look great in its latest performance report, there is a strong negative effect over the long term. When a supplier has no financial reason to continue working with a company, it will likely engage in the following practices:

- Look for alternative customers, and drop the company when it has found them
- Give the company's orders lower priority, in favor of more profitable orders
- Refuse to assist in new product development efforts
- Minimize investments for equipment, since it cannot afford the cost
- Minimize attention to quality and employee training, since it cannot afford the cost

All of these practices work against the interests of the company. Consequently, it pays to investigate the financial needs of a supplier, and work with it to develop a fair price that will make the supplier want to work with the company. This is a particular concern once a company has determined which suppliers it wants to work with over the long term. For these key suppliers, negotiations must result in contracts that present benefits to both sides. Otherwise, a company is taking short-term gains in exchange for alienating suppliers that may be crucial to its long-term interests.

The reverse situation may arise, where the supplier is in a monopoly position, being the only entity that can supply what the company needs. This situation creates a power imbalance that greatly favors the supplier, and which usually means that the company is forced to take the terms demanded by the supplier. In this situation, consider the following options:

- *Consolidate purchases*. If the company has many operating units, each of which is placing orders with the same supplier, it can make sense to aggregate these purchases into a small number of large orders, which gives the company more negotiation clout.

- *Encourage an adjacent-market supplier.* If there are qualified suppliers located in adjacent markets, consider approaching them about entering the market as competitors to the recalcitrant supplier. For example, a supplier located in a nearby state could be persuaded to expand its sales into the geographic region in which the company is located.
- *Lock in prices for the supplier.* If the supplier's market routinely experiences major price fluctuations, offer a multi-year contract at a fixed price, or at a price that fluctuates within a relatively narrow band. By doing so, the supplier is assured of making a profit over the long term, and so is more willing to negotiate with the company.
- *Offer entry into a new market.* If the company plans to expand into a new market, offer to buy the supplier's products in that market. For example, a company is planning to set up dozens of retail stores in a new country, and offers to buy a supplier's unique camera-based automated selling system in that country. Since doing so gives the supplier a highly visible product placement in a new market, the supplier may be more willing to work with the company on pricing and other negotiation points.
- *Unbundle purchases.* If the company already places significant orders with the supplier for multiple items, investigate whether these purchases can be unbundled. It is possible that, while some items must be acquired from the supplier, other items can be sourced elsewhere. The threat of shifting the procurement of these latter items to other suppliers can be an effective negotiating point.

Negotiation Failures

There will be instances in which negotiations break down. It is possible that a failure could have been predicted from the outset, because there is no overlap between the positions of the parties that allows for a median point that is agreeable to both parties. In this case, the least acceptable position of one party is still higher than the desired outcome for the other party. A few rounds of negotiations will likely clarify that neither party is willing to concede more than what has already been offered. If so, there are several ways to deal with the failure:

- See if there are other issues that can be discussed, and which could yield a favorable outcome for both parties. For example, a distributor might not be able to negotiate a reasonable price point from a manufacturer for one consumer appliance, but can do so for a different product.
- If it appears useful to do so, provide additional information regarding the reason for one's position. For example, a demand to sell at a price point below a supplier's variable costs is not tenable for the supplier, so it could be worthwhile to present variable cost information. This could result in the other party modifying its position.
- Break off the negotiations. There are instances in which the positions of the two parties are simply too far apart. This does not necessarily mean that the

parties will never negotiate a settlement. It may be possible to float an inquiry a few months later, to see if the other party has any interest in reopening negotiations. If so, the reason could be that there has been a reevaluation of the original bargaining position, which has now been adjusted. If not, there is no harm done; the company would have otherwise been forced to accept a contract with unfavorable terms that could have damaged it over the long term.

Negotiation Follow Up

During a contract negotiation, an assistant should be taking notes about the progress of the talks. These notes can include the identities and titles of all parties, their roles in the negotiations, the initial and subsequent positions of the parties, and the concessions that were given away at each phase of the negotiations. These notes should be assembled into a coherent package at the end of the negotiations, along with a summary, and archived. This information can be valuable if the organizations elect to engage in negotiations over a new contract at a later date. It is quite possible that the same people will attend, and that the relative importance of the various issues discussed during the last negotiations will appear again. In particular, the concessions brought up and later discarded by the other party will likely be repeated in the future, which gives the next negotiation team a good idea of which initial positions of the other party are likely to be throwaways, and which are important.

One thing that the negotiation process will certainly generate is a great deal of time working (or jousting) with the party on the other side of the table. While it is possible that the other party's negotiator is focused on no other activity than negotiating agreements, it is just as likely that the individual will go back to working on other tasks. The result might be that the negotiators end up working with each other on a regular basis. If so, their deeper knowledge of each other might contribute to a higher-than-usual level of cooperation, which can assist in developing a successful working relationship between the two entities.

Conversely, if animosity built up between the negotiators and they are then forced to work together to implement the resulting contract, this can lead to difficulties. If the personal relationship appears to be interfering with the contract, one or both of the original negotiators may want to remove themselves from the contract implementation.

The relations between the parties at the end of a negotiation can be important, since it is likely that the same negotiators will be asked to settle the terms of subsequent contract negotiations. The main reason for using the same negotiators is that it takes quite an effort for a negotiator to learn about the other party for the first time – its financial situation, operational characteristics, products, and so forth. If a different negotiator were to be assigned to a prospective new contract with the same company, then the new negotiator has to invest in this initial learning phase again. Consequently, it is useful for the two principals in a negotiation to part on reasonable terms, since they may be seeing each other again in the future.

When a contract negotiation has been completed, it must be linked to the company's operating systems, so that the supplier's performance under the terms of the contract can be monitored. This may mean generating a contract-specific report that is shared with the supplier, noting the performance terms in the contract and comparing them to actual results. Also, if there is a contract management system (CMS), the terms of the contract should be loaded into the CMS.

Summary

The ability to negotiate effectively with suppliers is a fundamental skill of the purchasing professional. This is not one of the easier skills to acquire. To be an effective negotiator, a person must observe and learn from the behavior of more experienced negotiators, participate in training sessions, and be willing to accept constructive feedback. The result is a skilled professional who prepares carefully for all negotiation sessions, has a flexible attitude to dealing with counterparty proposals, and is willing to explore alternatives that will yield benefits for both sides. The best negotiators have a long-term outlook, where they help to build relations with the best suppliers, with the expectations that these suppliers will want to work with the company for a long time to come.

Chapter 8
Contract Management

Introduction

Contracts define the terms and conditions under which two entities agree to do business with each other. The intent of a contract is for both organizations to engage in activities that are beneficial to them. However, a poorly-designed or incorrectly managed contract can result in acrimonious relations, so it makes sense to be aware of the implications of every clause in a contract, as well as how contracts should be monitored on an ongoing basis. In this chapter, we cover contract terms and conditions, contract pricing, when to issue contracts, dispute resolution, document retention, and related matters.

Contract Terms and Conditions

The terms and conditions included in a contract define the rules for how a contract is to be administered. Terms and conditions typically include the following subjects:

Header

- *Date*. States the date of the contract. This can be of some importance, if the contract spans a certain number of days. Setting the date back can reduce the effective span of a contract.
- *Parties*. States the legal names of the entities entering into the contract, along with their addresses. Can be important if only the name of a subsidiary is used, since it reduces the legal liability of the parent entity.

Terms and Conditions

- *Definitions*. There will be many terms in each contract; they are defined at the beginning of the contract, where all parties can easily reference them. Definitions can be surprisingly useful since even a common term may be mis-interpreted. For example, it may be necessary to define the word "price," because it could refer to just the base price of an item, or it may also include discounts, sales taxes, rush charges, freight, and so forth.
- *Acceptance criteria*. This clause notes the criteria that will be applied when the company examines the supplier's deliveries. The criteria can be quite detailed, and so may be expanded upon in an accompanying schedule.
- *Arbitration*. This clause requires the parties to accept arbitration if there is a dispute, thereby avoiding the expense and delay associated with using the court system. Alternatively, there may be a clause mandating the prior use of

mediation before taking a dispute into the court system. See the Contractual Disputes section for more information.

- *Confidentiality*. This clause notes that all information shared by the parties is not to be shared with other parties. This is of most concern when a company is sending intellectual property to a supplier, and does not want a competitor to see it, or to have information leaked to the public.
- *Currency*. This clause states the currency in which payments will be made. This can be a useful way to avoid foreign currency risk, by forcing the supplier to accept payment in the company's home currency.
- *Effective dates*. This clause states the start and ending dates of the agreement. An issue in this clause is any automatic extension, stating that the contract will automatically renew unless proper notice is given by one party to the other. This can be a contract management issue, involving monitoring the contract termination date well in advance.
- *Force majeure*. This clause identifies those events that are considered outside of the control of the parties, such as wars, hurricanes, fires, and floods, which relieve the parties from having to perform under the terms of the contract.
- *Governing law*. This is a designation of the court of law in which any disputes between the parties will be settled. The company usually wants the court to be located nearby, to reduce its travel costs. If both parties are located close to each other, then this clause is a minor one.
- *Insurance*. The company may not want any supplier liabilities to spill over onto it, and so will be quite specific about the types and amounts of insurance that it wants a supplier to maintain. This clause may also state that a supplier forward certificates of insurance to the company, proving that the mandated insurance is currently valid. A large company can force these terms onto a smaller supplier, but this can be a more contentious issue when the bargaining positions of the parties are more even.
- *Intellectual property*. A potentially major issue is which of the parties owns any intellectual property that arises from work performed under a contract. The company usually wants to take ownership of any intellectual property created, so that a supplier cannot sell it to a competitor. If the rights are split, this clause needs to specify the nature of the split rights. This clause is much less of a concern when commodity-grade goods are being purchased, since there should be no associated intellectual property.
- *Liabilities*. The company typically uses this clause to make the supplier responsible for any losses and liabilities arising from the contract. The supplier will probably want to limit its liability to the replacement of the goods being sold to the company. The company may attempt to expand the liability to include lost profits or other damages or injuries caused by the supplier's goods or services; this presents a much greater liability for the supplier. Several variations on the range of liabilities are:
  - o *Actual damages*. These are the actual losses incurred by the company within the range of circumstances defined within a contract.

- o *Consequential damages.* These are losses arising as a consequence of the actions of a party to a contract.
- o *Cover damages.* This is the incremental additional cost incurred by the injured party to replace goods that should have been provided by the other party.
- o *Incidental damages.* This is essentially reimbursement for the incidental expenses incurred by the damaged party to cover for the breach of contract by the other party.
- o *Liquidated damages.* This is a predetermined amount to be paid if there is a breach of contract. The amount is specifically stated in the contract. The amount must be reasonable, or else the courts will likely throw out the award.

- *Payment terms.* This clause states the prices that will be paid, and any adjustment factors, such as pricing changes based on the passage of time or changes in the amount of units purchased. Prices may also be adjusted based on changes in pricing indexes or foreign exchange rates.
- *Performance.* Depending on the nature of the contract, there may be a clause outlining the circumstances under which a supplier is considered to have unusually poor or excellent performance, and the penalties or extra compensation associated with each condition. For example, an engineering firm constructing a runway could be penalized for late delivery and paid a bonus for early delivery.
- *Purchase orders.* This clause establishes the linkage between the contract and any purchase orders issued by the company to a supplier during the term of an agreement. The usual terms indicate that any purchase orders issued during the term of the contract are assumed to fall under the terms and conditions set forth in the contract. There may also be language regarding what to do if the terms in a purchase order vary from the contract terms (the contract terms typically override the purchase order terms).
- *Risk of loss.* If a supplier is being asked to stock inventory at a company location, a clause should define which of the parties is responsible for any inventory damage or losses occurring while the inventory is being stored at the company location.
- *Severability.* This is a boilerplate statement that the rest of the contract is still enforceable even if one or more clauses are subsequently proven to be void or unenforceable.
- *Subcontracting.* The company may not want a subcontractor to handle the work it is assigning to a supplier. This can be a particular issue if the goods being produced have unusually tight tolerances, and the company is uncertain of the ability of a subcontractor to deliver goods within the designated specifications.
- *Termination.* This clause states the conditions under which either party can terminate the contract. This clause is always worth a close examination, to determine how tightly the parties are being bound to the terms of the contract.

There may be additional language stating any payments to be made in the event of an early contract termination; for example, the company may need to pay the supplier if a certain purchasing volume was not attained as of the termination date.

- *Transfer of ownership.* If a supplier is being asked to stock inventory at a company location, a clause should define the circumstances under which there is a transfer of ownership from the supplier to the company.

Footer

- *Signatures.* Authorized signatories for both parties sign and date the agreement. The key point here is "authorized," since an unauthorized person could sign a contract. Accordingly, it is customary for both parties to state their job titles in the signature block.

Any of the preceding terms and conditions may refer to a schedule that is attached to the back of a contract. These schedules provide additional detail that clarifies the basic terms, such as the specific measurement calculations to be used to evaluate the performance of a supplier, or the unit volumes at which volume discounts will begin to apply. The schedules deserve at least as much attention as the main clauses of the contract, since they are the least likely to be boilerplate; instead, they will have been written specifically for a contract. The types of schedules integrated into a contract can vary substantially; the following are more likely to be found in a purchase contract:

- Expected unit volumes to be ordered
- Prices to be paid and mechanisms for adjusting those prices
- Product quality assurance guidelines
- Product specifications or statement of work
- Required lead times for orders
- Shipping methods to be used

The negotiation of each paragraph in the terms and conditions of a contract can require an inordinate amount of time. To make better use of the purchasing staff's time, it is better to adopt the industry-standard terms and conditions, and then only adjust those specific items that need to be tailored to a specific purchase.

Commercial Terms

The contract terms and conditions described in the preceding section can be considered the basic, low-level legal minutiae of a contract. They are simply a requirement of doing business, and are always present in order to deal with a range of issues that commonly arise. The more important part of a contract is its commercial terms. These terms address the quality, price, delivery, and other key aspects of an arrangement that are unique to that arrangement.

Commercial terms are not boilerplate. Instead, they are based on a lengthy discussion of the business arrangement that both parties are contemplating entering. In particular, commercial terms should be crafted only after there has been a discussion of the full range of conditions that may arise during the contract term, and the burdens that these conditions may place on either party. The ideal commercial terms are ones that will keep a contract from failing, where the terms will change to accommodate a party that is being negatively impacted by an alteration in conditions. For example:

- Rather than requiring the buyer to purchase a minimum of 1,000,000 units in each of the next ten years, the requirement starts at 1,000,000 units and then declines by 10% per year. Doing so accommodates the buyer, which may be increasingly uncertain about its need for 1,000,000 units in the later years of the contract.
- A utility needs a long-term source of coal, but the supplier is concerned about being locked into a long-term fixed price arrangement. To accommodate the supplier, the contract states that the contract price will be compared to the market price at annual intervals, with a maximum price adjustment of 5% occurring at each of these intervals. Doing so mitigates the total amount of the maximum price change for the utility, while providing some relief to the supplier.

If it seems like a waste of time to go over all possible contingencies with a supplier as part of the contract development, consider that *not* doing so may lead to a lawsuit, which will be far more expensive.

The Employee or Contractor Designation

An area of particular concern when developing a contract is to clearly identify whether a supplier is considered a company employee. If an individual is considered an employee, then any intellectual property developed by that person becomes the property of the company. If an individual is instead considered an independent contractor, then ownership of this property is less clear, and should be defined further in the contract.

To determine whether a person can be classified as an independent contractor, review the entire working relationship between the company and the person, and arrive at a decision based on the complete body of evidence. There are three categories of facts to consider, which are:

- *Behavioral control.* A person is an employee if the business has the right to direct and control how the person does the task for which he was hired. The amount of control is based on the level of instruction regarding such issues as when and where to work, what equipment to use, which employees to use, where to buy supplies, what sequence of tasks to follow, and so forth. Behavioral control can include training by the company to perform services in a particular way.
- *Financial control.* Facts indicative of financial control by the company are the extent to which a worker is reimbursed for business expenses, the amount

of investment by the worker in the business, the extent to which the worker sells his services to other parties, whether the amount paid to the person is based on time worked rather than for a work product, and whether the worker can participate in a profit or loss.

- *Type of relationship.* A person is more likely to be considered an independent contractor if there is a written contract describing the relationship of the parties, the business does not provide benefits to the person, the relationship is not permanent, and the services performed are not a key aspect of the regular business of the company.

EXAMPLE

Mr. David Stringer is a securities attorney who specializes in the issuance of bonds. He has been paid on an hourly basis for the last ten years by his sole client, Heavy Lift Corporation (HLC), and is reimbursed by HLC for expenses incurred. The CFO of HLC does not attempt to control the work habits of Mr. Stringer. There is no contract between the two parties; instead, Mr. Stringer simply issues an invoice to HLC at the end of each month, and the company pays it. HLC does not pay any benefits to Mr. Stringer. HLC is not in the business of selling bonds – it only does so periodically in order to raise capital.

The cumulative evidence in this situation is in favor of Mr. Stringer being an independent contractor. HLC does not exercise behavioral control, though there is some evidence of financial control that would be reduced if Mr. Stringer had any additional clients. The type of relationship is more firmly in favor of independent contractor status, since HLC does not pay benefits and Mr. Stringer's area of specialization is outside of the regular business of the company.

EXAMPLE

Waylon Price has signed a contract with Milford Sound to provide concrete pouring services for several of Milford's public stadium projects. Under the terms of the contract, Mr. Price's firm will be paid a flat fee once specific tasks have been completed, and is liable for any subsequent issues with the concrete through a one-year warranty period. Mr. Price carries workers' compensation insurance for his business, and he employs several people. Mr. Price is an independent contractor.

EXAMPLE

Hubble Corporation lays off Red Miller, and then agrees to pay him a flat fee to design trajectory tracking software for one of Hubble's telescopes. Hubble does not provide Mr. Miller with any specific work instructions, and only sets a target date for delivery of the software. He is not required to attend any meetings of the programming department. He has signed an agreement with Hubble, which specifically states that he is an independent contractor, and will receive no benefits from the company. Mr. Miller is an independent contractor.

Contract Pricing Arrangements

The type of pricing incorporated into a contract can vary substantially, depending on the extent of risk sharing between the parties. In the following sub-sections, we note the different pricing arrangements that can be incorporated into a contract, with commentary on the effects of each one and the situations in which they are used.

Firm Fixed Price

The most common pricing arrangement is the firm fixed price, where (as the name implies) the supplier commits to provide goods or services in exchange for the payment of a specific, unvarying price. Buyers like to use firm fixed pricing, because all risks of cost fluctuations are shifted to the supplier. These fluctuations can include the costs of new labor contracts with unions, spikes in commodity prices, and adverse foreign exchange rates, so a supplier may be taking on a substantial risk of loss under this arrangement. However, suppliers can also benefit handsomely from a firm fixed price, if all of the risk variables turn in favor of the supplier. Also, if there are few or no competitors to drive down the price, a supplier can bid a firm fixed price that guarantees it a generous profit.

Besides the offloading of risk, buyers also like the firm fixed price arrangement because there is no need to review the costs of the supplier (as is the case with the following cost plus pricing arrangement). Instead, the buyer simply confirms that the contracted goods or services have been received, and then pays the designated price.

The firm fixed price concept can be risky for either party when incorporated into a long-term contract, depending on future changes in market conditions. For example, a utility may contract for a 20-year supply of coal from a coal mine, at a price that is 10% below the current market price. Initially, this arrangement benefits the buyer. However, a few years later, the federal government places a tax on coal, which reduces demand and thereby cuts its market price to a level 20% below the contract price. At this point, the contract favors the supplier over the buyer. Thus, the use of this type of pricing over long periods of time can have unintended effects for the participants.

When a firm fixed price arrangement clearly places the risk on the supplier, it is not uncommon for the supplier to then boost its bid price. The intent of doing so is to give it some profit cushion to offset the potential risk of loss that it would otherwise incur.

Firm fixed price arrangements work best for short-term delivery schedules, where it is unlikely that market prices will change significantly.

Fixed Price with Adjustments

As just noted, the basic problem with a firm fixed price arrangement is that the supplier is taking on a number of risks that could result in losses. There are several ways to equalize the sharing of these risks by modifying the contract. Consider the following alternatives:

- *Escalation clause.* The contractual price to be paid is compared to a price index at regular intervals. If the linked price index changes, then so too does the contractual price. The assumption is that the price index will increase, which allows a supplier to charge higher prices. However, it is not impossible that the price index could decline, resulting in lower contractual rates. An escalation clause is fair to both parties when a long-term pricing arrangement is contemplated.

- *Incentives clause.* A variety of incentive payments for a supplier can be built into a fixed price contract. The intent is to give the supplier a good reason to increase its production efficiencies or to accelerate the delivery of goods. If certain targets are met, this triggers additional payments to the supplier. This clause can work well when the buyer expects a supplier to reduce its costs over time as it improves a production process, and wants to share in these cost reductions.

- *Revision clause.* There are situations where the production process for a new product is so new that the supplier cannot create a reasonable bid price for the work. Perhaps there is a new process that has only been attempted in a small pilot plant, and no one knows what costs will be incurred to produce at a higher level. Whatever the case may be, the parties can insert a clause in the contract to re-examine the supplier's production costs once a certain production volume has been achieved, and re-set the fixed price at that time. The resulting pricing revision may be complex, so it makes sense to include a schedule that provides additional detail about the revision calculation, as well as an example revision scenario.

Cost plus Pricing

Cost plus pricing is a price-setting method under which the direct material cost is added to the direct labor cost and overhead cost for a product, after which a markup percentage is added in order to derive the contract price. In a contract, the buyer reimburses the supplier for all costs incurred and also pays a negotiated profit in addition to the costs incurred.

EXAMPLE

A government agency contracts with Failsafe Containment to develop a containment vessel for a new fusion reactor model. The work involves a large amount of research and is highly risky, so Failsafe insists on a cost plus pricing arrangement, where it is guaranteed a 6% profit on all costs incurred.

Over the course of the contract, Failsafe incurs costs of $50,000,000, which includes related overhead costs of $8,000,000. The government reimburses Failsafe for the full $50,000,000, plus a 6% profit, which is another $3,000,000.

The following are disadvantages of using the cost plus pricing method, from the perspective of the buyer:

- *Assured contract profits.* Any supplier is willing to accept this method for a contractual agreement with a customer, since it is assured of having its costs reimbursed and of making a profit. There is no risk of loss on such a contract for the supplier. Instead, the buyer takes on all risk.
- *Contract cost overruns.* The supplier has no incentive to curtail its expenditures - on the contrary, it will likely include as many costs as possible in the contract so that it can be reimbursed. This is a particular problem when a supplier has a large amount of corporate and factory overhead, where it is difficult to determine how these costs can be allocated. Thus, a contractual arrangement should include cost-reduction incentives for the supplier.

From a paperwork perspective, cost plus pricing has the following advantages for both parties:

- *Justifiable.* In cases where the supplier must persuade its customer of the need for a price increase, the supplier can point to an increase in its costs as the reason for the price increase.
- *Simple.* It is quite easy to derive a billable price using this method, though both parties should define the overhead allocation method in order to be consistent in calculating how much overhead will be charged to a contract.

When entering into a cost plus arrangement, the classification of which costs are allowable should be carefully reviewed. It is possible that the terms of the contract are so restrictive that the supplier must exclude many costs from reimbursement, and so can potentially incur a loss.

A cost plus arrangement works well when the buyer and supplier have a long history of working together, since this means they are more likely to have mutually agreed to a policy regarding which costs are to be billed, and the buyer trusts the supplier in regard to which costs are submitted.

A variation on the cost plus pricing arrangement is the cost plus fixed-fee contract. Under this approach, the supplier is reimbursed for all qualifying costs incurred, and is also paid a fixed profit amount that is based on the original budgeted cost of the item to be constructed. This variation is usually not recommended from the perspective of the buyer, since there is no incentive for a supplier to reduce its costs – instead, all risks have been shifted to the buyer.

Time and Materials Pricing

Time and materials pricing is used in service industries to bill customers for a standard labor rate per hour used, plus the actual cost of materials used. The standard labor rate per hour being billed does not necessarily relate to the underlying cost of the labor; instead, it may be based on the market rate for the services of someone having a certain skill set. Thus, a computer technician may bill out at $100 per hour, while costing $30 per hour, while a cable television mechanic may only bill out at $80 per hour, despite costing the same amount per hour. The cost of materials charged to the customer is for any materials actually used during the performance of services for the customer. This cost may be at the supplier's actual cost, or it may be a marked-up cost that includes a fee for the overhead cost associated with ordering, handling, and holding the materials in stock.

Under the time and materials pricing methodology, a single hourly rate may be charged irrespective of the experience level of the person performing the services, but usually there are different rates for different experience levels within the company. Thus, an associate consultant will have a lower billing rate than a consulting manager, who in turn has a lower billing rate than a consulting partner.

Industries in which time and materials pricing are used include:

- Accounting, auditing, and tax services
- Consulting services
- Legal work
- Medical services
- Vehicle repair

If a company chooses to base its labor rate under time and materials pricing on its underlying costs, rather than the market rate, it can do so by adding together the following:

- The cost of compensation, payroll taxes, and benefits per hour for the employee providing billable services
- An allocation of general overhead costs
- An additional factor to account for the proportion of expected unbillable time

---

EXAMPLE

Hammer Industries has an equipment repair group that charges out its staff at a level that covers the cost of labor, plus a profit factor. In the past year, Hammer incurred $2,000,000 of salary expenses, plus $140,000 of payroll taxes, $300,000 of employee benefits, and $500,000 of office expenses; this totaled $2,940,000 of expenses for the year. In the past year, the company had 30,000 billable hours, which is roughly what it expects to bill out in the near future. Hammer wants the division to earn a 20% profit. Based on this information, the division charges $122.50 per hour for each of its repair personnel. The calculation of the labor price per hour is:

$2,940,000 annual costs ÷ (1 - 20% profit percentage) = $3,675,000 revenue needed

$3,675,000 revenue needed ÷ 30,000 billable hours = $122.50 billing rate

---

The following are disadvantages to using the time and materials pricing method, from the perspective of the buyer:

- *High prices*. The billing rates charged may far exceed the underlying costs of the supplier, resulting in inordinately high fees.
- *High risk situations*. This pricing method is similar to cost plus pricing, in that a supplier has no responsibility for the outcome of the work product, thereby shifting the risk of the final outcome of the contract to the buyer.

If a buyer is willing to negotiate, it is possible to substantially reduce the hourly billing rates being charged, especially if the company is planning to pay for many hours of work. If so, include a pricing schedule in the contract that notes the percentage discounts that will be applied as the unit volume of hours worked increases. The following are additional possibilities for controlling the price paid:

- Include a "not to exceed" cap in the contract, so that the company will not be egregiously overbilled.
- Negotiate the maximum margin added to any materials supplied under the contract.
- Insist on periodic reviews of project status and the activities of all billable personnel, to monitor project progress. This can be coupled with a termination clause that allows the company to escape from a contract if project progress is inadequate.

Summary of Pricing Arrangements

The variety of pricing arrangements available represents a full continuum of risk management possibilities. Firm fixed pricing shifts risk to the supplier, while any cost reimbursement arrangement shifts risk onto the buyer. A company might be tempted to always use firm fixed pricing, especially when it is large enough to impose pricing conditions on a small supplier. This is not always a good idea, since it imposes a burden on the supplier base. The realization of any of these risks could result in a financially weaker group of suppliers, which hurts a company in the long run. A wiser approach is to examine the inherent risks in each contract, and engage in mutual risk mitigation and hedging activities with suppliers – especially those suppliers considered critical to the welfare of the company. This approach can also engender a notable amount of supplier loyalty.

It is entirely possible that one or even both parties to a pricing arrangement in a contract will be confused by it. A simple description of a pricing arrangement may be subject to interpretation, which could result in serious disputes between the parties. To avoid this problem, consider adding a schedule to the contract that clarifies the arrangement in greater detail. For example, it could describe the date and source of any inflation index to be used to alter prices, the definitions of each element of a pricing formula, and an example that includes one or more hypothetical pricing situations.

Contract Templates

A company could use a standard contract template for all of its purchasing requirements. However, the terms and conditions associated with one arrangement, such as the purchase of commodities, might not apply to an arrangement involving the design of a new process flow, or a strategic consulting agreement. Consequently, it can make sense to develop a set of contracts that are applicable to different purchasing situations, each with a different set of terms and conditions. This is done in order to standardize contracts for specific purposes, which minimizes the amount of contract customization that may be required. For example, there may be separate contract formats for the purchase of goods, services, and transportation. Each of these standard contracts should contain clauses that answer the following questions:

- Does it identify what is being acquired?
- Does it address the shipment and installation of the item being acquired?
- Does the recipient need to examine and formally accept the delivered goods or services?
- If the delivered goods or services do not meet expectations, what are the consequences for the seller?
- Is there is a need for a product or service warranty, what should it cover, and for what period of time?

Duration-Based Contractual Issues

The many terms, conditions, and other clauses noted in an earlier section are mostly applicable to longer-term contractual arrangements. In these arrangements, the intent is for a company to develop relations with suppliers that are expected to last through a number of purchases, possibly including the sharing of intellectual property. These can be rewarding arrangements, but require much more time to craft a contract that accommodates the needs of both parties. Conversely, a short-term contract is usually needed to fulfill a one-time requirement, after which there is no expectation that a company will continue to need the services of a supplier. Given the impact of these different scenarios, we include in the following table the contractual issues to consider, based on contract duration.

Contractual Issues Based on Contract Duration

	Short-Term Contract	Long-Term Contract
Commitment	There is no expectation that a company will need to deal with a supplier again	There is an expectation that the two parties will work together on a regular basis
Industry capacity	When the industry is nearing full capacity, suppliers are more interested in short-term contracts, so that they can charge at the higher spot rates	When an industry has lots of excess capacity, suppliers are more willing to lock in long-term deals, thereby assuring the use of some portion of their available capacity
Operating cost information	The company does not expect a supplier to share any operating cost information with it, with the intent of setting prices based on underlying costs	The supplier is willing to share its operating cost information with the company, so that the parties can jointly determine a reasonable price to pay, as well as opportunities for cost reduction
Product development	Raw materials and components are purchased in standard configurations	The two parties work together to create new components and non-standard parts, possibly jointly developing intellectual property
Production schedule	The company does not intend to share its production schedule with the supplier	The company insists that the supplier continually accesses its production schedule, in order to determine when and where goods are to be delivered
Purchasing centralization	The company may only purchase a single item from a supplier	The company is interested in placing orders for multiple types of goods with a supplier
Reserved capacity	The supplier will ship to the company when it can find the time to fill an order	The supplier is willing to set aside capacity for the company, which gives the company preferential shipment dates; this can be critical when raw material supplies can be easily disrupted
Supplier finances	The company is not overly interested in the long-term viability of the supplier, only in obtaining low prices for commodity items	The company anticipates such a close relationship that the supplier must have a robust financial situation; the company cannot afford to have the supplier go bankrupt

	Short-Term Contract	Long-Term Contract
Supplier progressiveness	If the supplier does not appear interested in continuing improvement, it cannot reduce its costs or develop more advanced products	When the supplier's management team is constantly driving toward more efficient operations and enhanced products, the company will benefit from its pricing and product enhancements
Technology sharing	Neither party expects to have access to the technology of the other party	Both parties expect to use each other's intellectual property to develop cutting-edge goods; especially useful when doing so can block a supplier's technology from competitors
Unpredictable volumes	When the company is not certain of the volume of units needed, it is more likely to use short-term contracts until the volume requirements are more clear	When there is a high level of predictability in the number of units needed, it is safer to obtain them through a long-term contract where the company is obligated to buy in certain volumes

The points raised in the table should make it clear that only a minority of contracts need to be set up as long-term arrangements. The purchasing team should discuss the pros and cons of a long-term arrangement before engaging in any discussions with a supplier to do so. In many cases, the advantages of a long-term contract will not be apparent, in which case it will be more cost-effective to write a short-term contract using mostly boilerplate terms and conditions.

A particular concern when selecting a supplier for a long-term contract is the risk of a "false positive," which arises when the wrong supplier is picked for a long-term contract. If so, the purchasing team may find that a supplier is unable to deliver on time, produces sub-standard goods, is not willing to work together on product development, and so forth. This is a major concern when a contract mandates that the two parties work together for a number of years. This concern may introduce a great deal of hesitation about entering into long-term contractual arrangements. A reasonable way to allay this concern is to first work with suppliers on short-term joint collaboration arrangements, and only progress to a long-term contract when the management team is convinced that doing so presents few downside risks.

Contract Approval Process

The amount of time spent reviewing and approving contracts with suppliers should strike a balance between the risk of allowing unfavorable terms, the time required to complete a review, and the delay that a review introduces into the process of obtaining goods and services. The general guideline for contract approvals is that the purchasing staff is assigned a monetary threshold, below which no additional approvals are required. If a staff person has considerable experience, the approval threshold might be raised to a higher level. Above this threshold, the approval of the purchasing manager might be needed, as long as the standard terms and conditions are used in the contract. If the contract amount both exceeds the review threshold *and* contains altered terms and conditions, then the legal staff must also review and approve the document. This approval process flow focuses attention on those contracts that could potentially result in unusually high expenditures for the company.

Contracts and Purchase Orders

A contract defines the overall relationship with a supplier. However, it does not contain purchasing specifics, such as exactly how much of which items will be purchased within what period of time. These details are set forth in one or more purchase orders.

Purchase orders are used as the link between contracts and the accounting system. When a supplier sends a shipment to a company, the shipment documentation may reference the authorizing purchase order. If so, the receiving staff can call up the purchase order on a computer terminal and log in the delivery as having been received, after which the payables system automatically issues a payment to the supplier. Alternatively, a supplier invoice may reference an authorizing purchase order, which the accounts payable staff uses to manually compare the invoice to the purchase order and receiving documentation (known as three-way matching). No matter which of these systems is used, the purchase order is a reference that is needed to pay a supplier.

If a contract is identified by a contract number, then each purchase order issued will reference the contract number, so that orders can be traced back to the authorizing contract. This is a useful way to build a clear linkage between contracts and purchase orders, and is especially useful when one contract has expired and been replaced by another; one can then use the contract number reference on a purchase order to decide which contract it belongs to.

In short, a relationship with a supplier is defined by a contract. The tactical implementation of this relationship is the purchase order. From the perspective of many people in a company, the only supplier-related document they may ever see is the purchase order, since they are only concerned with suppliers at the level of the individual purchase transaction.

Change Order Management

When a project involves a fixed fee arrangement, there is a strong likelihood that the scope of the project will change over time. If so, it will be necessary for the supplier and buyer to mutually agree upon a change order that specifies the extent of the scope change, as well as the related alteration in the amount that the supplier is now allowed to bill to the buyer.

A change order management process involves a supplier committee that is comprised of the project manager, a buyer representative, and the project accountant. The manager and buyer representative must approve each change order, while the accountant processes the paperwork for the change order and bills it to the buyer. Various technical personnel from the project team will be brought in to discuss the financial and timing impact of proposed changes to the existing project scope. The committee is also responsible for maintaining the most current listing of project requirements, and for monitoring the project's actual status in comparison to these requirements.

Change requests should be documented on a standardized form, which ensures that the same set of information is provided to the committee whenever a change is proposed. The form should include space for the following information:

- *Change request number.* Needed to uniquely identify each request made. This is useful for ensuring that no requests are lost.
- *Name of the individual requesting the change.* Needed in order to report back the committee's decision, as well as who to contact for more information. This field can include contact information for the requester.
- *Date of the request.* Needed to establish the amount of time that has elapsed before a request is dealt with.
- *Description of the change.* Summarizes the requested change, possibly including an estimate of the impact on project cost, scope, or time of completion.

When the committee receives a change request, it should enter the request into a change order log, so that no forms are inadvertently lost. The log should also state when the committee dealt with each request, and the outcome of that analysis. Once a change order is approved by the committee, the project accountant should enter it into a separate log that is used for billing purposes, to ensure that each change order is billed to the buyer when the related work is completed.

From the perspective of the buyer, it is useful to inquire about the change order management system that a supplier uses before a contract is signed, in order to anticipate the process flow and determine how to respond to it.

Contractual Disputes

Over time, a purchasing professional is likely to be involved in any number of contractual disputes. They might be caused by the fundamental intransigence of the parties to a contract, but it is also possible that a dispute hinges on the interpretation of a contract clause, or someone's opinion of the goods or services being provided. If so, it is possible that settlement of a dispute will require an inordinate amount of time and money, as the parties establish their positions and debate points of law in court. There are alternative ways to settle disputes that can keep a company and its suppliers out of the courtroom. These alternatives also allow for a greater degree of privacy, rather than the public forum of a courtroom dispute. The alternatives are as follows:

- *Mediation.* The parties jointly hire a mediator, whose task is to work with both sides to arrive at a compromise position. The parties do not have to accept a solution suggested by the mediator.
- *Arbitration.* The parties agree to allow a third party to examine the facts of the dispute, and make a ruling that both parties agree in advance to accept (known as binding arbitration). This arrangement is relatively inexpensive and can be completed quickly.

- *Rent-a-judge.* A court refers a pending lawsuit to a neutral third party, who conducts what is essentially a private trial. The third party, who may be a retired judge, then renders an opinion, which the parties may or may not accept.

The choice to use mediation and/or arbitration should be built into each contract. This clause describes the situations in which these methods can be used, and the method by which the parties will agree on a mediator or arbitrator. The rent-a-judge option does not appear in contracts, since this is essentially a referral from the court system.

A potentially significant issue to address in a contract if the parties are located far apart is where hearings will be held. Since it may be necessary for several people to travel to a mediator or arbitrator more than once, this can be a moderately expensive proposition for the more distant of the two parties.

Contract Auditing

Contract auditing involves an examination of the written arrangements with suppliers. The intent behind a contract audit is to ensure that the amount and quality of goods and services delivered to the customer was correct and that the customer was billed an appropriate amount. A possible result of a contract audit is that the supplier is required to deliver additional goods and services, or that it must rebate a portion of its billings. The threat of a contract audit is a useful deterrent to keep suppliers from overbilling or under-delivering to a customer.

Document Retention

A larger purchasing department may have hundreds or thousands of contracts and related documents on file. Given the expense of office space, what is the best way to manage them? There are several issues to consider that can reduce the storage burden.

One issue is the existence of a formal document destruction policy. This policy is designed to ensure that all contracts are retained for a certain period of time, after which their status will be reviewed, and they will be destroyed if no longer needed. Doing so ensures that there is a regular process in place for examining and dispositioning old contracts. For example, there may be a policy that mandates contract destruction 10 years after the termination date of a contract. Whatever policy is implemented, be sure to first consult with legal counsel, to ensure that there are no statutes that will be violated if a contract is destroyed too early. The following table notes several types of purchasing documents for which different retention periods might be mandated.

Types of Purchasing Documents

Document Type	Retention Period
Contracts	Legal counsel should make a determination of the most appropriate time period over which contracts should be retained after they have been closed
Inventory records	Normally maintained by the warehouse staff, not the purchasing department; the retention period should be relatively short
Project documentation	Normally maintained by the department that was responsible for the project; retention is based on company policy – there are not usually any legally-mandated retention periods
Purchase orders	Open purchase orders are always retained; closed purchase orders should be retained for at least six years
Supplier report cards	There is no legal reason to retain report cards, but should be retained as long as a supplier is active, to provide background on historical performance

Another issue is when to shift contracts off-site. Once a contract's termination date has been reached, it may still make sense to keep it on-site if there is a successor contract, as there may be a need to consult the arrangement in the prior contract. However, once any pressing need for on-site contract retention has passed, shift it to a secure off-site storage location, and enter its storage location in an index, so that it can be readily located if needed.

A variation on the off-site storage concept is to purchase contract management software, and enter the essential elements of each contract into the software. By doing so, the original document can be immediately shifted off-site. In addition, the information in each contract is now accessible to anyone having access to the software, so it can be reviewed in multiple locations at the same time.

A final issue is whether the purchasing department is responsible for contract storage at all. It is quite possible that the legal department will take responsibility for all contracts, while the purchasing department only has to store non-contract documents.

Summary

Contracts are an essential part of the documentation generated by the purchasing department, and are the basis for many of its transactions. Given their importance, the purchasing professional should be familiar with the basic contents of a contract, when a contract should be used, how to update it for change orders, and what types of pricing arrangements it should encompass. A lesser issue is to set up a document retention system, so that contracts and purchase orders are retained for a legally appropriate period of time, and in a manner that does not clutter up the department.

Chapter 9
Inventory Management Issues

Introduction

A key factor that drives profitability is the amount of inventory that a business holds. If the investment in inventory is too high, this increases the amount of funds needed to operate the company, while also resulting in substantial inventory holding costs and an enhanced risk of inventory obsolescence. However, too small an amount of inventory can also be dangerous, since it may mean that customer orders cannot be readily fulfilled.

In this chapter, we explore the different types of inventory, why a business tends to maintain too large an investment in inventory, and the techniques available for reducing inventory, with an emphasis on the effective use of the supply chain to assist in these efforts.

Related Podcast Episodes: Episodes 186 and 192 of the Accounting Best Practices Podcast discuss inventory variances and cycle counting, respectively. They are available at: **accountingtools.com/podcasts** or **iTunes**

Types of Inventory

Before discussing the issues associated with inventory, we will first address the types of inventory that a business may deal with. There are quite a few more types than might initially be apparent. They are:

- *Raw materials and components inventory.* This is unfinished inventory that must be transformed before it is ready for sale. Most entities buy their raw materials and components from suppliers, but a vertically-integrated business may produce a selection of its more critical raw materials for its own use. The procurement of raw materials and components inventory is a primary task of the purchasing department.
- *In-transit inventory.* This is inventory either in transit to the company from suppliers, or in transit from the company to its customers. Depending on the terms of the freight arrangements being used, in-transit inventory could belong to the company or its suppliers or customers. The purchasing staff may monitor the progress of inbound raw materials and merchandise to company facilities, in order to predict when it will arrive.
- *Work-in-process inventory.* This is inventory that has entered the process of being converted into finished goods, and has not yet completed the conversion process. Most of the time, work-in-process inventory is not actually undergoing any conversion work. Instead, it is waiting in queue in front of a work

station for processing work, or is piling up on the other side of a work station, waiting to be moved elsewhere for another processing step.

- *Finished goods inventory.* This is inventory that has completed all processing steps, and is ready for sale to customers. The investment in finished goods inventory can be massive when sales are seasonal, and production begins well in advance of the selling season. It can also be large when a business is ramping up for a major product launch, or when inventory is produced to a forecast.
- *Merchandise inventory.* This is goods that are acquired as finished products from suppliers. The company may repackage them for final sale, but no transformational activities occur. In some situations, known as *drop shipping*, a supplier may deliver merchandise straight to a company's customers, thereby taking the company out of the inventory-handling process entirely. The purchasing staff is deeply involved in sourcing merchandise inventory.
- *Consignment inventory.* This is inventory owned by one entity, but which is being sold by another. For example, a manufacturer may retain title to goods that are on display in a retailer's store, and will be paid by the retailer when the goods are sold. This approach may be used when a company wants to shift the funding burden of owning inventory back onto its suppliers.
- *Rework inventory.* When goods fail an internal quality review or are returned by customers as defective, they must be routed back through the production process for additional processing work. In some cases, they may be returned to suppliers for rework, in which case the purchasing staff must monitor their status.
- *Maintenance, repair and operating supplies (MRO) inventory.* This is the myriad of items that are not physically included in finished goods, but which are needed to support company operations. Examples of MRO are cleaning supplies, lubricants, copier paper, repair parts, and tools. Quite a large amount of funds can be invested in MRO, and yet this cost may be hidden, since the purchases are charged to a number of departments. The purchasing department is responsible for obtaining MRO items. This category of inventory is covered in more detail in the Cost Management chapter.

The work-in-process and finished goods inventory classifications may not directly impact the purchasing department, but it is involved with all of the other inventory classifications. The purchasing manager should have a detailed knowledge of the impacts of excessive inventory levels, the cost of inventory, and how inventory levels can be lowered – all of which are covered in the following sections.

Excessive Inventory Issues

Why would an organization maintain inventory levels that are clearly too high? There are a number of reasons for it, many of which relate to management's unwillingness to address operational problems. Here are several of the underlying causes:

- *Batch sizes*. The production process may be set up in such a manner that an outbound box next to a work station must be filled before a materials handler moves it to the next work station that is scheduled to work on the in-process materials. The inventory contained within these boxes is unnecessary. Instead, the batch sizing concept could be altered by installing conveyors between work stations, so that each unit is immediately passed to the next work station as soon as processing work on it has been completed.

- *Engineering change order issues*. The engineering department may periodically issue an engineering change order (ECO), under which part of a product is replaced with a different configuration. If an ECO is issued when there is still a large amount of the materials and components in stock that are being replaced, there is no longer a need for these items, and they will languish in stock.

- *Expediting*. A major customer may insist that its orders be given priority in the production process. To allow for this demand, management may assign an expediter to the customer's production job and run it straight through the production process. Doing so likely entails setting aside other jobs, and possibly even robbing required materials from other jobs. The end result will likely be a much higher investment in work-in-process than is necessary, which is comprised of the cast-aside jobs littering the shop floor.

- *Inaccurate forecasting*. A business may suffer from an unusually poor sales forecasting system. While all forecasting is inherently inaccurate, a forecast that is excessively optimistic or contains the wrong mix of expected product sales will lead to over-ordering of the wrong goods from suppliers. These goods may remain in stock for lengthy periods, until they are eventually dispositioned.

- *Incorrect bills of material*. A bill of material is the official list of the materials contents of a product. It is used to calculate the amount of goods to buy from suppliers. If a bill of materials is incorrect, the purchasing staff may unknowingly order too many units of certain goods.

- *Incorrect inventory records*. If the warehouse does not maintain highly accurate records of on-hand balances, there is a heightened risk of stockout conditions arising. To avoid this situation, management may authorize the purchase of excessive amounts of inventory.

- *Lengthy production runs*. There may be lengthy setups involved in switching over production equipment to run a different product. If so, there is a temptation to keep manufacturing the same products for longer periods of time. The result is *a lot* of finished goods sitting in the warehouse, which is also at risk of becoming obsolete.

- *Low quality materials*. When suppliers deliver materials that are of low quality, a business must keep extra inventory on hand to compensate for the proportion of inventory that it must throw away as scrap.
- *Multiple product configurations*. The marketing department may claim that a business can sell more units if it offers its products in every possible configuration. While quite possibly true, this also means keeping all of the finished goods variations in stock, which may result in extra inventory costs that outweigh the profits from the extra product sales.
- *Pilferage*. The inventory records may be incorrect due to pilferage of the inventory by employees or outsiders who gain access to the inventory. This means that the inventory records are overstated for those items that have been stolen. When the records are inaccurate, it may be necessary to place rush orders for replacements when there is a sudden need to fill a customer order and there are not enough units to complete the order.
- *Unreliable deliveries*. When suppliers have a history of making deliveries late, an organization must keep an unusually large safety stock of inventory on hand to guard against stockout conditions. This is a particular problem when management focuses excessively on buying low-priced goods from overseas, and does not realize that there is a lengthy delivery period associated with these goods.
- *Unstable production schedule*. When a company constantly alters its production schedule at the last minute, it is much more difficult for suppliers to react to these changes with an altered set of raw materials. In this case (which is entirely the fault of the company), it may be necessary to maintain extra stocks of raw materials to ensure that the latest permutation of the production schedule can be achieved.
- *Unwillingness to eliminate inventory*. Managers may not be willing to recognize a large write-down of the inventory asset in order to purge obsolete inventory from the warehouse. This is usually driven by financial issues involving not reporting a loss.
- *Variable yields*. The production process may generate usable production at a rate that is difficult to predict, perhaps with acceptable batches being followed by ones with much higher scrap rates. Given the level of uncertainty, the materials management staff would likely elect to maintain a raw materials inventory level that will cover for the lowest yield rate that can be expected.
- *Volume purchases*. The purchasing manager may focus too much on volume discounts, and so orders far more units than are immediately needed in exchange for a low per-unit cost.

In all of the preceding cases, there is a specific problem area that can be fixed if management pays attention to the underlying issue. If not, the only alternative is to simply keep more inventory on hand. The management team might pay more attention to the overabundance of inventory if it understood the costs associated with holding inventory. Here are the general categories of costs that will be incurred when inventory must be stored:

- *Facility cost.* This is the cost of the warehouse, which includes depreciation on the building and interior racks, heating and electricity, building insurance, and warehouse staff. This is largely a fixed cost; it does not vary if there are small changes in the amount of inventory stored in the facility.
- *Cost of funds.* This is the interest cost of any funds that a company borrows in order to purchase inventory (or, conversely, the foregone interest income). This can be tied to a specific unit of inventory, since selling a single unit immediately frees up funds which can then be used to pay down debt. This cost of funds varies with the market interest rate.
- *Risk mitigation.* This is not only the cost of insuring inventory, but also of installing any risk management items needed to protect the inventory, such as fire suppression systems, burglar alarms, and security guards. As was the case with facility costs, this is largely a fixed cost.
- *Taxes.* The business district in which the inventory is stored may charge some form of property tax on the inventory. This cost can be reduced by selling off inventory just prior to the date on which inventory is measured for tax purposes.
- *Obsolescence and damage.* Inventory may become unusable over time (especially for perishable items), or it may be superseded by technological advances. In either case, it may only be disposed of at a large discount, or have no value at all. This tends to be an incremental cost that is more likely to be associated with low-turnover goods.

EXAMPLE

Tsunami Products manufactures and sells a number of plumbing products targeted at the residential bathroom, including shower heads, faucets, and toilet fixtures. Tsunami maintains a large warehouse, in which are stored several thousand inventory items for all possible configurations and colors of the company's products. There is pressure from the president to reduce the company's product offerings, due to the high cost of storage. Before responding to the president's request, the materials manager decides to quantify the cost of inventory storage. She derives the following information:

Expense Item	Last Year Cost
Facility Cost	
Warehouse rent	$180,000
Depreciation on storage racks	80,000
Depreciation on fork lifts	50,000
Warehouse utilities	40,000
Staff compensation	600,000
Building insurance	25,000
Cost of funds (6% interest cost on $30,000,000 of inventory)	1,800,000
Risk Mitigation	
Inventory insurance	60,000
Depreciation on fire suppression system	15,000
Burglar alarm annual fee	4,000
Taxes (property taxes)	80,000
Damage (Inventory rendered unusable and scrapped)	25,000
Total cost	$2,959,000
As percent of $30,000,000 inventory investment	10%

The cost of inventory storage turns out to be 10% of the cost of the stored goods. The materials manager is particularly startled by the cost of funds, which comprises more than 60% of the total cost. The president points out that this cost of funds is unusually low, and will likely increase in a tighter credit market. Consequently, just to mitigate changes in the cost of funds, it is imperative that Tsunami reduce the cost of its inventory storage.

The significant cost associated with holding inventory brings up the question of whether inventory should be considered an asset at all. It has a high carrying cost, may become obsolete over time, and can be difficult to convert into cash within a reasonable period of time. While these characteristics are not representative of a liability, they do indicate that inventory has several negative characteristics that can lead to reduced financial results. The following example illustrates the point.

EXAMPLE

The managers of Grunge Motor Sports (maker of the famous Caveman XT dirt bike) are concerned about the financial results that the company has been producing for the past few years, which have led to complaints from investors that their return on investment is too low. The management team decides to set a goal of cutting the total inventory investment in half. To see what this would do to the return on investment, the company's controller creates the following before-and-after analysis of the company's financial results:

(000s)	Actual Results	Adjusted Results
Cash and investments	$650	$650
Receivables	2,050	2,050
Inventory	3,200	1,600
Fixed assets	4,100	4,100
Total assets	$10,000	$8,400
Equity	$7,500	$5,900
Sales	$12,000	$12,000
Profits	480	560
Return on investment	6.4%	9.5%

In the adjusted version of Grunge's financial results, the inventory investment is reduced by half, which is $1,600,000. The released funds are then used to buy back company stock from investors, which results in a reduced equity balance. In addition, it is assumed that the holding cost of the inventory was 10% per year; however, it would take all year to reduce the inventory by half, so a cost savings of half that amount is assumed for the full year. The result of the inventory reduction is therefore a cost savings of $80,000, which increases profits to $560,000. The net effect of the profit increase and equity decline is an improvement in the return on equity from 6.4% to 9.5%.

Inventory Record Accuracy

Of all the issues just listed that caused inventories to become bloated, the worst is inventory record accuracy. The purchasing staff must base its acquisition activities in large part on the company's records of on-hand inventory levels. When these records are unreliable, the staff is forced to order excess quantities to ensure that the company's usage needs are met.

The basis of a functional inventory recordkeeping system is the *perpetual inventory system*, where every addition to and withdrawal from the warehouse is logged into the inventory database as soon as the transaction occurs. These updates must be made religiously, or else the accuracy of the database will decline. The reliability of these updates can be enhanced by setting up bar codes for each inventory location and item, and using portable bar code scanners to record transactions throughout the warehouse. However, despite these improvements, there will be a gradual decline in record accuracy over time.

The method used to achieve and maintain the highest possible level of inventory record accuracy is called *cycle counting*. This is the ongoing daily counting of a small proportion of the total inventory by the warehouse staff. When a discrepancy between the actual quantity and the record quantity is found, the warehouse staff researches why the error occurred and how to correct the underlying problem, so that the risk of similar errors arising in the future is reduced. The staff also updates the inventory records to adjust to the actual count.

There are an immense number of issues that can cause inventory record accuracy problems, such as the loss of bar codes, missing scans, incorrect units of measure, poor lighting that makes it difficult to read inventory labels, inadequate employee training, and a backlog of data entry work in the warehouse. None of these issues are a direct concern of the purchasing manager, but it can be useful to be aware of the depth of the issues that must be overcome before a high level of inventory record accuracy can be achieved. The latest edition of the author's *Inventory Management* book contains an extensive review of the issues leading to record inaccuracy, and how to resolve them.

Operating with Reduced Inventory

The preceding discussion of excessive inventory issues should make it clear that high inventory levels result from a lack of attention to operational excellence. What would the situation look like if management decides to attend to these issues? The following sub-sections address the operational changes needed to effect inventory reduction at varying levels of difficulty.

Basic Inventory Reduction Activities

To achieve a reduced amount of inventory in the *company*, the purchasing department needs to insist on very high product quality, so the risk of having to scrap delivered goods is essentially zero. Deliveries would also have to be exactly on time, probably within a very narrow time window. This would reduce the need to keep extra inventory reserves on hand. To achieve a reduced amount of the inventory in the *supply chain*, a company would need to make its production schedule and related ordering needs completely transparent to suppliers, which means that they should be able to log into the company's production scheduling system. Doing so eliminates supplier uncertainty regarding what will be ordered and when, so there is no need for them to retain excess inventory levels to guard against unexpected orders.

Advanced Inventory Reduction Activities

The most in-depth reduction of inventory that can be achieved is through the use of a just-in-time (JIT) system. JIT is really a collection of production management techniques that work together to drive down inventory levels. The central tenet of the system is that production is only triggered by the receipt of a customer order. This has several implications, which are:

- The production system has a "pull" orientation, where a customer order triggers the authorization of the system to create the exact amount stated in the order. This is the reverse of the much more common "push" system, where a forecast generated by the company triggers production. This "pull" orientation extends back through the supply chain, where suppliers are requested to ship only the amounts needed for current production. This task is easier if suppliers are located close to a company's production or fulfillment facilities, and can make deliveries on short notice and in small amounts.
- If there are no customer orders, then no production occurs. In essence, it is better to incur the cost of having the production staff sit with no work to do, than to create additional units that may never be used. However, it can be more practical to create a uniform work load for the production staff, thereby preventing demand spikes from overloading the production system. This means there may still be some finished goods inventory that acts as a buffer between customers and the production area.

In order to react quickly to an incoming production order, the production area should be reconfigured. The traditional layout is oriented toward lengthy assembly lines or clusters of similar workstations that produce the same units in massive production runs. A better approach is to create a number of production cells in the manufacturing area. A cell arrangement is a cluster of people and equipment that are brought together to focus on the construction of a small group of related products. A production cell usually has the following characteristics:

- It is configured in a "U" shape, which is an efficient flow path for unfinished parts to follow as they move through the various conversion stages.
- There are few employees in each cell, perhaps as few as one person who is responsible for multiple finishing steps.
- The equipment in each cell must be capable of a fast changeover to handle different products in rapid succession.
- The ordering of goods between production cells is handled by an authorization to produce a specific quantity of goods, which is called a kanban. A kanban is simply a move signal, such as a card or an empty container, which is sent to the work station that must produce more units. When kanbans are in place, the amount of work-in-process inventory declines precipitously, since the kanbans only authorize the production of just enough units to ensure that an order is completed.

- An organization usually experiences a predictable number of units that it can expect customers to purchase within a given period of time. If so, the team in a production cell must ensure that it can maintain an average pace of unit production that ensures the number of items to be sold can be created. This concept is called operational takt time, which includes the expected amount of downtime from all possible causes.
- The quality of first-pass production must be extremely high. Otherwise, units must be scrapped and a kanban sent to the upstream workstation for more parts to be delivered.
- Suppliers may deliver raw materials and components directly into a production cell. If so, this calls for tight integration of the pull system with suppliers, so that they can deliver items within narrow time windows, and probably in small order quantities.

The characteristics just noted point toward the need for a high level of coordination between the ordering system, the production floor, and the supply chain. Nonetheless, if the systems reconfiguration and accompanying coordination levels can be implemented, the investment in inventory can be drastically reduced.

A Reduced-Inventory Environment for Suppliers

When an organization has made a commitment to reducing its investment in inventory, suppliers will likely be called upon to assist in the effort. This will involve creating a different set of requirements for suppliers, which will require that information be shared with them in an open manner. The following additional changes will be needed:

- *Frozen production schedule.* The production planning staff must lock down the production schedule for a period of time that encompasses the lead times of its suppliers, so that they can reliably produce and deliver the correct materials. Otherwise, the company must maintain a buffer stock of additional inventory to support its short-term needs when it alters the production schedule.
- *Information sharing.* The company must give on-line access to its production schedule and raw material requirements to all suppliers. In addition, it may be necessary to warn them via electronic messages of any changes to the short-term schedule. Doing so improves the ability of suppliers to conduct their own scheduling for the provision of inventory to the company.
- *Minimal number of suppliers.* The kind of close relationship required to create a reduced-inventory environment can only happen when there are a small number of suppliers. It is simply not possible to coordinate activities with several thousand suppliers.
- *Small deliveries.* Suppliers will need to make large numbers of small-unit deliveries, rather than the traditional full-truckload deliveries. This may call for an entirely different form of transport, such as side-loading trucks that can pull up next to a production facility and quickly offload a few units. This is

needed in order to keep large deliveries from languishing in the company's warehouse for long periods of time. Given the need for frequent deliveries, it will likely be necessary to associate with suppliers located a short distance from the company.

- *Zero defects.* Suppliers will need to alter their processes to arrive at a quality level where product defects are essentially zero. This is needed in order to keep from having to maintain extra inventory at the company to guard against arriving raw materials that must be scrapped.

Bottlenecks in the Supply Chain

In most organizations, there is a bottleneck somewhere within operations that impedes the business from generating more *throughput* (which is defined as revenues minus all variable costs). To increase profits, a business must increase its throughput, so bottleneck management is essential.

Bottlenecks can be located in a variety of places. Perhaps all manufacturing jobs must be run through a machine that is already operating at maximum capacity, or the sales staff is unable to respond to any additional customer requests for quotes, or perhaps the research staff is not developing enough new products. Another possibility that is of importance from the perspective of the purchasing staff is that the bottleneck might lie in the supply chain. It is entirely possible that a supplier has begun allocating the sales of a certain raw material, or it does not have sufficient capacity to supply a necessary sub-assembly. If so, the supplier is constraining the business from increasing its throughput and therefore its profits.

A bottleneck in the supply chain is a major issue for the purchasing manager, since it directly impacts overall corporate profitability. There are a number of actions that can mitigate the situation, such as:

- Adding other suppliers that can provide the same materials
- Paying the supplier to reserve a portion of its capacity for the company
- Entering into a long-term supply contract with the company to provide it with a certain minimum amount of materials per year
- Working with the engineering staff to design products that can use substitute products

While all of these workarounds can be quite effective, the real issue is simply recognizing that a bottleneck exists. For more information about how to locate bottlenecks and calculate their financial impact, see the author's *Constraint Management* book.

Reasons to Retain Some Inventory

The preceding discussion might lead one to believe that inventory should be driven down to zero. This is neither practical nor even possible. There will always be a certain minimum level of inventory that must be maintained for an organization to operate at an optimal level. Even in an environment in which all possible just-in-time measures have been implemented, some amount of inventory will always be flowing through the production facility. In addition, it is impossible to eradicate all hiccups in the production process, so some modest amount of reserve stock will need to be retained to keep these issues from halting production.

A larger issue is the extent to which senior management wants to please its customers by offering them rapid order fulfillment. The marketing argument in favor of fast order fulfillment is that customers will be more loyal and more likely to place repeat orders if they can be assured of very fast order fulfillment. However, this policy also requires that sufficient finished goods be kept on hand at all times to be able to fulfill orders. This can be quite difficult, especially when it entails a major increase in the inventory investment to meet all possible order requirements. A reasonable midway point is to determine the minimum inventory increase required to promise customers that most (perhaps 98%) of their orders can be fulfilled within one day, and the remainder within a few more days. The worst possible situation is to offer an immediate 100% fulfillment rate, since the associated inventory investment would be quite high.

Another valid reason for retaining inventory is to use it as a hedge against the risk of supply restrictions and price increases. There may be a valid risk that a certain raw material or sub-assembly will not be available from a supplier; for example, a supplier is expecting a strike by its production staff, or violence in a neighboring country may interrupt deliveries from a supplier in that country. Alternatively, there is expected to be heightened demand by consumers for a certain product, which will raise supplier prices for a key component. When these types of situations could arise, a reasonable reaction is to place orders for increased amounts of the impacted items from suppliers. If so, the additional amount that can realistically be ordered may not be that large, either because the company does not have sufficient storage capacity or the supplier does not have enough additional production capacity to fulfill the order.

Under certain circumstances, it can make sense to order in larger volumes in order to take advantage of volume discounts. This is not always the case, especially when the result is a large amount of inventory that sits in the warehouse for long periods of time. However, if there is a reasonable projected need for the inventory in the short-term, the benefit to be gained from the discount could make the transaction worthwhile. This is an especially valid option if the supplier will allow deliveries under the order to be spread out over a period of time, thereby delaying the payment of cash to the supplier.

Other Inventory Best Practices for Suppliers

Thus far, we have noted a number of actions that can be taken to extend a just-in-time system down into the supply chain, and emphasized the need to monitor bottlenecks. However, these concepts do not exhaust the range of supplier options available for managing inventory. In the following sub-sections, we make note of several additional opportunities, such as shortening lead times, delaying final product configuration, and altering product designs to yield more effective procurement activities.

Supplier Lead Times

A key part of the grief experienced by the purchasing staff is dealing with the ordering lead times required by suppliers. If a long lead time is required, the staff must plan well in advance for the production of goods that incorporate these components. An equally unpalatable option is to maintain a reserve of components on-site, thereby avoiding the lead time issue but requiring a large investment in inventory.

A concept that is rarely explored is the relevance of the lead times quoted by suppliers. In some cases, a supplier may be quoting a long lead time that has been used traditionally, but which has little basis in fact. There may instead be a considerably shorter actual lead time underlying the date range being quoted by a supplier's sales staff. When entering into a relationship with a new supplier, it can be useful to forcefully point out the company's need for a short lead time, so that it can maintain minimal buffer inventory and also quote short lead times to its own customers. This immediate emphasis on lead times may cause some suppliers to take themselves out of consideration, leaving only those suppliers capable of delivering on short notice. The same concept can be applied to existing suppliers, and may result in some turnover among those suppliers unwilling or unable to deliver within a short period of time.

The Total Inventory Concept

Many of the changes that a company makes to reduce inventory do not actually eliminate inventory – they just move inventory back to a supplier. The supplier is supposed to hold a larger amount of inventory off-site, and deliver it only when called upon. This approach increases the amount of working capital that the supplier must invest, and also shifts all the usual inventory holding costs onto the supplier. The result is a weakening of the finances of a company's supplier base. When suppliers earn a lower profit, they are less interested in working with the company, are at increased risk of bankruptcy, and cannot reinvest in their own operations to improve efficiencies. In short, shifting inventory back onto suppliers is a short-term proposition that does not help a company in the long run.

The only way to maintain a healthy group of suppliers is to strip inventory out of the *entire* supply chain. This approach requires a large amount of effort, working with primary suppliers to improve their systems and practices. One way to detect which suppliers to approach with this assistance is to measure total inventory. Total inventory is the sum of all inventories in all locations, for which the calculation appears in the following table.

Total Inventory Calculation

+	Inventory already located at the company
+	Inventory already produced for the company by suppliers
=	Total inventory

This calculation requires that the company ascertain the amount of company-specific inventory at suppliers, which can be difficult to obtain. Consequently, this may be a measurement that is only compiled once every quarter or year. However, the calculation effort can highlight the largest pockets of inventory, which are then targeted for reduction.

> **Tip:** The total inventory concept works best when inventory items are sole sourced. In this case, a company's engineers and procurement specialists only have to work with a single supplier to create reductions in total inventory. This work is multiplied if the company must work with several suppliers to reduce the same inventory item.

EXAMPLE

Mole Industries manufactures a variety of trench-digging machines. The company assembles components produced by five primary suppliers. The president of Mole is deeply interested in reducing the total inventory of the company, and so commissions the following total inventory measurement:

Inventory Specific to:	Inventory at Mole Industries	Inventory at Supplier	Total Inventory
Supplier A	$2,500,000	$1,250,000	$3,750,000
Supplier B	150,000	1,000,000	1,150,000
Supplier C	10,000	3,000,000	3,010,000
Supplier D	1,700,000	250,000	1,950,000
Supplier E	450,000	250,000	700,000
Totals	$4,810,000	$5,750,000	$10,560,000

The initial calculation reveals that there may be significant opportunities for inventory reduction by working with Suppliers A, B, and C. The most egregious case of excessive inventory appears to be related to Supplier C, where the company maintains essentially no inventory on site, having shifted a large inventory burden back onto Supplier C.

The concept of total inventory can be used to monitor inventory management techniques, to ensure that inventory is actually being eliminated from all parts of the supply chain.

Downstream Postponement

The postponement concept is that a company should store goods one level below their final configured form. The reason is that a far smaller number of inventory items can be maintained. For example, if a widget can be sold with five different attachments, maintain just the widget in stock, and add whichever of the five attachments are ordered just prior to shipment. By doing so, the company can maintain a single stock of base-level widgets, rather than its best guess as to the final configurations that customers may order.

The postponement concept can be encouraged among suppliers. By doing so, suppliers also have to maintain less inventory, which reduces their working capital requirements. A smaller amount of cash needed to run the business improves the financial prospects of a supplier, which in turn yields a stronger supply chain. The only downside for the company is that it may have to accept slightly longer supplier lead times, which they need to make final configuration adjustments to the goods to be shipped.

Suppliers Own On-Site Inventory

Have suppliers own their inventory in the company's warehouse until the moment when it is used or sold. This eliminates the holding period for inventory, thereby shifting the cost of the inventory to suppliers until the inventory is needed. Also, the company incurs no risk of inventory obsolescence, since suppliers will take back any unused inventory.

This approach is usually only possible if inventory is sole sourced to certain suppliers, so that they can be assured of more sales in exchange for taking on the inventory holding cost. Also, the goods cannot be customized, so that suppliers can take back their goods and sell them elsewhere if not used by the company.

This approach works best if the company tracks the on-hand unit levels for supplier-owned inventory, and suppliers are given access to this information. Better yet, give suppliers direct access to the company's production schedule, so they can plan for the exact amount of upcoming demand for the inventory items for which they are responsible. Another possible trigger is to send kanban notifications to the supplier when inventory levels reach a predetermined reorder point, which places responsibility for triggering replenishment activities on the company, not the supplier.

While this approach will reduce a company's investment in inventory, there may be an offsetting increase in the prices charged by suppliers. They are taking on an increased funding cost, and may also need to send their staff on-site to review inventory levels. However, a price increase may be avoided if a supplier can be the sole source of an increased number of inventory items. Another concern with supplier-owned inventory is that suppliers may want to overstock goods, in order to keep from making too many replenishment trips to the warehouse. If so, the company may find that it is allocating an excessive amount of warehouse space to the supplier's goods.

Suppliers Pre-Configure Goods

Some goods are ordered from suppliers that will then be sold straight to customers without modification. If so, request that suppliers deliver the goods in the same unit quantities in which they are ordered by customers. For example, if customers tend to order in quantities of 25, then have the supplier deliver the goods prepackaged in this size. If customers tend to order in several quantities, then order a mix of prepackaged sizes from the supplier. Doing so shifts the order preparation task back onto the supplier, while also allowing the company to pick and pack customer orders within the minimum possible period of time.

> **Tip:** Set price points to encourage customers to order in the quantities in which goods are prepackaged for delivery. For example, a sharp discount for orders of five units will likely yield a preponderance of orders for this unit size.

Parts Standardization

Product designers can develop products that share many of the same component parts. This is particularly likely across product families, where the same basic design is being used as the foundation for a cluster of products. By doing so, a business can eliminate a number of parts from raw materials inventory, while applying for volume discounts with suppliers for the remaining parts, which it will need in greater volume. This concept also tends to result in less obsolete inventory, since so few parts are solely linked to a single product. However, it typically requires at least one product cycle to build the parts minimization concept into the product design philosophy, so it can take years to implement this approach.

Design for Broad Tolerance

Some products are designed to work only with parts whose dimensions are very precisely defined. If a part does not exactly match the planned characteristics, it is designated as scrap and thrown away. This scrap cost can be reduced by designing products to operate with components whose characteristics can vary somewhat from specifications. A side benefit of this approach is that it may be less expensive to purchase parts that have a broader tolerance range, since suppliers do not have to be so exacting in manufacturing these items.

Design around Limited Availability Components

There may be cases where the components designed into a product are only available from a single supplier, or are heavily in demand. A possible outcome of this situation is that a company is put on allocation when it orders goods. If so, this limits the ability of the company to generate products, which constrains its profitability. Another possibility is that suppliers react to high demand by massively increasing their prices. If the cost of such a component comprises a large proportion of the total cost of a product, this can severely impact its profitability.

To avoid the limited sourcing issue, the product development staff can work with the purchasing department during the design phase of a new product to identify components that may not be readily available. It is much less expensive to design replacement parts into a product during the initial design phase, rather than in a later engineering change order, after the product has already been released.

Design around Lifetime Buy Decisions

A lifetime buy is when a needed part is no longer going to be provided by a supplier, so a company is forced to buy a large quantity of the part right now, to ensure that the part is in stock for what may continue to be a lengthy usage period. A lifetime buy is not a good decision to make, since it ties up working capital in inventory for an extended period, and eventually puts a company at risk of an obsolete inventory writedown. There are a number of ways to reduce the frequency with which lifetime buys must be made. Possible alternatives include the following:

- *Increased communications.* When a part is first designed into a product, communicate with the supplier the expected volume to be purchased per year, and for how long the purchasing is expected to continue. If substantial, this information may persuade the supplier to put off its product termination.
- *Design for common parts.* When there is a choice between designing a standard or non-standard part into a product, always go with the standard version. By doing so, the company can buy the part from multiple suppliers.
- *Design for new parts.* If a part is extremely new, then a supplier is likely to let it run for a reasonably long life cycle. Conversely, designing in an old component, such as an older model computer chip, puts a business at risk of having a supplier eliminate the part quite soon.
- *Shorten the product life cycle.* If a part used in a product is to be shut down soon, use this as a trigger to shut down the product in which the part is used, in favor of a replacement product. If there is a history of part life cycles that are quite short, this may be the best option – the company designs all of its products to have roughly the same product life cycles as the parts that go into them.

Advance Material Purchase Issues

A company may focus on rapid product releases, so that it can beat its competitors to market with new designs. Sometimes, the products they are designing include components that have unusually long lead times. In order to compress their product launch dates, a design team may authorize the purchase of these components before the final designs are completed. This approach is possible when a sub-assembly is considered to be final, even though the remainder of the product design is still being tweaked.

While an advance material purchase may appear to be a clever way to compress product design time, it can run into trouble if there is a subsequent product alteration that *does* impact the material. If so, a large and expensive materials purchase will later arrive, and will not fit into the final product design. The following techniques can reduce the risk of this situation occurring:

- *Manual solution – purchasing review.* The product development team should include someone from the purchasing department who is specifically assigned to monitor any changes to items requiring advance material purchases. This is the easiest monitoring solution, but runs the risk of a prospective change getting past the attention of the designated person.
- *Manual solution – drawing updates review.* If there is a change to an item requiring an advance material purchase, the change will be reflected in an altered engineering drawing, which should contain the date of the revision. Have someone periodically compare the drawing dates to the dates on which

advance material purchases were made. If the drawing date is later than the purchase date, there may be a problem.

- *Automated solution - tag advance items*. The design team should maintain an ongoing series of preliminary bills of material, one for each version of a prospective product. Always tag those items in the bill that require advance purchases, and require password access to the system to alter these items. If a change is subsequently made, have the computer system issue a notification message to the team leader. However, few bill of materials systems contain this feature. Also, a bill may not be changed, even though an underlying engineering drawing is changed. Consequently, the preceding drawing updates review is the better control.

Inventory Disposal

The purchasing department is routinely tasked with disposing of excess or obsolete inventory. This can be a significantly profitable activity, especially when alternatives can be found that improve upon the receipts generated by simply selling off the inventory to a scrap dealer. The following alternatives are presented in order by the size of return that will be generated, with the first alternatives being the most productive:

- *Reserve as spares*. If there is a history of spare parts orders from customers, set aside a sufficient amount of the inventory to deal with these orders. This is one case where full pricing can still be obtained from sale of the goods, and probably for a fairly long period of time.
- *Move to different location*. If the company has multiple locations, it is possible that demand is higher at a different location. If so, estimate the long-term demand in the alternate location, and shift a sufficient amount of inventory there to cover the demand.
- *Return to suppliers*. Suppliers are typically reluctant to take back goods, especially if the value of the goods has declined over time. Still, it may be possible to do so in exchange for a restocking fee. This option is most attractive when a supplier is willing to pay the company for any credit granted. Conversely, if a credit is granted and the company no longer does business with the supplier, the value of the credit is minimal.
- *Marketing campaign*. If the obsolete inventory is finished goods, the marketing department can roll out a discount program that offers the goods to customers at a steep discount. This approach should be used with caution, in case the goods being sold at a lower price will cannibalize sales of the company's full-price products.
- *Product integration*. If the obsolete inventory is raw materials, the engineering manager may be able to design them into new products. However, this is quite a long-term proposition, and is usually only feasible for a small number of items.
- *Third party reseller*. A number of third party resellers maintain cut-rate distribution channels through which they sell obsolete inventory. They may be

willing to buy obsolete inventory, though only at a large discount. In this case, there is a risk that goods resold through these alternative distribution channels will cannibalize sales of the company's full-priced products.

- *Donation*. It may be possible to donate obsolete inventory to a not-for-profit entity. By doing so, the company can recognize the fair value of the donated goods as a tax credit. This approach works best for supplies and foodstuffs, for which there are a number of charities willing to accept donations.
- *Break down*. It may be possible to break down finished goods into their constituent parts, which can then be used in other products. However, doing so can damage the parts salvaged from this process.
- *Sell to salvage contractors*. There are third party salvage contractors that will periodically pick through a company's unwanted inventory and offer to purchase selected items. The price obtained will be low, but may be higher than what can be obtained from a scrap dealer. If this route is taken, consider offering goods in batches, rather than allowing contractors to buy only the best items. Doing so may not result in much additional revenue, but will clear out a fair amount of valuable storage space in the warehouse.
- *Scrap*. A small amount of cash can be gleaned from scrapping inventory, if it contains a sufficient amount of residual metal to be worth selling to a scrap dealer. Scrapping inventory may also make sense if the company wants to prevent its branded products from appearing in the marketplace.

As can be seen from the list, the purchasing department does not actually have to be involved in the disposal of inventory until several potentially more profitable alternatives are addressed internally. Also, it can make sense to work with the engineering and marketing departments on the internal alternatives before looking at outside disposal options.

Summary

It is possible to interpret the level of management commitment to the inventory asset simply by comparing the inventory asset to the sales of a business. A high proportion of inventory probably means that there are a number of flaws within the product design, production, materials management, and recordkeeping systems of a business that are being offset by retaining too much inventory. This represents a major opportunity to cut back drastically on inventory levels, while still maintaining high customer service levels.

An increased amount of inventory management certainly impacts the purchasing department, since it is responsible for obtaining large amounts of raw materials and merchandise from suppliers. This can be achieved with several techniques, including improved communications, rapid deliveries, kanban notifications, and compressing supplier lead times. A full implementation of these concepts will likely require that the supplier base be reduced in size, to just the highest-quality suppliers that are willing to assist the company in its inventory management efforts.

Chapter 10
Logistics

Introduction

From the perspective of the purchasing department, logistics at its most basic level refers to the process of bringing goods into a company from suppliers. This simple definition is most likely to apply to the delivery of commodities to a company from suppliers with which the company does not have a close working relationship. When the relationship is more integrated, logistics can also refer to the prepositioning of goods for immediate company use, as well as the creation of sub-assemblies at supplier locations prior to delivery to the company. The total cost of logistics can be the third largest corporate expense, after direct materials and compensation. If so, it is deserving of significant attention from the purchasing department.

In this chapter, we discuss the range of logistics responsibilities that the purchasing department may take on, the different types of freight terms and how they alter the focus on logistics, the process flow for setting up a logistics system, and several related topics.

Purchasing Responsibilities

The bulk of all deliveries from suppliers will arrive in a timely manner, and will dovetail into a company's production and distribution systems. However, other deliveries will *not* arrive on time, and for any number of reasons – such as weather delays, road closures, incorrect information on a purchase order, a supplier's bankruptcy, or a delay in a supplier's production process. Or, goods may arrive but were damaged in transit, and so are no longer usable. When these delays arise, the purchasing department may resolve the problem. In addition, the purchasing staff will likely evaluate third party shippers and enter into long-term freight hauling contracts with the best of this group. Given these responsibilities, the department can be expected to engage in the following activities:

- *Pricing.* The purchasing staff evaluates the routes along which it expects to receive goods, and possibly also ship them to customers, and then determines the mix of prices offered by suppliers to handle the related inbound and outbound freight. This is a specialized function, which may be assigned to those purchasing staff with expertise in logistics.
- *Alternative sourcing.* It may be possible to obtain alternative goods on the spot market on extremely short notice, and have them air freighted to the company. This is an expensive alternative, but does allow a business to keep functioning.

- *Insurance claim.* If the freight terms state that the company owns the goods while they are in transit to the company (see the next section), an insurance claim must be filed that states the particulars of the situation. There may be a number of these claims outstanding at any time, requiring a modest amount of monitoring. The receiving department may file these claims.
- *Internal scheduling change.* When there is no way to work around a delayed receipt, the purchasing department contacts the internal materials planning coordinator to discuss altering the production or shipping schedule to accommodate the missing goods.
- *Split orders.* If a supplier can only deliver part of an order and has backordered the remainder of the order, purchasing works with the materials planning coordinator to decide whether to accept a split order, or to wait until the entire order can be fulfilled with one delivery.
- *Status checks.* In situations where it is essential for goods to arrive on time, or when a supplier has a history of late deliveries, the purchasing staff may need to engage in status checks to ascertain the current status of a pending delivery.

Though a number of purchasing responsibilities have been listed in this section, it does not mean that the purchasing department is responsible for all inbound transportation; that is the responsibility of the transportation department or materials management department. The purchasing staff only inserts itself to obtain the best terms, and again to obtain alternate sourcing when it is apparent that a delivery will be late.

Free on Board Shipping Terms

The discussion in the next section involves the evaluation of the logistics function. A central part of this discussion is the point at which a company takes possession of inbound goods, so we will first address the FOB concept. FOB is an acronym for Free on Board. The term originated with the delivery of goods from suppliers to their customers by ship. The type of FOB assigned to the delivery of goods states whether the supplier or the buyer will pay shipping expenses. Also, the type of FOB shows which party takes legal responsibility for the goods being shipped, and at what point during transport that responsibility is transferred.

There are two types of FOB, which are FOB destination and FOB shipping point. The type of FOB to be used is typically designated in a buyer's purchase order, and is also stated on the supplier's invoice to the buyer.

FOB Destination

FOB destination means that the buyer takes delivery of goods being shipped to it by a supplier once the goods arrive at the buyer's receiving dock. There are three variations on FOB destination terms, which are:

- *FOB destination, freight prepaid.* The supplier pays the freight charges and owns the goods while they are in transit.

- *FOB destination, freight collect.* The buyer pays the freight charges, though the supplier still owns the goods while they are in transit.
- *FOB destination, freight collect and allowed.* The buyer pays for the freight costs, but deducts the cost from the supplier's invoice. The supplier still owns the goods while they are in transit.

If the goods are damaged in transit, the supplier should file a claim with the insurance carrier, since the supplier has title to the goods during the period when the goods were damaged.

It might initially appear that a company should always insist on FOB destination terms, since this reduces the time period over which the company has ownership of any goods arriving from suppliers. Any damage caused in transit is therefore the responsibility of someone else – not the company. While this position is true, the real issue is that goods may be damaged in transit, and so are not available to the company. Thus, the real issue is how to prevent in-transit damage, which is covered later in the Additional Logistics Topics section.

FOB Shipping Point

The term FOB shipping point is a contraction of the term Free on Board Shipping Point. It means that the buyer takes delivery of goods being shipped to it by a supplier once the goods leave the supplier's shipping dock. Under FOB shipping point terms, the buyer is responsible for the cost of shipping the product.

If the goods are damaged in transit, the buyer should file a claim with the insurance carrier, since the buyer has title to the goods during the period when the goods were damaged.

Creating a Logistics System

When evaluating logistics, the main involvement of the purchasing department in the process is the negotiation of transportation rates and service levels. This is by no means the first step in the process of creating a cost-effective logistics system. The following steps describe the full systems creation process:

1. Decide whether to have suppliers ship goods to the company (FOB destination) or have the company's transport contractors pick up goods at supplier locations (FOB shipping point). The FOB shipping point concept requires much more complexity for the company, but also gives it better control over inbound logistics, as well as better visibility into the locations of trucks, trains, and ships carrying inbound goods to the company.

2. Determine the logistics performance goals that the company needs to succeed. For example, it may be necessary to have frequent delivery intervals, or deliveries that occur within narrow time slots, or short transit times, or the lowest possible freight rates. The mix of performance goals needed drives the selection of the transportation mode to be used. For example, the fastest possible transit time and no particular emphasis on freight cost might point

toward the use of air freight, while the reverse situation might lead one to select rail transport.

3. Select the mode of transport that meets the company's logistics performance goals. The following table can help to narrow down the available choices.

Mode of Transport Options

Situation	Most Applicable Transport
Bulk commodities	Rail transport, pipeline, or ocean vessel; low cost in all cases
Fluids	Pipeline for long-term supply situations, ocean vessel if longer lead times are acceptable, trucks for lower volumes and where higher cost is acceptable
Hazardous materials	Rail transport
Overseas deliveries	Ocean vessel when transport cost is an issue, and especially when goods are in bulk; air freight when cost is not an issue and the goods are high-value
Rapid delivery	Truck delivery for moderate volumes; air freight for high-value, smaller-size goods
Reliable delivery	Trucks are best; most other forms of transport are either subject to periodic delays or are not located near a company's facilities (as may be the case for rail transport)

The characteristics of the types of transport noted in the preceding table are as follows:

- *Air transport.* Can provide long-distance transport of smaller, high-value items on short notice. It can be especially useful for the transport of short-life products, since other modes of transport would limit their salability. However, its cost is significantly higher than for all other types of transport. Also, the nearest airport may be relatively far from a company location.

- *Barges and ocean vessels.* Can provide long-distance transport of oversized and bulk items at low cost, such as automobiles built in other countries, or grain intended for a different state. This type of transport can be shut down due to weather conditions on the oceans, or due to freezing on inland waterways. Transport times tend to be quite lengthy, so this is certainly not a good choice for time-sensitive deliveries. Another issue is that the nearest port facility may be quite distant from the intended company delivery point.

- *Pipelines.* Can provide reliable, high-volume transport of petroleum products and natural gas to fixed points. Given the environmental and high fixed costs of constructing pipelines, they are only directly accessible to companies buying these products in large volumes.

- *Rail transport.* Can provide long-distance transport of oversized and bulk items at low cost, such as coal and agricultural products.

However, the lead times required to schedule rail transport are significant, and rail lines do not always pass near a company facility. Also, transit times can be lengthy, as rail cars may be switched to several different trains as they move from a supplier to the company.

- *Trucks*. Able to move goods anywhere, and can deliver within narrow delivery windows. They can be used to move goods on short notice. However, load sizes are limited and the cost of transport is moderately high. Also, delivery reliability is affected by traffic, seasonal weather, and the quality of the road system. Generally, trucks will be part of the overall transport solution, if only to provide the final transport link from a seaport, airport, or rail line to a company's location.

It is quite common for the routing of goods to involve a mix of different types of transport, which is known as *intermodal transport*. For example, a Chinese supplier may load goods onto a container ship, which delivers the goods to a port, at which point the containers are loaded onto a train for transport to a rail spur in the middle of the country, where they are offloaded to a truck and delivered to the end customer. A single carrier will handle the logistics for intermodal transport, so that a company's transportation department only has to schedule a single transaction – the carrier handles the freight transfers among the different transport providers, and issues a single consolidated billing to the company.

4. Once the best mode of transport has been chosen, select the specific carrier best able to fill the company's needs. There are a number of possible options to choose from. The choices are greatest for transport by truck, including the following:

- *Common carrier*. This is a general carrier of goods that charges based on a standard pricing schedule. There are a number of common carriers that provide transport services over broad regions.
- *Contract carrier*. This is a carrier that can be hired to serve a company's specific needs, such as to make large numbers of frequent delivery runs between the business and its suppliers. Prices with a contract carrier are negotiated.
- *Private fleet*. A company may maintain its own fleet, which gives it absolute control over deliveries. This may not always be a cost-effective option (since trucks may be empty for a large part of the time), so a variation is to use a private fleet for specific delivery runs, and common or contract carriers for other deliveries.

5. Negotiate pricing and service levels with transport suppliers. This is where the purchasing department is most likely to become involved, though it is also possible that a buyer might enter into the preceding stage, where a specific carrier is chosen. The reason for involving the department earlier in the

process is that a carrier is less likely to haggle if it already knows it has been chosen as the designated transport provider.

The inclination of the purchasing staff will be to concentrate service with the smallest possible number of transport providers, to take advantage of volume discounts. The level of price discounting that can be obtained represents a tradeoff with delivery reliability, since a freight carrier may be able to offer quite a low price, but only if the company's deliveries are used as filler on deliveries primarily intended for other companies. Also, the company may have particular delivery requirements that will *increase* the price charged, such as the need for less-than-truckload (LTL) deliveries and being able to deliver within tight time windows.

As the preceding steps indicate, there is not an immediate need for purchasing to be involved until a number of planning steps have been completed. Once pricing and service levels have been agreed upon, the purchasing department switches to a monitoring role, to verify how well a transport provider is complying with its contractual obligations.

Transportation Brokers

A company may find that the logistics function is not a core competency, and so outsources the entire function to a transportation broker. This entity acts as the company's agent in negotiating for best prices and deliveries, in exchange for a service charge. There are several advantages to using a transportation broker, including the following:

- The purchasing staff can hand off pricing negotiations with freight companies to the broker, who may be able to obtain better rates by negotiating on behalf of all of its clients.
- The broker may specialize in getting inbound goods through customs, which could accelerate transit times.
- The broker can arrange for the temporary storage of inbound goods, if they have arrived too soon for the company to house them.
- The broker provides access to its monitoring systems, so that a company can review the status of deliveries; the best brokers will also issue alerts whenever a delivery will be delayed.

A broker should also be able to provide a variety of metrics to a company as part of its ongoing services, to give management a better idea of the extent of its logistics involvement. Examples of these metrics are the proportion of FOB destination to FOB origin shipments, the performance of individual carriers used by the broker, and expenditures by carrier.

Some brokers specialize in certain areas, such as international logistics or domestic freight, so it may be necessary to maintain relations with several brokers. If so, it can make sense to keep the number of brokers used down to a minimum level, so that the company can concentrate on achieving maximum coordination with the few brokers used. If there are too many brokers, it is too difficult to coordinate operations with all of them, resulting in some inefficiencies and occasional system breakdowns that result in late deliveries.

The advantages noted here are especially appealing for a smaller business that does not have the staff to handle its own logistics, as well as for firms of any size that only deal with goods on an occasional basis. However, handing off logistics to a third party also means that a company will lose its in-house expertise in this area, and lose any direct control over logistics.

Just-in-Time Deliveries

When a company engages in just-in-time manufacturing, one aspect of this system is to have suppliers only deliver goods on an as-needed basis. This has the following implications from the perspective of logistics:

- Deliveries may be needed in very small unit quantities.
- Given the small quantities needed, suppliers or their warehouses may need to be located quite close to the company's facility, thereby reducing total travel times.
- It is easier to deliver from a small delivery van than from the traditional trailer, so either suppliers need to use a different transport system or the company should provide them with one.
- If the company provides transport service to its suppliers, the vans should be on a regular schedule, where they visit all supplier locations for pickups at certain scheduled times of the day.
- Given the use of delivery vans by either suppliers or the company, there is less need for third party shipping services.
- Deliveries from smaller vans cannot be made through the traditional loading bays in the receiving area, which may call for a different receiving dock configuration.

Also, a just-in-time system requires extremely consistent deliveries, where deliveries are made within a narrow time window, perhaps just a couple of hours. If some suppliers are located at a long distance, this means that the company will still need to employ third party freight haulers, but only those that are extremely reliable. This has the following implications:

- There will be few transport services that can meet the company's more rigorous standards, so expect a consolidation of a company's transport spend with a small number of providers.
- Once business has been concentrated with just a few transport services, it is best to formalize these relationships with long-term contracts.
- The purchasing staff will need to know exactly when goods will arrive at the shipping dock, so arrange for advance shipping notices (see the Applicable Information Technology chapter). A transport service may be willing to

install GPS transponders on its vehicles, so that their exact locations can be tracked.

Additional Logistics Topics

There is a cost management opportunity if a company is willing to take on the ownership of inbound goods at a supplier's receiving dock, using FOB shipping point terms. In exchange for the increased amount of complexity to arrange for this transport, a company does not run the risk of having a supplier incur excessive freight costs and then bill them through to the company. This is a particular concern when a supplier is adding a profit percentage to its freight billings. In addition, a company can greatly increase its volume of freight services by taking on these shipping chores, which gives it greater sway with its transport suppliers.

If a company does not want to engage in the additional management chores associated with taking over inbound logistics, it can at least provide its suppliers with a "short list" of approved freight carriers to be used. Doing so keeps inbound freight with carriers that have a proven record of on-time deliveries and not damaging goods while in transit.

During the transport process, there are a number of opportunities for goods to be damaged. The reasons for damage can likely be traced to a small number of causes which occur on a regular basis. The purchasing staff could institute a tracking log of damage to received goods, and trace the reasons for the damage. Examples of the findings of such a system could be inadequate packaging of incoming goods, broken pallets, and not using an air ride truck. These issues can then be mitigated by imposing additional conditions on the applicable transport service. If the service does not comply, then the purchasing staff can shift the company's logistics business to a more amenable supplier.

Summary

The level of involvement that the purchasing department can take in the logistics area depends on the corporate structure, the amount of logistics-related spending, and the amount of expertise that the department can bring to this area. If there is a separate and well-staffed transportation department, this separate group may be quite qualified to handle all logistics contract negotiation issues. Also, logistics is a specialized area, to which a buyer with only generalized training might not be able to bring any value; only employees with detailed logistics training and experience will be able to negotiate effective agreements with suppliers. And finally, it may not be cost-effective to delve into the logistics area if the amount of spend is minimal to moderate. Instead, management may make the decision to leave this area alone, in favor of concentrating the attention of the purchasing department on other areas where there are greater opportunities for improvement.

Another way of looking at the involvement of the purchasing function in logistics is whether a company wants to be reactive or proactive. In reactive mode, a company leaves logistics issues up to its suppliers, and only gets involved when there is a late delivery situation. In proactive mode, a company configures logistics to strike a balance between costs and attaining the appropriate level of service needed to run the business.

Chapter 11
Spend Management

Introduction

In a typical organization, the amount spent on all types of materials and services is usually spread among many suppliers. The situation is compounded in a multi-division company where each division conducts its own purchasing activities. The result may be purchases of approximately the same items from a multitude of suppliers, with each purchase at a different price and likely in small quantities. This means that a business is wasting money by paying more for goods and services than it could achieve by employing the principles of spend management.

Spend management is the process of collecting spend information, aggregating it to discern possible purchasing opportunities, acting on this information, and monitoring compliance with the new, better-managed purchasing process. This chapter covers all aspects of spend management.

The Spend Database

One aspect of spend management involves the aggregation of information about a company's expenditures into a database, which can then be sorted in a variety of ways to uncover opportunities for cost reductions, primarily through the concentration of purchases with a smaller number of suppliers.

The spend management database lies at the center of the spend management system. Information from the company's purchasing departments in all of its subsidiaries is pulled into the database. Once the information is assembled, it must be cleaned up with the following techniques:

- *Name linkages.* It is extremely likely that each subsidiary uses a different supplier identification code for its suppliers, so the aggregated information probably contains information about purchases from a single supplier that are listed under several different names. A table must be constructed for the database that links all of these name variations to a single supplier name. Thus, purchases from ATT, AT&T, and AT&TWIRELESS would all be linked to the same phone company.
- *Description linkages.* As was the case for supplier names, the descriptions of items purchased may vary wildly from each other at the subsidiary level, and so must be standardized in the spend database. To do so, have the suppliers always load the official supplier part number for each item into their purchasing software, so that this can be ported into the spend database. Then attach a file to the database that contains all supplier part numbers and part descriptions. Once supplier part numbers are identified in the data feeds from subsidiaries, they can be linked to the supplier descriptions.

- *Commodity code linkages*. Every purchase made should have attached to it a standard commodity code, which assigns a spend category to the purchase. This information is useful for aggregating purchases by commodity type, which can then be used to concentrate purchases with preferred suppliers for volume discounts. It is best to have all subsidiaries record purchases using the same standard commodity code system, such as the North American Industry Classification System (NAICS). If commodity codes are not being entered, then there should be a feedback loop to the subsidiary purchasing departments to remind them to do so.
- *Credit rating linkages*. The database should include a data feed from a third party credit rating service, which contains the credit rating for each supplier. This information is useful for determining which suppliers may be in financial difficulty, so that spending can be shifted to more reliable suppliers.

A spend database can be enormous, which means that all of the preceding data cleansing and enhancement activities must be performed through automated routines. It is not even remotely cost-effective to engage in these activities manually.

> **Tip:** Do not use an excessively detailed system of commodity codes. When a massive number of codes are used to "slice and dice" spend into potentially thousands of different classifications, the coding process takes too long and is subject to error. In addition, it can create confusion when a supplier has a number of offerings that could be classified in several alternative ways.

> **Tip:** The purchasing staff can review the information resulting from the various automated routines just described, and recommend additional automated routines to further clean up the information.

Spend Management Activities

Once information has been fully aggregated into the spend database, sort the information by commodity code to determine spend levels for all of the various types of commodities. The resulting reports can be used to drive down costs by any of the following means:

- *Consolidate suppliers*. While each subsidiary may proudly point out that it has already consolidated its supplier base, each one may have consolidated around a different group of suppliers. The database can reveal that the subsidiaries have few suppliers in common at the commodity code level, which represents an opportunity for *all* of the subsidiaries to consolidate their purchases with the same group of suppliers. The net result can be a remarkable decline in the overall number of suppliers from which purchases are made. For example, if there are five subsidiaries and each one purchases from five suppliers, of which only 20% are commonly used by all subsidiaries, this means a total of 20 suppliers could potentially be stripped away from a pool of 25 suppliers, which is an 80% reduction.

- *Consolidate professional services.* There is a tendency for each department or subsidiary to hire their own professional services firms, such as consultants, tax accountants, attorneys, and auditors. The spend report will aggregate professional services, so that management can see the overall extent of purchasing in this area, and especially the large number of services firms used. A likely outcome is a general retrenchment of the purchasing function in this area, where work can be centralized with a much smaller number of services firms. Doing so may also result in the discovery that some services were being duplicated in several company locations. However, centralization in this area can be taken too far, since there are some firms with unique expertise that cannot be found elsewhere. The ideal outcome is the identification of those specialists whose offerings are unique, with all other work being centralized with a small number of larger service firms.
- *Source through distributors.* The spend report may reveal that the company is spending a relatively small amount with a large number of suppliers in certain commodity code categories. When this is the case, the easiest solution may be to locate a single distributor through which all of the items can be purchased. The result could be a massive reduction in the number of suppliers, which reduces the administrative and accounting burden of the purchasing and accounting departments.
- *Source overseas.* If certain commodities have high labor content, there may be an opportunity to source them from overseas locations where labor rates are extremely low, which can yield significant cost reductions.

It can take a long time to gradually work through the information provided by a spend database, shifting purchases to a smaller and smaller pool of suppliers. Over time, the categories of unaddressed commodity codes will shrink, in which case the emphasis should always be on the next largest remaining spend by commodity code. It is possible that the lowest-spend commodity codes will never be addressed, because the potential savings are so small that they are not worth investigating.

Spend Compliance

Once purchases have been shifted to a small group of preferred suppliers, the company must ensure that it is obtaining the full amount of volume discounts from these suppliers. Accordingly, monitor the amount spent with each supplier and compare the aggregate spend with the contractual trigger points at which volume discounts will be achieved. The company should remind suppliers whenever volume discounts have been earned.

This level of spend analysis is made easier if the database contains a listing of the trigger points at which volume discounts and other rebates will be earned, by supplier. This listing is essentially a summarization of the key elements of each supplier contract. The primary data items to include in the listing for discount tracking purposes are:

- Contract start and stop dates
- Discount thresholds and amount of discounts
- Rebate thresholds and amount of rebates

When this contract information is matched against the spend database, you may find that suppliers are not following the terms of their own contracts, and that the company is entitled to volume discounts right now, before any supplier consolidation activities have commenced. Consequently, matching contract terms against the spend database should be one of the earlier activities to engage in, once the database has been created.

Another rich opportunity source for spend compliance is maverick spending. This is the purchase of goods and services from unauthorized sources. Maverick spending can result in paying excessively high prices for items that the purchasing staff could have sourced elsewhere for a lower price. This is a particular problem when the spending is occurring in a commodity code for which there is already a contract with a preferred supplier, since the spending could have contributed toward a volume discount. In commodity codes where no volume discount has yet been negotiated, maverick spending has less of an impact.

It is relatively easy to track down maverick spenders, since their names are on the offending purchasing documents or sales receipts. Once located, there are several ways to deal with them, including the following:

- *Formal meeting*. Schedule a meeting with the individual, and discuss the implications of their actions on total cost savings. This is much more effective than an impersonal memo.
- *Feedback*. Send a periodic report to the person, as well as his or her supervisor, detailing the nature of all maverick spending that occurred in the preceding period.
- *Chargeback*. Charge the person's department an inter-company fee for each maverick spending situation.
- *Reimbursement rejection*. Note in the employee manual that requests for the reimbursement of maverick spend items will be rejected.
- *Annual review*. Include a discussion of their spending behavior in their annual performance reviews.

Implications of Spend Management

The following points relate to additional spend management concepts that can be used to drive down costs further:

- *Standardize parts*. The spend database may indicate that subsidiaries are purchasing slight variations on the same parts. If so, there may be an opportunity to redesign products so that exactly the same parts are used in multiple locations. Though such redesigns can drive down costs through bulk purchases, they also involve years of redesign work, and so may not be worth the effort.

- *New supplier additions*. Compare the approved supplier list to the most recent additions to the spend database, to see if any new suppliers have been added that were not approved. Use of these new suppliers should be curtailed, so that purchases are more heavily concentrated with preferred suppliers. This can mean that the supplier base tends to centralize around the existing suppliers – it is more difficult for new suppliers to break in.
- *Purchase order receiving requirement*. Have the receiving staff reject any deliveries for which there is no authorizing purchase order. If the purchasing system is configured to only issue purchase orders to suppliers on the preferred supplier list, this means that all other purchases not being acquired with procurement cards are effectively blocked. However, it can also result in annoyed employees who are wondering why their purchases were turned away at the receiving dock.
- *Audit billed prices*. The sales staff of suppliers may not route new contracts with the company to their billing departments, which means that the company will be billed at old price points. This issue can be detected by conducting regular audits of supplier invoices, where billed prices are matched against contract prices. If the audit reveals continuing pricing issues for a supplier, designate that supplier for more frequent audits.

Rollout of Spend Management

The construction of a spend management system is one of the more expensive database projects that a company can engage in. To accelerate the payback period, consider the following ways in which to roll out the system:

- Initially include in the database the purchasing information for just the largest subsidiaries. Doing so accumulates the bulk of the information needed for the database, without wasting an undue amount of time creating interfaces to the smaller purchasing systems.
- Estimate which commodity codes comprise most of the company's spending activity, and focus all of the data cleanup efforts on purchases within these codes. Doing so allows you to take more immediate action to engage in volume purchasing in these areas.

These actions should yield relatively rapid results, which may encourage management to provide additional funding for a more complete rollout of the system.

Summary

The up-front cost of a spend management database is considerable. To gain a reasonable return on investment from it will require a great deal of focused attention from the purchasing department. To obtain this return, consider setting up a permanent team of buyers who work their way through the database, continually targeting new commodity codes to explore. Given the size of the potential payback, this group cannot be diverted by any other activities, so the purchasing manager will need to protect them from stray work assignments. As this group completes its analysis of commodity codes and signs agreements with preferred suppliers, a follow-on task is to engage in spend compliance activities, which requires the active involvement of a smaller group of purchasing analysts. In short, there needs to be a reorientation of the purchasing staff to properly employ its new spend management database tool. Otherwise, a large investment will be wasted or at least underutilized.

Chapter 12
Quality Management

Introduction

An inexperienced management team might believe that the quality of goods provided by suppliers is at most a modest issue, one that is ranked well below other concerns, such as achieving the lowest possible product costs. A more experienced team will realize that the cost of quality is so enormous that quality management must be one of the cornerstones of ongoing supplier relations. In this chapter, we define quality, elaborate upon its cost, and note a number of paths to follow to improve the quality of the goods provided by suppliers.

Quality from a Supplier's Perspective

Quality involves the creation and delivery of a product that meets the expectations of a customer. Thus, if a customer spends very little for an automobile, he will not expect leather seats and air conditioning - but he will expect the vehicle to run properly. In this case, quality is considered to be a vehicle that functions, rather than a luxury experience. When this concept of quality is applied to a supplier, it means that a quality product is one that reliably meets the specifications of the buyer in all respects. For example:

- If a widget must have a specific width with a plus or minus variation of .005%, then a quality widget is one that falls anywhere within this allowable range of variation.
- The term "in all respects" means that all parts of the buying experience meet a buyer's expectations, including the product installation, maintenance, field service, and warranty.

A supplier's view of quality could be formed by the contents of the scorecard that a buyer applies to it. As noted in the Supplier Management chapter, a scorecard can include measurements for quite a large number of issues, such as on-time delivery, billing accuracy, and conformance with specifications. As companies gradually rationalize their supply chains, they use these scorecards to determine which suppliers will stay and which will be dropped. Thus, if it can be assumed that the scorecard is a way of defining quality, then quality can be considered an essential element of supplier survival.

The quality of the goods that a supplier delivers to a buyer does not have to include superior materials and unusually tight tolerances. If a company designs its products to incorporate components that work fine at a lower level of conformance to specifications, then the supplier has just gone to extra effort to provide something that the buyer did not need. Thus, exceeding the expectations of a buyer does not necessarily equate to providing higher-quality goods, as viewed from the perspective of the buyer.

A more accurate view of supplier quality is that a supplier must be able to meet expectations with *absolute* consistency. This means that no parts should be delivered that are out of specification, that no deliveries should be even one minute outside of the designated delivery window, and so forth.

Quality from the Company's Perspective

The buyer should also understand that the quality levels displayed by a customer are, in part, based on the operations of the company. For example, if the company routinely alters its production schedule at the last minute, a supplier may be so rushed to meet the associated purchasing requirements that it produces out-of-spec parts or delivers them late. Or, if the company routinely alters its products using engineering change orders that are enacted on short notice, suppliers will also be rushed, and so may not be able to meet the company's quality standards. Another situation is when the engineering department releases product specifications for which there has been no prior attempt to receive input from suppliers – who might have pointed out that certain aspects of the design are bound to fail. In short, the cause of supplier quality problems may not reside at the supplier.

The purchasing department must be quite careful in defining quality for its suppliers through its measurement systems. An old adage is that anything measured will improve, so including a measurement in the department's supplier scorecard system will likely result in a gradual increase in supplier performance for that measurement. However, one must look at the downside of this situation. If the purchasing staff has added a measurement to the scorecard that is not really necessary (perhaps tightening the delivery window from four hours to two hours), it will find that suppliers are now expending resources to meet a fake quality target. Consequently, it makes sense to only modify the contents of the supplier scorecard after a great deal of deliberation.

When a buyer is reviewing the quality of a supplier, it is not sufficient to only examine its historical performance. In addition, the buyer should delve into the supplier processes that are allowing it to provide goods at the designated quality levels. If the underlying processes are excessively primitive, this means that the supplier may not be able to continue providing a high level of quality if the company increases the size of its orders. This forward-looking view of supplier quality could mean that a supplier will be dropped, despite its current adherence to quality standards.

Quality Costs

It is helpful to understand the types of costs associated with quality. These costs are associated with preventing, detecting, and remediating product issues related to quality, and become increasingly expensive as they are found later in the production and distribution processes. The quality cost classifications are as follows:

- *Prevention costs.* Prevention costs are incurred in order to keep a quality problem from occurring. It is the least expensive type of quality cost, and so is highly recommended. Prevention costs can include proper employee training in assembling products and statistical process control (for spotting processes that are beginning to generate defective goods), as well as a robust product design and supplier certification. A focus on prevention tends to reduce preventable scrap costs, because the scrap never occurs.

- *Appraisal costs.* As was the case with a prevention cost, an appraisal cost is incurred in order to keep a quality problem from occurring. This is done through a variety of types of inspection. The least expensive is having production workers inspect both incoming and outgoing parts to and from their workstations, which catches problems faster than other types of inspection. Other appraisal costs include the destruction of goods as part of the testing process, the depreciation of test equipment, and supervision of the testing staff.
- *Internal failure costs.* An internal failure cost is incurred when a defective product is produced. This appears in the form of scrapped or reworked goods. The cost of reworking goods is part of this cost.
- *External failure costs.* An external failure cost is incurred when a defective product was produced, but now the cost is much more extensive, because it includes the cost of product recalls, warranty claims, field service, and potentially even the legal costs associated with customer lawsuits. It also includes a relatively unquantifiable cost, which is the cost of losing customers.

The quality costs noted here can be extravagantly expensive when they occur as either internal or external failures, and are much less expensive when they occur earlier, as prevention or appraisal costs. Ideally, this means that quality issues associated with goods delivered from suppliers are dealt with at supplier locations, so that there is never a quality issue for a company to deal with at all.

Quality Improvement Considerations

When investigating a supplier's ability to improve the quality of its deliverables, there are a number of factors to review. All of the following points (which are culled from the various philosophies of quality management) are indicators that a supplier understands the need for and commitment to quality:

- *Management commitment.* The entire management team must not only have a firm commitment to the need for quality, but must also consistently spread the message to employees, so that there is no question anywhere in the organization that quality must be pursued.
- *Understand process variation.* Everyone at a supplier must understand that a core reason for quality problems is that a process creates variable outcomes, and that the range of this variation must be reduced. One cannot simply station an inspection person at the end of a production line, who throws out all nonconforming goods. Instead, the process itself must be revised to keep from producing any nonconforming goods.

- *Focus on the process, not the product.* When there is an understanding that process variation is the root cause of nonconformance, there is less need to waste resources examining in-process and finished goods, and more emphasis on examining variations in the process itself.
- *Design for quality.* A large part of the process variation that occurs is because the underlying product design or manufacturing process is causing nonconforming outputs, perhaps due to inadequate processes, equipment, or layouts. This means that the product engineers and industrial engineers must consider quality up-front, as part of the design process.
- *Constant improvement.* Everyone understands that there is a long-term need to continually improve processes to drive down quality issues. There is no end point at which a quality campaign can be stopped, since quality issues will simply crop up as soon as the campaign is over. Instead, the improvement drive never ends.
- *Train everyone.* It is not sufficient to simply talk about a need for quality. Instead, employees must receive both initial and ongoing training in process improvement tools and techniques.
- *Focus on total system cost.* A supplier's buyers cannot focus on just acquiring goods at the lowest price. A low price may be associated with low quality, which introduces nonconforming materials into the supplier's processes. Instead, it may be necessary to pay a significantly higher price in order to obtain goods that always meet the supplier's specifications.
- *Eliminate quotas.* If production quotas are foisted upon supplier employees, their incentive is to ship a certain volume of goods, irrespective of the quality of the goods being shipped. Instead, incentives should be used that encourage a proper level of attention to discovering nonconforming goods and fixing underlying problems.

Six Sigma

In order to arrive at extremely high levels of product quality, suppliers need a tool for driving down the incidence of nonconformance. A general concept that can be of assistance is *six sigma*, which sets a standard of driving down problems to just 3.4 defects per million opportunities (an opportunity is defined as a chance of not meeting a required specification). The main reason for setting such a high target is the cost associated with correcting problems. A business that does not attend to its quality program will likely spend somewhere between 25% and 40% of its revenue just fixing quality-related problems. On the other hand, those entities that have achieved six sigma performance spend an amount on problem resolution that is essentially a rounding error.

There are many tools under the six sigma banner that can be used to achieve this remarkably low defect rate, including statistical analysis, cause and effect diagrams, control charts, cost-benefit analysis, design of experiments, root cause analysis, and value stream mapping. These tools are employed by six sigma "black belts," who are highly-trained experts who know when to use these tools, given the varying circumstances that they may find. They operate within a five-step process, which is:

1. *Define*. Articulate the nature of the problem to be addressed.
2. *Measure*. Establish a baseline from which subsequent improvements will be measured.
3. *Analyze*. Examine the data to determine the root cause of the targeted problem.
4. *Improve*. Test and implement a solution.
5. *Control*. Sustain the achieved gains by developing and implementing a plan to control the newly-altered process.

This five-step process may be repeated many times, as an organization works its way through a large number of issues that cause its quality levels to be too low.

International Quality Standards

A possible area in which to encourage supplier involvement is for them to apply for certification under the ISO 9001:2008 standard. This standard is promulgated by the International Organization of Standardization (ISO). ISO 9001:2008 lays out the requirements for a quality management program. According to ISO, more than 1,000,000 organizations have been certified under this standard. The standard is based on the following eight principles, which are condensed from the ISO's Quality Management Principles:

- *Customer focus*. Organizations depend on their customers and therefore should understand current and future customer needs, meet customer requirements and strive to exceed their expectations.
- *Leadership*. Leaders establish unity of purpose and the direction of an organization. They should create and maintain an environment in which people can become fully involved in achieving the organization's objectives.
- *Involvement of people*. People at all levels are the essence of an organization, and their full involvement enables their abilities to be used for the organization's benefit.
- *Process approach*. A desired result is achieved more efficiently when activities and related resources are managed as a process.
- *System approach to management*. Identifying, understanding and managing interrelated processes as a system contributes to the organization's effectiveness and efficiency in achieving its objectives.
- *Continual improvement*. Continual improvement of an organization's overall performance should be a permanent objective of the organization.
- *Factual approach to decision making*. Effective decisions are based on the analysis of data and information.
- *Mutually beneficial supplier relationships*. An organization and its suppliers are interdependent, and so a mutually beneficial relationship enhances the ability of both to create value.

The ISO publishes additional materials about the standard, which are available at www.iso.org. Be aware that the requirements of this program are quite detailed, and so it can take a significant amount of time to achieve compliance.

A company could use a supplier's ISO certification as evidence of the existence of a quality program, without delving deeper into its processes with an on-site visit. If so, encouraging prospective suppliers to pursue ISO certification could greatly compress the time (and minimize the expense) required to evaluate new suppliers. This certification can be useful for those suppliers who have already been accepted by the purchasing department, for two reasons. First, it may indicate areas of weakness that have been overlooked by the purchasing department's review process. And second, the certification can be used as a selling point when the sales staff of a supplier is pursuing business with its other customers. Consequently, the ISO certification can be quite a useful tool for all parties involved in a quality management program.

The Quality Message to Impart

When a company wants to acquire high-quality goods from its suppliers, it needs to send a message to them regarding the need for quality. This must be a consistent message, so that suppliers are not conflicted by differing signals, only some of which give them an incentive to focus on quality. Here are several points regarding the message being sent:

- *Initial review.* When the purchasing department is reviewing a prospective new supplier, a key part of the review checklist should be comprised of topics regarding the quality focus of the supplier, quality training, and the commitment to process improvement. This gives new suppliers an immediate message regarding the priorities of the company.
- *Supplier quality manual.* A company can issue a supplier quality manual to its approved suppliers, which delineates such matters as the minimum amount of inspections that suppliers should engage in, as well as the mandated use of statistical process control and sample evaluations. The manual also notes the examination criteria that the company will employ on received goods, how suppliers will be measured for the quality of their output, and how the parties will communicate when there is a nonconformance event. At a more expanded level, the manual can outline how the company conducts its quality audits of suppliers, and how these results are used to evaluate suppliers for certification as preferred suppliers. All related procedures and forms are included in the manual.
- *Supplier certification.* There is a certification program in place, under which the company's quality engineers audit a supplier's facility, examining its processes and methods to determine whether they can consistently produce goods that conform to the company's quality criteria. At a more detailed level, a company might insist on separately certifying each product that a supplier delivers. If a supplier is certified, this is considered a threshold requirement for being classified as a preferred supplier, and may also allow a supplier to bypass a company's receiving process.

- *Corrective action process*. When the receiving department finds a nonconformance in goods delivered from a supplier, it initiates a corrective action process that requires the supplier to submit a written explanation for the nonconformance, as well as a corrective action plan to eliminate the underlying process issue.

- *Supplier involvement in designs*. The company actively recruits suppliers to participate in its new product design process, with a particular emphasis on advising regarding the quality of prospective designs and of the components to be used. For example, a supplier can advise on the component tolerances that can be built into a product, and which most closely match the supplier's production capabilities.

- *Pricing*. The company will not pursue aggressive price negotiations with its suppliers. Instead, it ensures that they have sufficient profitability to maintain their quality programs.

- *Inspections*. The company sends out review teams at regular intervals, both to review the current status of supplier quality programs, and to provide assistance in enhancing these programs.

- *Measurements*. The primary focus of supplier scorecards are measurements that track the quality of delivered goods. These measurements are then used to determine which suppliers will be retained and which will be dropped. The contents of scorecards can therefore be a very effective message to suppliers regarding the main orientation of a company.

- *Supplier elimination*. The purchasing department should be clear with its suppliers about the reasons why they may be eliminated, of which a key consideration is quality. As the supply base shrinks, this means that the remaining suppliers will have strong quality programs that routinely produce goods that are always in conformance with specifications.

This multi-layered approach to dealing with suppliers gives them a comprehensive message that quality is a major consideration, one that will be the focus of any decisions to drop or retain them.

Summary

A massive part of the cost structure of a business is devoted to the correction of problems that arise in its processes; this cost is rarely recognized, since it falls outside of the manner in which costs are normally accumulated and identified in an accounting system. If managers were to understand the true extent of these costs, they would likely expend far more effort on developing an environment that supports all types of quality initiatives – including the delivery of quality goods from suppliers. If a large part of an organization's cost of goods sold is comprised of purchased goods, then it is evident that quality must be infused into the supply chain in order to reduce the costs of problem correction.

One of the actions causing product quality to be such an issue with some suppliers is the excessive emphasis that buyers place on purchasing at the absolute lowest price.

When suppliers are being forced to give away a larger share of profits to their customers, they may offset this loss by reducing expenditures related to quality, and by enforcing price cuts on their suppliers. In the second case, a possible outcome is that quality lapses at second-tier suppliers will trickle into the goods shipped to a company by its own suppliers. Given this issue, the purchasing staff should consider that pushback from a supplier about a price cut may be more than a negotiating tactic – they may really be sending a signal that further cuts could lead to negative consequences.

Chapter 13
Cost Management

Introduction

Customers may place value on a company's products based on many factors, such as their fit and finish, styling, servicing, innovative features – and price. While there are many ways to provide value, the overriding one in the eyes of customers is usually price. A reasonable price in relation to all of the other value factors is necessary in order to be competitive. To offer reasonable prices while still maintaining a decent profit margin, a business must manage its costs. Much of this cost management task falls on the purchasing department, especially when a large part of a company's total spend is with its supplier base. In this chapter, we cover many cost management tools and best practices, including commodity cost management, price analysis, target costing, and several related topics.

> **Related Podcast Episode:** Episode 257 of the Accounting Best Practices Podcast discusses how to present cost control information. It is available at: **accounting-tools.com/podcasts** or **iTunes**

Types of Analysis

The first step in cost management is deciding how to evaluate the prices being proposed by suppliers. The simplest approach is *price analysis*, where the prices offered by suppliers are compared to those of others who offer the same products. Other factors are also included in price analysis, such as matching up prices based on the unit quantities being requested, delivery times, product quality, and the reputation of the supplier. This type of analysis is commonly applied to the purchase of commodities.

A somewhat more detailed analysis method is *total cost analysis*, where other costs of ownership are added to the price being offered by a supplier. These additional costs may include the following:

- *Shipping.* The costs to transport the goods to the company's location may include considerable freight charges and tariffs. This is particularly common when materials are being sourced from distant suppliers.
- *Financing.* It may be necessary to incur extra costs to pay certain suppliers, such as the costs associated with a letter of credit when dealing with foreign suppliers.
- *Hedging.* If goods must be purchased in a foreign currency, it may be necessary to enter into a hedging transaction to offset any possible changes in the exchange rate before the company issues payment. The cost of the hedge should be included in the total cost.

- *Inventory storage.* Some suppliers may only ship in large unit quantities, in which case the company must incur additional costs to store the inventory until such time as it has been consumed.
- *Quality costs.* The quality specifications offered by a supplier may be somewhat lower than usual, which may lead to a heightened scrap level, along with the costs of identifying and disposing of the items being scrapped.
- *Training.* If equipment is being purchased, the supplier may include the related training for free, or it may be necessary to pay for this training separately.
- *License fees.* If software is being purchased, the supplier may require that a hefty annual license fee also be paid. If so, include the present value of these fees in the total cost analysis.

Total cost analysis is highly recommended for larger spend items, since it can reveal that what may initially appear to be low price points being offered by suppliers may actually result in the highest total costs to the company.

A more detailed (and difficult) approach to analyzing supplier prices is *reverse price analysis*, where the purchasing staff instead estimates the costs incurred by the supplier to construct a product. This analysis is not comprised of just an estimation of the direct materials, labor hours, and labor rates required to create a product, since this is only part of the cost structure of a business. It is also necessary to estimate the other operating costs of a supplier, and make a reasonable allocation of them to the product in question, plus a profit allocation. The result of this analysis is a much better understanding of the costs being incurred by a supplier, which can lead to more fully-informed pricing negotiations.

Commodity Cost Management

It is useful to understand when the items being purchased are commodities. When products are so standardized that there is no ready differentiation between the offerings of different suppliers, these products can be considered commodities. When sourcing commodities, purchases are usually made in a highly competitive market with many suppliers; their pricing strategies typically focus on low pricing, where profits are made by turning over inventory as rapidly as possible. In this environment, it is not necessary to understand the cost structures of suppliers, since they are assuredly already focusing on cost reductions themselves. Instead, look at the total delivered cost of the commodities. A supplier may initially appear to offer the lowest price, but only for high volumes of goods that must be stored, for which the company will incur inventory holding costs. Or, a distant supplier offers the lowest price, but the commodity is so bulky and/or heavy that the transport cost makes the total cost from this source prohibitively expensive.

> **Tip:** Some goods begin as specialty products that are highly differentiated. Over time, increased levels of competition reduce the amount of differentiation, which in effect commoditizes the products. Thus, it makes sense to periodically evaluate the entire list of goods purchased to see if any have become commodities. If so, the cost management strategy can switch from a detailed cost analysis of a supplier to a more modest effort involving the total delivered cost of goods.

Price Analysis

Price analysis involves gaining an understanding of the market factors and company pricing strategies that interact to create market prices. Pricing is essentially derived from the concept of supply and demand. However, there are many reasons why actual market prices do not adjust to obvious changes in supply and demand. Also, there are a number of pricing strategies that suppliers can use that may result in unusually high or low price points. These issues are covered in the following sub-sections.

Supply and Demand

Price analysis begins with the concept of supply and demand. Stated simply, if there is more customer demand than available supply, then this is considered a seller's market, and prices will increase until demand shrinks, thereby bringing supply and demand into equilibrium. Conversely, if there is more supply available than customer demand, then this is considered a buyer's market, and prices will decline until additional customer demand matches the amount of available supply, which also creates a state of equilibrium. This is the theoretical concept of supply and demand, but as we will find in the following bullet points, the reality can be quite different. Issues to consider include:

- *Stickiness of supply.* When there is an overabundance of supply, this is usually caused by the presence of too much production capacity in an industry. Producers are usually quite unwilling to shutter their facilities in order to bring down capacity, which means that a condition of oversupply tends to exist for long periods of time. This is a relatively common condition in three situations. In the first case, initially high prices convince suppliers to build more capacity under the assumption that the high prices will continue (which they will not, once the additional capacity floods the market). In the second case, the level of investment in the additional capacity is so large that managers are afraid to write off the investment, thereby creating a massive loss for their businesses. And the third situation is when the incremental cost required to keep a facility running is relatively low, so managers decide to tolerate the low prices and wait for someone else to shutter *their* facilities. In this situation, the purchasing manager can reasonably conclude that costs have declined to levels near the variable costs of suppliers, and can likely take advantage of this pricing for a long period of time.
- *Perception of supply changes.* For some commodities, the mere perception of a halt in supply can send prices skyward, even though there is no current

change in demand. A classic example is the market for crude oil. If there is even a rumor of pirates attacking oil tankers, possible quarrels in the Middle East, or of proposed regulations regarding refineries, the markets tend to react by spiking prices. Changes in these perceptions can arise on a daily basis, which makes the purchasing staff's job quite difficult. Possible solutions are an ongoing series of hedging transactions to mitigate the risk of price swings, or simply entering into long-term contracts at fixed prices. The risk in the latter case is that the prices mandated under a long-term contract may prove to be higher than the market rate over the long term.

- *Impact of outsiders.* The amount of supply and demand may appear to be relatively fixed, based on the recurring set of suppliers and customers that have interacted with each other over the years. However, this can change suddenly when new players enter the field from outside the traditional group. To continue with the crude oil example, the demand for it declined somewhat when farmers decided to grow corn to convert into ethanol. Or, the spurt in electric cars reduced the demand for oil. These disruptive changes tend to occur at relatively long intervals, and so may not impact the purchasing staff for many years at a time.

- *Patent restrictions.* If a supplier has strong patent protection for its products, it can block competitors from entering a market, thereby restricting the possible sources of supply. In this case, buyers may be forced to pay inordinately high prices for the duration of the relevant patent. This issue can be mitigated by designing products to use components that are not subject to such a high level of patent protection.

A point of long-term interest to the purchasing manager is the level of interest rates. When interest rates are low for a prolonged period of time, the cost of money for suppliers is low, and they are therefore more likely to use borrowed funds to build capacity. Thus, it can make sense to avoid entering into long-term, fixed-price contracts with suppliers when interest rates are low. Conversely, when interest rates are high, additional capacity is less likely to be built, so the price of goods will generally increase. In the latter case, it makes more sense to enter into a contract to lock in prices for a longer period of time.

The points noted here result in conditions in many industries where prices are either depressed or inordinately high for long periods of time, or else jitter up and down at a rapid pace that is not justified by underlying changes in supply and demand. It is likely that any purchasing department must deal with at least a few supplier markets where these anomalies are present.

Supplier Pricing Strategies

It is useful for the purchasing staff to understand the pricing strategies that are being employed by suppliers. This knowledge can be used to form a negotiation plan for obtaining a reasonable price, or it may drive one to look elsewhere for a better deal. The pricing strategies employed occupy quite a broad range, some being based on costs, and others on entirely different factors that are not related in any way to the underlying costs incurred. The pricing strategy used will likely fall into one of the following categories:

- *Cost based pricing.* Prices are derived from the costs of the underlying products.
- *Strategic pricing.* Pricing is set to drive away competitors or position a supplier within a market.
- *Value based pricing.* Prices are based on customer perceptions of the value of products.

The following pricing strategies are clustered under the classifications just noted.

Cost Based Pricing

- *Cost plus pricing.* This is a price-setting method under which the direct material cost is added to the direct labor cost and overhead cost for a product, after which a markup percentage is added in order to derive the price of the product. It can also be used under a contract with a customer, where the customer reimburses the seller for all costs incurred and also pays a negotiated profit in addition to the costs incurred. This pricing strategy can be an issue for the customer, since the supplier has no incentive to curtail its expenditures - on the contrary, it will likely include as many costs as possible in the contract so that it can be reimbursed. Thus, a contractual arrangement should include cost-reduction incentives for the supplier. It will also be necessary for the purchasing staff to negotiate which costs will be included in overhead, and the amount of the markup percentage.
- *Time and materials pricing.* This method is used in service industries to bill customers for a standard labor rate per hour used, plus the actual cost of materials used. The standard labor rate per hour being billed does not necessarily relate to the underlying cost of the labor; instead, it may be based on the market rate for the services of someone having a certain skill set. The cost of materials charged to the customer is for any materials actually used during the performance of services for the customer. This cost may be at the supplier's actual cost, or it may be a marked-up cost that includes a fee for the overhead cost associated with ordering, handling, and holding the materials in stock. The purchasing staff can negotiate reductions in the billable rate per hour, eliminate any mark-up on materials, and impose a "not to exceed" clause in any time and materials contract, thereby limiting the profits of the supplier.
- *Marginal cost pricing.* This is the practice of setting the price of a product at or slightly above the variable cost to produce it. This may be done when a

company has a small amount of remaining unused production capacity available that it wishes to use to maximize its profits, or when it is unable to sell at a higher price. In either case, the sales are intended to be on an incremental basis; this is not intended to be a long-term pricing strategy. The purchasing staff should certainly take advantage of any supplier offers where marginal cost pricing is being used.

<u>Strategic Pricing</u>

- *Breakeven pricing.* This is the practice of setting a price point at which a supplier will earn zero profits on a sale. The intention behind the use of breakeven pricing is to gain market share and drive competitors from the marketplace. By doing so, a supplier may be able to increase its production volumes to such an extent that it can reduce costs and then earn a profit at what had been the breakeven price. Alternatively, once it has driven out competitors, the company can raise its prices sufficiently to earn a profit, but not so high that the increased price is tempting for new market entrants. One can never tell how long these ultra-low prices will last, so it can make sense to pursue longer-term pricing deals when it is apparent that breakeven pricing is being offered.
- *Price leadership.* This is a situation where one company, usually the dominant one in its industry, sets prices which are closely followed by its competitors. This firm is usually the one having the lowest production costs, and so is in a position to undercut the prices charged by any competitor who attempts to set its prices lower than the price point of the price leader. Competitors could charge higher prices than the price leader, but this would likely result in reduced market share, unless competitors could sufficiently differentiate their products. In this case, it can be difficult to obtain price points from suppliers that vary much from the "going rate" in the industry.
- *Price skimming.* This is the practice of selling a product at a high price, usually during the introduction of a new product when the demand for it is relatively inelastic. This approach is used to generate substantial profits during the first months of the release of a product, usually so that a supplier can recoup its investment in the product. However, by engaging in price skimming, a supplier is potentially sacrificing much higher sales than it could garner at a lower price point. Eventually, a supplier that engages in price skimming must drop its prices, as competitors enter the market and undercut its prices. Thus, price skimming tends to be a short-term strategy. From a purchasing perspective, it can pay to initially purchase in minimum volumes, in anticipation of the arrival of other market entrants within a short period of time who will offer lower prices.
- *Dynamic pricing.* Under this approach, suppliers constantly monitor the amount of their remaining available capacity, and charge more as the available capacity declines. Conversely, they may drastically drop prices if they have an excessive amount of residual capacity. An example of this situation is a hotel, which could mark up its prices for the last few remaining rooms, or

cut prices during slow weeks to bring in more customers. This approach is also heavily used by airlines. From a purchasing negotiation perspective, the best option is to aggregate purchases with a small number of providers and negotiate volume discounts well in advance, thereby sidestepping the more pernicious effects of dynamic pricing.

Value Based Pricing

- *Premium pricing.* This is the practice of setting a price higher than the market price, in the expectation that customers will purchase a product due to the perception that it must have unusually high quality. In some cases, the product quality is not better, but the seller has invested heavily in the marketing needed to give the *impression* of high quality. This approach works for suppliers when their products have been heavily branded, there are strong barriers to entry, there is patent protection, and/or there are no substitutes available. The cost structures of suppliers following this strategy tend to be bloated, since they have heavy expenditures on marketing, and little incentive to pare away at their expenses. The result can be quite a difficult pricing negotiation, since there are few alternatives to their products. From a purchasing perspective, the best approach may be a long-term one, where there is an ongoing search for alternative products. In those cases where there are substitute products but there is an internal perception among employees that the branding efforts of a supplier have value, the negotiation task is instead directed inward, to convince employees that generic alternatives will be acceptable.
- *Value based pricing.* This is the practice of setting the price of a product or service at the perceived value to the customer, which tends to result in very high prices. This approach does not take into account the cost of the product or service, nor market prices. Value based pricing is usually applied to very specialized services. For example, attorneys skilled in initial public offerings can use value pricing, since clients might not otherwise raise millions of dollars without their services. Other areas where value based pricing may be used include bankruptcy work outs, cost reduction analysis, lawsuit defense, and product design. These suppliers typically gain approval for their services from senior management, thereby circumventing the purchasing department entirely.

Volume Discounts

We list volume discounts as a discussion topic immediately after the pricing topic, because it helps to understand cost-based pricing before negotiating for volume discounts. In essence, a supplier that is focused on its long-term viability must sell at prices that cover its variable costs (materials and labor), plus its factory overhead and administrative overhead, plus a reasonable profit. A supplier may incur significant marketing costs to acquire new customers, and also wishes to avoid small customer orders, which are more expensive to process, resulting in higher overhead costs. The ideal situation for a supplier is to obtain the bulk of its sales from a small number of customers that place large orders at regular intervals. A company can become one of these most favored customers by placing large orders. A supplier that routinely receives large orders can spread its overhead costs over a large number of units sold, making it much easier to generate a profit. Customers can reasonably request a share of these profits by requesting volume discounts. This is one of the best ways for a purchasing department to manage costs.

There are a number of ways to arrive at a position where a business can place large-volume orders with its suppliers. They are as follows:

- *Centralize procurement.* When each subsidiary or location of a business is allowed to do its own purchasing, the company as a whole does not benefit from the concentration of purchases with a small number of suppliers that can generate volume discounts. The issue can be mitigated by centralizing the negotiation of purchasing contracts with a small number of suppliers, and then forcing local buyers to only use these designated suppliers. The purchasing of specific goods does not have to be centralized, as long as the local buyers only purchase from the designated suppliers. The company will need to aggregate the amount of its annual spend with each supplier across the entire company in order to negotiate its volume discounts.

- *Centralize spending by commodity.* Suppliers tend to specialize in selling a certain category of commodity, so aggregate the company's spending in the same way, to obtain volume discounts. For example, have representatives from each subsidiary agree on which supplier will be used for all purchases of fuel oil, and then approach that supplier about a volume purchasing discount. The arrangement is typically formalized in a master purchase agreement, which all parts of the company reference when ordering from a particular supplier. The master purchase order number is then tracked by both parties to aggregate the total amount of purchases made. This information is also used as the basis for the next round of volume discount negotiations. Purchases for a number of commodity groups can be arranged in this manner, usually starting with the largest-expenditure commodities and then working through the list of commodities in descending order by purchasing volume.

- *Minimize the number of suppliers.* When there are many suppliers being used for fulfillment in each commodity area, this implies that the opportunity for volume discounts is being dispersed among the suppliers. To concentrate purchases with the minimum number of suppliers, engage in an ongoing process of paring down the number of suppliers used, thereby shifting purchases to a select few suppliers.

The downside of volume discounts is that a company is committing to a large purchase volume – a volume that it may not need, based on future changes in its sales. Consequently, the purchasing staff must be able to recognize situations where the discount should be pursued, and when it should not. Here are several scenarios to consider:

- *Min-max delivery range.* If the company projects a continuing need for large volumes of an item over an extended period of time, it can safely commit to a large purchase volume. To make the promised order quantities fit within its production schedule while still qualifying for the discount, enter into a min-max agreement with the supplier. This means that the company will maintain a certain range of production volume that will mandate deliveries from the supplier within a minimum and maximum unit range. By making this arrangement, the supplier can tailor its own production processes to manufacture goods at sufficiently high volume levels to still earn it a profit within the indicated volume range.

- *Contract-based purchases.* If the company is relying on a contract with a large customer as the justification for a volume purchase discount, only negotiate the discount for the volume of purchases indicated by the current contract. It can be exceedingly dangerous to commit to a larger quantity in expectation of a contract renewal, which may not happen. An alternative is to make a supplier aware of the situation, and then negotiate for a lower volume discount based on the current contract and a higher discount if the company gains a renewal of the contract.

- *Expanded purchases.* It may be possible to obtain a volume discount by committing to a broad range of purchases, rather than the purchase of just one or two specific items. It is much more likely that a company can follow through on a commitment of this type, as opposed to being forced to buy large quantities of just a few items for which demand has declined.

- *After-the-fact discounts.* If a company cannot make a binding commitment to a specific purchasing volume, an alternative is to wait until the end of the annual measurement period, and retroactively calculate the volume discount based on whatever the volume turned out to be. This may not yield as large a discount, since the supplier cannot rely upon steady demand from the company through the contract period.

Contract Duration

If there is a long-term downward trend in the price of a particular commodity, expect suppliers to offer longer-term contracts, which allows them to garner larger profits over time as the company is locked into a fixed price while their costs decline. In such cases, it is better to steer clear of these offers. Alternatively, if there is a long-term upward trend in the price of a commodity, attempt to lock in the longest-term pricing arrangement possible. However, doing so may put a supplier at risk of becoming unprofitable, so consider including a cost-sharing clause in the contract that allows the supplier to continue to be financially viable.

It is more important to maintain a mutually profitable, long-term arrangement with suppliers than to reduce their profits with clever anticipation of pricing trends. Nonetheless, this is an area to consider when devising ways to reduce the cost of purchases.

Materials Sourcing Considerations

Though a key focus of the preceding sections has been cost management, there are other considerations that can be of greater importance than cost. Consider the following:

- *Availability*. A supplier must be able to provide goods in a timely manner. If not, the buyer cannot properly schedule them into its own production processes. Needless to say, promises to customers may be severely impacted. This problem is most common among those suppliers that pare away their internal support staffs in order to offer the lowest possible prices to their customers. Availability is a massive concern when the materials are only available from a small number of suppliers, and the overall supply of goods is constrained. In this case, it pays to use the highest-availability supplier, rather than the lowest-cost one.

- *Capacity*. Does the supplier have the production capacity available to meet the buyer's requirements? In some cases, the buyer is not the supplier's highest priority, and so is only allocated a small amount of capacity once the needs of more important customers are met. In other cases, a supplier's capacity is maxed out, and so it must put all customer orders on an allocation basis. In this situation, the best supplier may be the one that charges the highest price, but which can effortlessly provide large unit volumes on short notice.

- *Delivery*. If the company requires that materials be delivered within a specific time slot on a certain day, the supplier must be able to meet that requirement on a consistent basis. If not, the result is likely to be an inoperable production schedule. Alternatively, if the buyer is simply forwarding supplier deliveries to customers, delays directly impact customers. This issue can arise because of the supplier location – a long transport distance from a low-cost supplier in another country is nearly guaranteed to eventually result in a delayed delivery. In many cases, a strong emphasis on reliable delivery times may mandate that suppliers all be based near the company's production and/or distribution facilities. If so, the cost of materials is a lesser consideration.

- *Quality*. A supplier's goods must meet the buyer's specifications. This means that all specifications, such as for product dimensions, appearance, and material content, be met with such reliability that there is essentially no point in inspecting the goods at the receiving dock. If a supplier cannot meet this standard, being the low-cost provider is nearly an afterthought. Indeed, suppliers with the best product quality are in such high demand that they can routinely charge much higher prices than their counterparts – and buyers are willing to pay the price.

- *Foreign suppliers*. Many companies buy from foreign suppliers, which have access to such low labor costs that they can routinely underbid domestic suppliers. However, a low-cost international supplier may not be the best alternative. If a foreign supplier demands payment in a local currency, the buyer is at risk of an unfavorable swing in foreign exchange rates. If the buyer does not want to incur this risk, then it must buy a foreign exchange hedge, which increases the cost of the overall transaction. In addition, the buyer may have to pay additional administrative costs to monitor the transaction, as well as customs duties. Consequently, it is useful to examine the total cost of international transactions before engaging the services of a supplier in another country.

There are situations where being the low-cost provider of goods is still the most important consideration for end users. This situation typically arises for a subset of customers that are willing to tolerate late delivery times and uneven product quality in exchange for rock-bottom prices. However, a much larger proportion of companies have a higher regard for the other factors noted here, and so are willing to accept higher price points.

Unique Product and High Value-Added Cost Management

There are usually a small number of suppliers that provide unique goods and services, or goods with a high value-added component. These items are certainly *not* commoditized, and may represent a significant part of the total corporate spend. If so, the purchasing staff should target these suppliers for a detailed analysis, to see if a pricing reduction can be achieved.

In this case, the tool used is called *reverse price analysis*. In essence, it is designed to formulate an approximation of what a supplier's product should cost. This information can be difficult to obtain, but here are some possibilities:

- *Public company information.* If a supplier is publicly-held, it must file its financial statements with the Securities and Exchange Commission (SEC); these reports can be downloaded from the SEC's website at www.sec.gov. If such a business has a relatively limited product line, one can determine from its income statement the proportions of materials, labor, and overhead costs that probably apply to the product in question. However, a larger supplier may have so many product lines that this aggregated information at the level of the income statement will not reveal much information that pertains to the cost of a specific product.
- *Materials estimates.* Consult with the company's engineering staff to obtain an estimate of the cost of materials that a supplier includes in its products. This will be a rough estimate, but can be refined by calling on the services of an expert who routinely breaks down products and provides costing estimates.
- *Labor estimates.* Run an Internet search to locate the Annual Survey of Manufacturers (ASM) report. The results of the ASM are posted by the United States Census Bureau on its website, sorted by NAICS code (the North American Industrial Classification System). The report lists the aggregated costs reported for each NAICS code in many areas. Calculate the ratio of the total production workers wages to the total cost of materials in the survey. For example, the relevant figures for manufacturing for 2010 yielded a ratio of 10.9% of production labor to the cost of materials. So, if the engineering staff

were to estimate that the cost of a product's materials component was $10, the related labor would be $1.09.

- *Overhead estimates.* Pull from the SEC website some of the financial statements of publicly-held companies that operate in the same industry as the supplier, and extract from these documents their administrative overhead expenses. Then convert these numbers into a percentage of sales. These percentages can be applied to the supplier in question.
- *Estimate residual profit and factory overhead.* Subtract the estimated costs of materials, labor, and administrative overhead developed in the preceding points from the product price. Any residual margin should cover the profit and factory overhead costs of the supplier.

The preceding points form a reasonable basis for a reverse price analysis, but can still be incorrect to a significant degree. A supplier may have an unusual cost structure due to its geographic location, contracts with its employees or its own suppliers, and so forth. Also, the average proportion of labor to materials could be well away from the actual situation. Nonetheless, this examination can result in a reasonable basis from which price negotiations can be launched.

EXAMPLE

Mole Industries builds trench digging equipment. The company is privately-held, but a number of its competitors are publicly-held. Eskimo Construction wants to buy several of its trench digging machines. The machines are quite expensive, and so warrant the time required to conduct a reverse price analysis. The purchasing manager has an outside consultant derive the materials cost of a ditch digger, which is $18,250. The relevant labor-to-materials cost ratio extracted from the Annual Survey of Manufacturers reveals a ratio of 1:3, which translates into an estimated production labor cost of $6,083. Finally, a review of the financial statements of several publicly-held companies in the same industry as Mole reveals that the administrative overhead as a percentage of sales is about 18%.

Given these inputs and a $50,000 list price for the desired trench digger, the purchasing manager derives the following reverse price analysis:

Price	$50,000
Direct materials cost	-18,250
Direct labor cost	-6,083
Administrative overhead cost	-9,000
Profit and factory overhead residual	$16,667

The percentage of profit and factory overhead to the list price is 33%. It is still necessary to estimate the amount of factory overhead applied to the product, but this analysis gives the purchasing manager a reasonable idea of the proportion of the total product price that may be subject to negotiation.

When attempting to negotiate a better price with a supplier, it is useful to consider several additional points, since they may impact the willingness of the supplier to negotiate. These points are:

- *Capacity usage*. If the supplier is currently operating at a point close to its maximum capacity utilization, it will be very unlikely to negotiate on price. In this situation, the chances are good that the supplier has an order backlog, and can simply reject the company's attempts at negotiation in favor of an in-hand order at the list price. Conversely, if a supplier is mired in a slump and has lots of excess capacity, it may be willing to operate close to its variable costs, and so could accept a price that is far below its list price.
- *Constraints*. A supplier may have a constraint in its own raw material supplies that does not allow it to increase its rate of production, even though its production capacity might initially appear to have ample available room. Or, the prospective order may impinge upon a particular production step within a supplier's manufacturing processes that is already operating at full capacity, or which requires skilled employees who are in short supply. Conversely, if a prospective order does not impinge upon *any* supplier constraints, the supplier might be more willing to entertain an offer of a low-priced order.
- *Order timing*. A supplier might currently be operating at or near full capacity, but is anticipating a decline in its order backlog in the near future. If the company is willing to wait for delivery, it may be possible to negotiate a lower price so that the supplier can slot the order into a weak order period in its projected backlog.

An alternative way of looking at the situation is to reduce the number of cases in which customized product specifications are sent to suppliers. Whenever customization is involved, a supplier must spend time reviewing the proposal, and may also need to alter a product's design, change molds, alter tooling, and so forth. The result can be substantially higher prices than would have been the case if industry-standard specifications had been ordered. Consequently, it makes sense to only order unique product specifications when the outcome will provide a clear product differentiation for the buyer when selling its own products. This requirement should drastically reduce the number of purchases of custom products.

Target Costing

A notable cost control concept that can reduce the cost of new products is target costing, under which a company plans in advance for the product price points, product costs, and margins that it wants to achieve. If it cannot manufacture a product at these planned levels, then it cancels the product entirely. With target costing, a management team has a powerful tool for continually monitoring products from the moment they enter the design phase and onward throughout their product life cycles. The purchasing department plays a key role in target costing.

Related Podcast Episode: Episode 57 of the Accounting Best Practices Podcast discusses target costing. It is available at: **accountingtools.com/podcasts** or **iTunes**

The Basic Steps of Target Costing

Target costing has been in existence for a number of years and is used by many companies, so the primary steps in the process are well defined. They are:

1. *Conduct research.* The first step is to review the marketplace in which the company wants to sell products. The team needs to determine the set of product features that customers are most likely to buy, and the amount they will pay for those features. The team must learn about the perceived value of individual features, in case they later need to determine what impact there will be on the product price if they drop one or more of them. It may be necessary to later drop a product feature if the team decides that it cannot provide the feature while still meeting its target cost. At the end of this process, the team has a good idea of the target price at which it can sell the proposed product with a certain set of features, and how it must alter the price if it drops some features from the product.

2. *Calculate maximum cost.* The company provides the design team with a mandated gross margin that the proposed product must earn. By subtracting the mandated gross margin from the projected product price, the team can easily determine the maximum target cost that the product must achieve before it can be allowed into production.

3. *Engineer the product.* The engineers and purchasing personnel on the team now take the leading role in creating the product. The purchasing employees are particularly important if the product has a high proportion of purchased parts; they must determine component pricing based on the necessary quality, delivery, and quantity levels expected for the product. They may also be involved in outsourcing parts, if this results in lower costs. The engineers must design the product to meet the cost target, which will likely include a number of design iterations to see which combination of revised features and design considerations results in the lowest cost.

4. *Ongoing activities.* Once a product design is finalized and approved, the team is reconstituted to include fewer designers and more industrial engineers. The team now enters into a new phase of reducing production costs, which continues for the life of the product. For example, cost reductions may come from waste reductions in production (known as *kaizen costing*, which is the process of continual cost reduction after a product is being manufactured), or from planned supplier cost reductions. These ongoing cost reductions yield enough additional gross margin for the company to further reduce the price of the product over time, in response to increases in the level of competition. Kaizen costing does not generate the size of cost reductions that can be achieved through initial design changes, but it can have a cumulatively significant impact over time.

EXAMPLE

SkiPS is a maker of global positioning systems (GPS) for skiers, which they use to log how many vertical feet they ski each day. SkiPS conducts a marketing survey to decide upon the features it needs to include in its next generation of GPS device, and finds that skiers want a device they can strap to their arm or leg, and which does not require recharging during a multi-day vacation.

The survey indicates that skiers are willing to pay no more than $150 for the device, while the first review of costs indicates that it will cost $160 to manufacture. At a mandated gross margin percentage of 40%, this means that the device must attain a target cost of $90 ($150 price × (1 – 40% gross margin). Thus, the design team must reduce costs from $160 to $90.

The team decides that the GPS unit requires no display screen at all, since users can plug the device into a computer to download information. This eliminates the LCD display and one computer chip. It also prolongs the battery life, since the unit no longer has to provide power to the display. The team also finds that a new microprocessor requires less power; given these reduced power requirements, the team can now use a smaller battery.

Finally, the team finds that the high-impact plastic case is over-engineered, and can withstand a hard impact with a much thinner shell. After the team incorporates all of these changes, it has reached the $90 cost target. SkiPS can now market a new device at a price point that allows it to earn a generous gross profit.

Value Engineering Considerations

The product engineering process noted above in step three involves many considerations. Here are examples of ways to reduce the cost of a product in order to meet a target cost:

- *Revise the manufacturing process*. The industrial engineering staff may be called upon to create an entirely new manufacturing process that uses less labor or less expensive machinery. It is entirely possible that multiple processes will be entirely eliminated from the production process. In particular, there may be an opportunity to eliminate various quality reviews from the process if product quality can be ensured by other means.
- *Reduce durability*. It is possible that the preliminary product design incorporates a product durability level that is actually *too* robust, thereby creating an opportunity to carefully decrease the level of product durability in order to cut costs. The typical result of this change is to completely eliminate some types of structural reinforcement from the product, or to at least downgrade to a less durable material in some parts of the product.
- *Reduce product features*. It may turn out to be quite expensive to offer certain features in a product. If so, the team needs to decide if it can delete one or more of these features while accepting a lower projected product price for which the net effect is an improved product margin. This type of value

engineering must be carefully weighed against the problem of eliminating so many key features that the product will no longer be attractive to customers.

- *Reduce the number of parts.* It may be possible to simplify the design by using fewer parts, especially if doing so reduces the cost of assembling the final product. However, this concept can be taken too far, especially when many standard parts are replaced by a smaller number of customized (and therefore more expensive) parts.
- *Replace components.* It is possible that slightly different components are available at a substantially reduced cost; if so, the design engineers can modify the product to accommodate the different components. This is an especially common avenue when a product is initially designed to include components that have a high per-unit cost, and which can be replaced with components on which the company already earns significant volume discounts by using them across multiple product lines.
- *Design for easier manufacture.* To avoid time-consuming mistakes in the manufacturing process, consider designing the product so that it can only be assembled in a single way – all other attempts to assemble the product in an incorrect manner will fail. By doing so, there will be fewer product failures or recalls, which reduces the total cost of the product. It may be necessary to *increase* the cost of a product in order to create the optimum design for manufacturing, thereby reducing the total cost of the product over its full life span.
- *Ask suppliers.* Suppliers may have significant insights into how to reduce the costs of the various components they are contributing to the final product design, particularly in regard to altering material content or changing the manufacturing process. Suppliers may be willing to serve on design teams and contribute their expertise in exchange for being the sole source of selected components.

If the project team finds that it can comfortably meet the target cost without engaging in all of the preceding steps, then it should work through the activity list anyways. By doing so, it can generate sufficient room between the actual and target gross margins that management now has the option to reduce the product price below the target level, which may attract additional sales.

The Cost Reduction Program

The methods used by the design team are more sophisticated than simply saying, "folks, we need to cut $150 in costs – anyone have any ideas?" Instead, the team uses one of two approaches to more tightly focus its cost reduction efforts:

- *Tied to components.* The design team allocates the cost reduction goal among the various product components. This approach tends to result in incremental cost reductions to the same components that were used in the last iteration of the product. This approach is commonly used when a company is simply trying to refresh an existing product with a new version, and wants to retain the same underlying product structure. The cost reductions achieved through this approach tend to be relatively low, but also result in a high rate of product success, as well as a fairly short design period.

- *Tied to features.* The product team allocates the cost reduction goal among various product features, which focuses attention away from any product designs that may have been inherited from the preceding model. This approach tends to achieve more radical cost reductions (and design changes), but also requires more time to design, and also runs a greater risk of product failure or at least greater warranty costs.

Of the two methods noted here, companies are more likely to use the first approach if they are looking for a routine upgrade to an existing product, and the second approach if they want to achieve a significant cost reduction or break away from the existing design.

The Milestone Review Process

What if the project team simply cannot meet the target cost? Rather than completing the design process and creating a product with a substandard profit margin, the correct response is to stop the development process and move on to other projects instead. This does not mean that management allows its project teams to struggle on for months or years before finally giving up. Instead, they must come within a set percentage of the cost target on various milestone dates, with each successive milestone requirement coming closer to the final target cost. Milestones may occur on specific dates, or when key completion steps are reached in the design process, such as at the end of each design iteration.

EXAMPLE

Milagro Corporation is developing a new espresso machine that only works with its specially-developed strain of coffee bean. Milagro conducts market research and concludes that the product cannot sell for more than $200. At the company's required gross margin of 40%, this means that the target cost of the product is $120. Management sets a maximum design duration of six months, with milestone reviews at one-month intervals. The results of the month-end milestone reviews are:

Review Date	Cost Goal	Actual Cost Estimate	Actual Cost Variance from Goal	Allowance Variance From Cost Goal
Jan. 31	$120	$150	25%	30%
Feb. 28	120	143	19%	20%
Mar. 31	120	138	15%	15%
Apr. 30	120	134	12%	10%
May 31	120	Cancelled	--	5%
June 30	120	Cancelled	--	0%

As the table reveals, the Milagro project team was able to stay ahead of the cost target at the end of the first two months, but then was barely able to meet the allowable variance in the third month, and finally fell behind in the fourth month. Management then cancelled the project, saving itself the cost of continuing the project team for several more months when it was becoming obvious that the team would not be able to achieve the target cost.

Though management may cancel a design project that cannot meet its cost goals, this does not mean that the project will be permanently shelved. Far from it. Instead, management should review old projects at least once a year to see if the circumstances have changed sufficiently for them to possibly become viable again. A more precise review approach is to have each project team formulate a set of variables that should initiate a product review if a trigger point is reached (such as a decline in the price of a commodity that is used in the product design). If any of these trigger points are reached, the projects are immediately brought to the attention of management to see if they should be revived.

Problems with Target Costing

Target costing is difficult to initiate, because of the uncertainty surrounding the eventual release of a product. A company that allows its engineering department sole responsibility for creating products will achieve product releases on a fairly consistent schedule, even though some of the products may not be overly profitable. Under target costing, it is quite possible that a company may cancel a series of projects before they reach fruition, resulting in a frantic marketing department that sees no new products entering the pipeline. The solution is a combination of firm support by senior management and ongoing questioning of whether the target gross margin is too high to be achievable. It is entirely possible that an overly enthusiastic management team sets an excessively high gross margin standard for its new target costing process, and then sees no products survive the process. Consequently, it may take some time before management understands what gross margin levels will result in a target costing process that can churn out an acceptable number of products.

Another problem with target costing is the unwillingness of management to cancel a project. They do not want to see their investment in a project thrown away, and so they keep funding it for "just one more month," hoping that the team will find a way to achieve the target cost. The end result is a very long design process that absorbs more design costs than expected, and which still does not achieve the target cost. The only way to resolve this issue is an iron resolve to terminate projects in a timely manner.

Finally, a design team needs a strong leader to keep control of the opinions of the various departments that are represented on the team. For example, the marketing department may hold out for certain product features, while the design engineers claim that those same features introduce too many costs into the product. The best team leader is not one who unilaterally decides on the product direction, but rather one who can craft a group decision, and if necessary weed out those who are unwilling to work with the rest of the group.

The Members of a Design Team

The members of the design team are drawn from multiple disciplines, and their contributions are all essential to the success of a product launch. These positions are:

- *Design engineering.* The design engineers play the most prominent role on the team, since they must create a series of product iterations that incorporate the cost reductions needed to achieve the target cost.
- *Industrial engineering.* A significant part of a product's cost arises during the production process, so industrial engineers must become involved in order to give feedback to the design engineers regarding which design elements should be used that require the lowest production costs.
- *Purchasing.* The purchasing department is a valuable contributor to the team, since many components will likely be sourced to third parties, and an experienced purchasing person can have a significant positive impact on the cost of purchased components.
- *Cost accounting.* A cost accountant should be with the team at all times, constantly compiling the expected cost of a design as it goes through a series of iterations. The cost accountant also compares the expected cost to the target cost, and communicates the status of the product cost situation to both the team members and management on a periodic basis.
- *Marketing.* The marketing department is particularly useful during the initial stages of target costing, where it investigates the prices of competing products and conducts polls to determine the value of specific product features.

Data Sources for Target Costing

It may be difficult to obtain data from which to develop the cost of a new product design. Here are some of the data sources needed for a target costing project:

- *New components.* The design team may be creating entirely new components from scratch, so there is no cost information available. In this case, locate roughly comparable components and extrapolate from them what the new components might cost, including tooling costs.
- *Materials sourcing.* Some materials that the design team wants to include in a product may be difficult to obtain, or be subject to significant price swings. Highlight these issues, particularly by using outside sources of historical commodity prices to note the range of price swings that have occurred in the recent past. It is dangerous to only report to management the current market price of these materials, since management may decide to continue product development when it might otherwise drop the project in the face of large potential cost increases.
- *Competitor costs.* It is extremely useful to disassemble competing products to determine what they cost to produce. This information can be assembled into a database, which is useful for not only calculating the likely gross margins that competing products are earning, but also for comparing the design team's

choice of components to those used by competitors. In many instances, the design team can copy some aspects of a competing design in order to quickly achieve a lower cost.

- *Production costs*. If a company has engaged in product design for a number of years, it may have developed a table that contains the cost to produce specific components or the cost of the production functions used to create those components. This type of information is difficult to obtain, and requires a great deal of analysis to compile, so having the information available from previous design projects is a significant advantage in the design of new products.

- *Downstream costs*. When the design team modifies a product design, there is a good chance that it will cause modifications in other parts of the design, in a ripple effect. The only source of information for what these changes may be is the design team itself, which must regularly discuss the cost effects of these changes.

- *Supplier performance data*. Suppliers are likely going to provide a significant proportion of the components of a new product, so obtain access to the company's database of supplier performance to see if key suppliers are capable of supplying goods within the performance constraints required by the new design. This is less of a cost issue than a qualitative review of the ability of a supplier to perform within the company's specifications.

These data sources frequently do not contain a high degree of data accuracy, so the result is likely to be a significant degree of uncertainty in costing information, especially during the initial stages of product design.

The Product Life Cycle and Target Costing

Target costing generates a significant and immediate cost reduction at the beginning of a product's life cycle. Kaizen costing then generates an ongoing series of smaller cost reductions that gradually decline as the number of cost reduction opportunities is eliminated. A company that wants to stay competitive with its product offerings should carefully track the gradual decline in product costs, and replace the original product with a new one when there are minimal cost reductions still to be garnered from the old product. The new product is subjected to the same target costing approach in order to create a new value proposition for the consumer, to be followed by another round of kaizen costing.

In order to remain competitive over the long term, it is clear that a company must be aware of where its products stand within their product cycles, and be willing to replace them when there are minimal costs to be eliminated from the old designs.

Target Costing Summary

Target costing is most applicable to companies that compete by continually issuing a stream of new or upgraded products into the marketplace (such as consumer goods).

For them, target costing is a key survival tool. Conversely, target costing is less necessary for those companies that have a small number of legacy products that require minimal updates, and for which long-term profitability is more closely associated with market penetration and geographical coverage (such as soft drinks).

Target costing is an excellent tool for planning a suite of products that have high levels of profitability. This is opposed to the much more common approach of creating a product that is based on the engineering department's view of what the product should be like, and then struggling with costs that are too high in comparison to the market price. Given the extremely cooperative nature of target costing across multiple departments, it can be quite a difficult change for the engineering manager to accept.

Inter-Entity Price Reductions

Cost management usually involves the examination of costs *within* entities, but it can also involve the costs that arise because of the interactions *between* a company and its suppliers. Here are several examples:

- *Receiving elimination.* If a supplier has proven to be a reliable provider of quality products, why bother to put its deliveries through a receiving inspection? Instead, if the supplier already has a high-quality production process, allow its deliveries to bypass incoming inspections, thereby reducing the need for an inspection staff.
- *Automated ordering.* There is not always a need to have a purchasing person at the company contact a salesperson at a supplier in order to place an order. It may be possible to use on-line ordering that automatically creates an order in the company's materials management system and sends an electronic message to the order entry system of a supplier. This removes the need for manual labor on both sides of the transaction.
- *Order visibility.* A company can give its suppliers direct access to its database of projected materials requirements. By doing so, suppliers no longer need to maintain large reserves of inventory to guard against unexpected orders, which reduces the overall investment in inventory throughout the supply chain.
- *Supply chain compression.* It may be possible to reduce the number of layers of suppliers. By doing so, there is less need to transport goods between suppliers, which also reduces the number of touches and therefore the risk of inventory damage.

These cost management suggestions can only be achieved if there is a high degree of communication between a company and its suppliers.

Maintenance, Repair, and Operations Cost Management

Part of the maintenance function that seems to defy cost reduction is expenditures on maintenance, repair, and operations (MRO) items. These can be comprised of a vast number of items that are frequently bought in very low volumes, and for which there may be only a small number of available distributors. Also, MRO items are usually charged to expense, rather than being recorded in a tracking database, so there is little usage information about them. Further, there is rarely any system in place for identifying or storing MRO items. All of these factors make MRO one of the more difficult purchasing areas in which to institute cost management concepts. Nonetheless, the following points could be of assistance:

- *Consolidate MRO items.* If there are multiple places within a company where MRO items are stored, consolidate them into one place. Doing so makes it easier to see if any items have been purchased in excessively large quantities. They can then be drawn down to a more reasonable level over time through ongoing usage.
- *Systematize storage.* Create a storage bin system, in which the same MRO items are stored in the same locations on a repetitive basis. This reduces the time required to locate items, and also makes it easier to conduct a visual inspection of the items on hand, to determine whether any items should be reordered.
- *Assign a responsible party.* Assign specific responsibility to a staff person for monitoring the MRO inventory and warning the purchasing department when items must be restocked. Though this and the immediately preceding bullet point may seem like primitive enhancements, they are needed because computerized monitoring systems are usually not applied to MRO items, given that there is usually open access to the inventory that makes it more difficult to keep accurate records.
- *Ask the distributor.* Distributors have a very good knowledge of the availability of any substitute products, and can recommend whether the company should use these substitutes, rather than what is currently being purchased. To gain the cooperation of a distributor in this area, consider allocating the bulk of the company's MRO spend with a single distributor. This is an excellent improvement, since the bulk of the investigative labor is being provided by a third party for free.
- *Buy generic.* The parts sold by original equipment manufacturers are typically much more expensive than their generic equivalents, even though their quality is not noticeably different. Consequently, make it standard practice to always purchase generic equivalent parts and supplies, as long as the underlying quality meets the company's specifications.
- *Buy in economy sizes.* Many types of supplies are substantially less expensive on a per-unit basis when bought in large unit quantities, as specified by the manufacturer. If so, and there is a reasonable expectation of eventually using all of the goods ordered, it may be cost-effective to buy in the larger quantities and simply set aside more storage space for these items. Conversely, buying in very small unit quantities may be inordinately expensive, and is not justified if there is a reasonable expectation for using more units over time.
- *Consolidate items.* It may be that slight variations on the same basic MRO item have been acquired over time. The result is greater risks of item

obsolescence, lower purchasing volumes per item that reduce any chance for volume purchase discounts, and more manual tracking of more items. If this is the case, conduct an ongoing review of similar purchases, and pare away any extraneous items. Though an obvious cost management improvement, this suggestion can meet with resistance if employees prefer a specific brand of product.

- *Concentrate purchases*. Distributors do not earn large profits on an individual order basis, instead relying on large order volumes from their customers to generate reasonable profit levels over the long term. Consequently, a company can gain the favorable attention of a distributor by concentrating most of its purchases with just that one distributor. The distributor can return the favor by granting modest discounts, and providing advice about which MRO items are the most cost-effective purchases.

- *Match purchases to specifications*. A close examination of the requirements for certain MRO items may reveal that what is being purchased is of much higher quality or contains more features than what is actually needed. For example, the percentage of a solvent in a cleaning solution could be higher than required. If so, only buy in accordance with specifications, which can reduce costs.

- *Monitor costs only for high-volume items*. There are an enormous number of MRO items that are purchased in such small quantities that any type of cost reduction analysis is inherently not cost-effective. Instead, restrict all analysis to only the highest-volume MRO items. All other analysis is likely to be a waste of staff time.

- *Packaging credits*. When MRO items are delivered, they may be on pallets or contain spools, spindles, cores, or similar items that the distributor is interested in taking back in exchange for a credit against future purchases. If so, accumulate these items on an ongoing basis and hand them over to the delivery person whenever a new delivery arrives.

- *Reduce safety stocks*. One of the reasons why a business maintains significant amounts of MRO items on hand is because the delivery time from the distributor is excessively long, and there must be a sufficient number of these items on hand to fulfill the company's needs until the next delivery arrives. If a company can arrange with its distributor for faster delivery, it can reduce the amount of safety stock kept on hand, thereby reducing its overall investment in MRO inventory.

- *Shift ownership to a distributor*. Some distributors may be willing to own the MRO inventory positioned on the company premises, and to only charge the company for these items when they are actually used. This represents an additional inventory holding cost for the distributor, as well as a monitoring cost, so this approach will probably only be acceptable if the company agrees to sole source its MRO requirements, and has a large amount of MRO spend per year.

- *Tool replacement.* Many tools are sold with lifetime warranties. To take advantage of these warranties, have the tool crib staff routinely examine tools for damage and apply for free replacements as needed.

A particular concern with many of the MRO suggestions just noted is that some of the items purchased will change, which may not go over well with employees at outlying locations who may be attached to particular brands. To mitigate these issues, allocate any resulting cost savings back to the locations, so the local staff can see that there is a benefit to be gained from accepting different MRO items.

Product Recycling

A commonly ignored aspect of cost management is that it may be possible to achieve savings by offering to recycle products. There are several areas in which savings can be achieved, which are as follows:

- *Trade-in program.* The real point may not be accepting back old products, but rather using this as an opportunity to retain customers by offering to replace the old products with new ones. Some discount off the standard price will be required to entice customers to engage in this program, but as long as the margin on the new product is large enough, the transaction should still create a tidy profit.
- *Refurbish products.* There is an after-market for many products, where customers are eager to buy refurbished goods for a discount. If so, it can make sense to route all returned products to a supplier that specializes in refurbishment and resale activities.
- *Recycle components.* Some component parts (such as toner cartridges) can be used over again. If so, create a free-freight offer to customers, requesting them to return these parts to the company. An inspection phase is used to eliminate damaged returns, after which all other items are refurbished and sent back into the market as sellable component parts.
- *Scrap.* Worst case, the products submitted for recycling can be broken down and sold to a scrap dealer. The resulting scrap receipts will not be large, but still constitute a modest gain for the company.

A product recycling program can also be viewed from the perspective of reducing the total cost to the environment, since items returned to active use are being kept out of landfills.

Cost Management Failures

There are a few activities within a business that can cause costs to increase, and which certainly work against the cost management efforts of the purchasing department. Some of the more pernicious of these activities are:

- *Engineering works alone.* We noted earlier that target costing teams can jointly develop new products for which costs have been minimized. The reverse of this situation is the more traditional approach of allowing the engineering department to design products by itself, with no cross-department support. When this happens, suppliers have been selected and the product design has been finalized before the purchasing department is ever involved in the process. In this environment, suppliers already know that they have been selected, and may have made substantial investments in designing the components; they will not be willing to disgorge their future profits through price decreases, especially since the purchasing staff has no bargaining leverage over them.

- *Suppliers create requests for quotes.* Someone outside of the purchasing department may be working with a supplier to develop specifications for a major purchase. For example, the information technology manager might want to install a new wireless network within the company, and contacts a supplier for advice. If the supplier volunteers to assist with writing the request for quote (RFQ) that will be sent out to prospective bidders, the supplier will likely configure the RFQ so that the only viable candidate that can meet all of the designated requirements is the supplier itself.

- *Maverick spenders.* There are usually a few people within an organization that step outside of the standard procurement process to buy whatever they want, from whichever supplier they want. These people are known as maverick spenders, and can get away with this behavior because they have positions of authority within the business. The trouble with this behavior is that maverick spenders do not always buy at the best price points and may not obtain the best payment terms.

In all three cases, the problem originates outside of the purchasing department. This means that controlling the issues will likely be outside of the control of the purchasing manager, who will not have sufficient authority over the problem areas. Only the support of a senior manager can bring about the improvement of these cost management failures.

Summary

We began this chapter with a discussion of several types of analysis, which are useful for negotiating the best possible prices with suppliers. We also noted several tactical offshoots of these analyses, such as the use of volume discounts and setting appropriate contract durations. In essence, this part of the chapter was designed to react to the prices being offered by suppliers.

We then switched to a lengthy analysis of target costing. This topic is more pro-active, since a business can design products to have certain costs, and work with suppliers to achieve those costs. The result can be a potentially large and favorable long-term impact on cost management. Though a high degree of inter-department cooperation is needed to make this program a success, the resulting profits can be so large that ignoring it is not an option.

We also described a number of ways to reduce MRO costs. This is one of the most unconsolidated and difficult to manage areas from a cost perspective, which is why the topic was listed. Our many cost management points should make it clear that, when properly addressed in a manner that is not overly time-consuming, it is possible to shave expenses in areas that may initially appear to be impenetrable.

Chapter 14
Purchasing Financial Analysis

Introduction

Besides its normal sourcing responsibilities, the purchasing department is routinely asked for recommendations of a more financial variety. Examples are whether to make or buy a product, or whether to lease or buy an asset. Other issues, such as the cost effects of the learning curve, volume pricing discount anomalies, and early payment discounts, may be incorporated into contract negotiations. In a larger organization, these questions may be shifted to a financial analyst or cost accountant, but the purchasing staff will probably be expected to address them when the financial support function is nonexistent or not heavily staffed. All of these types of financial analysis are described in the following sections.

The Lease or Buy Decision

Part of the negotiation to acquire an asset is whether the company wants to buy it or lease it. The purchasing staff should be familiar with the concept of a lease, its key terms, and how to determine whether it would be better to buy or lease.

A lease is an arrangement where the lessor agrees to allow the lessee to use an asset for a stated period of time in exchange for a series of fixed payments. The arrangement typically requires that the asset be returned after a stated interval, though the lessee may have the option to extend the lease or buy the asset at the end of the lease term. The two main types of leases are:

- *Capital lease.* The lessee records the leased asset on its books as a fixed asset and depreciates it, while recording interest expense separately. This option is only available if the lease terms have the characteristics of a long-term loan.
- *Operating lease.* The lessor records the leased asset on its books as a fixed asset and depreciates it, while the lessee simply records a periodic lease payment. This option is more common, and involves lease terms that essentially establish the ownership of the asset by the lessor.

There are a multitude of factors that a lessor includes in the formulation of the monthly rate that it charges, such as the down payment, the residual value of the asset at the end of the lease, and the interest rate, which makes it difficult to break out and examine each element of the lease. Instead, it is much easier to create separate net present value tables for the lease and buy alternatives, and then compare the results of the two tables to see which alternative is better from a cash flow perspective. The following example illustrates the use of net present value for this analysis.

EXAMPLE

Milford Sound is contemplating the purchase of an asset for $500,000. It can buy the asset outright, or do so with a lease. Its cost of capital is 8%, and its incremental income tax rate is 35%. The following two tables show the net present values of both options.

Buy Option

Year	Depreciation	Income Tax Savings (35%)	Discount Factor (8%)	Net Present Value
0				-$500,000
1	$100,000	$35,000	0.9259	32,407
2	100,000	35,000	0.8573	30,006
3	100,000	35,000	0.7938	27,783
4	100,000	35,000	0.7350	25,725
5	100,000	35,000	0.6806	23,821
Totals	$500,000	$175,000		$360,258

Lease Option

Year	Pretax Lease Payments	Income Tax Savings (35%)	After-Tax Lease Cost	Discount Factor (8%)	Net Present Value
1	$135,000	$47,250	$87,750	0.9259	$81,248
2	135,000	47,250	87,750	0.8573	75,228
3	135,000	47,250	87,750	0.7938	69,656
4	135,000	47,250	87,750	0.7350	64,496
5	135,000	47,250	87,750	0.6806	59,723
Totals	$675,000	$236,250	$438,750		$350,351

Thus, the net purchase cost of the buy option is $360,258, while the net purchase cost of the lease option is $350,351. The lease option involves the lowest cash outflow for Milford, and so is the better option.

The preceding lease or buy analysis was based on the concept of *discounted cash flows*. The foundation of this analysis is the concept that cash received today is more valuable than cash received at some point in the future. The reason is that someone who agrees to receive payment at a later date foregoes the ability to invest that cash right now. The only way for someone to agree to a delayed payment is to pay them for the privilege, which is known as interest income.

For example, if a person owns $10,000 now and invests it at an interest rate of 10%, then she will have earned $1,000 by having use of the money for one year. If she were instead to *not* have access to that cash for one year, then she would lose the $1,000 of interest income. The interest income in this example represents the time value of money.

To extend the example, what is the current payout of cash at which the person would be indifferent to receiving cash now or in one year? In essence, what is the amount that, when invested at 10%, will equal $10,000 in one year? The general formula used to answer this question, known as the *present value of 1 due in N periods*, is:

$$\frac{1}{(1 + \text{Interest rate})^{\text{Number of years}}}$$

The calculation for the example is:

$$\frac{\$10,000}{(1 + 10\%)^{1 \text{ year}}}$$

$$= \$9,090.91$$

In essence, if the person receives $9,090.91 now and invests it at a 10% interest rate, her cash balance will have increased to $10,000 in one year.

The effect of the present value formula becomes more pronounced if the receipt of cash is delayed to a date even further in the future, because the period during which the recipient of the cash cannot invest the cash is prolonged.

The following present value table states the discount factors for the present value of 1 due in N periods for a common range of interest rates. We have noted in bold the discount factors used for the preceding lease or buy analysis, where the presumed interest rate was 8%.

Present Value Factors for 1 Due in N Periods

Number of Years	6%	7%	8%	9%	10%	11%	12%
1	0.9434	0.9346	**0.9259**	0.9174	0.9091	0.9009	0.8929
2	0.8900	0.8734	**0.8573**	0.8417	0.8265	0.8116	0.7972
3	0.8396	0.8163	**0.7938**	0.7722	0.7513	0.7312	0.7118
4	0.7921	0.7629	**0.7350**	0.7084	0.6830	0.6587	0.6355
5	0.7473	0.7130	**0.6806**	0.6499	0.6209	0.5935	0.5674
6	0.7050	0.6663	0.6302	0.5963	0.5645	0.5346	0.5066
7	0.6651	0.6228	0.5835	0.5470	0.5132	0.4817	0.4524
8	0.6274	0.5820	0.5403	0.5019	0.4665	0.4339	0.4039
9	0.5919	0.5439	0.5003	0.4604	0.4241	0.3909	0.3606
10	0.5584	0.5084	0.4632	0.4224	0.3855	0.3522	0.3220
11	0.5268	0.4751	0.4289	0.3875	0.3505	0.3173	0.2875
12	0.4970	0.4440	0.3971	0.3555	0.3186	0.2858	0.2567
13	0.4688	0.4150	0.3677	0.3262	0.2897	0.2575	0.2292
14	0.4423	0.3878	0.3405	0.2993	0.2633	0.2320	0.2046
15	0.4173	0.3625	0.3152	0.2745	0.2394	0.2090	0.1827

To use the table, move to the column representing the relevant interest rate, and move down to the "number of years" row indicating the discount rate to apply to the applicable year of cash flow. Thus, if an analysis were to indicate $100,000 of cash flow in the fourth year, and the interest rate were 10%, you would multiply the $100,000 by 0.6830 to arrive at a present value of $68,300 for those cash flows.

Leasing Concerns

There is an undeniable attraction to acquiring assets with a lease, since it replaces a large up-front cash outflow with a series of monthly payments. However, before signing a lease agreement, be aware of the following issues that can increase the cost of the arrangement:

- *Buyout price.* Many leases include an end-of-lease buyout price that is inordinately high. If the lessee wants to continue using a leased asset, the buyout price may be so outrageous that the only realistic alternative is to continue making lease payments, which generates outsized profits for the lessor. Therefore, always negotiate the size of the buyout payment before signing a lease agreement. If the buyout is stated as the "fair market value" of the asset at the end of the lease term, the amount can be subject to interpretation, so include a clause that allows for arbitration to determine the amount of fair market value.

- *Deposit*. The lessor may require that an inordinately large deposit be made at the beginning of the lease term, from which the lessor can then earn interest over the term of the lease.
- *Deposit usage*. The terms of a lease may allow the lessor to charge any number of fees against the up-front deposit made by the lessee, resulting in little of the deposit being returned at the end of the lease.
- *Lease fee*. The lessor may charge a lease fee, which is essentially a paperwork charge to originate the lease. It may be possible to reduce or eliminate this fee.
- *Rate changes*. The lessor may offer a low lease rate during the beginning periods of a lease, and then escalate the rates later in the lease term. Be sure to calculate the average lease rate to see if the implicit interest rate is reasonable. In these sorts of arrangements, a rate ramp-up usually indicates an average interest rate that is too high.
- *Return fees*. When the lease term is over, the lessor may require that the leased asset be shipped at the lessee's cost to a distant location, and sometimes even in the original packaging.
- *Termination notification*. The lease agreement may require the lessee to notify the lessor in writing that it intends to terminate the lease as of the termination date stated in the contract. If the lessee does not issue this notification in a timely manner, it is obligated to continue leasing the asset, or to pay a large termination fee. Whenever this clause appears in a lease agreement, always negotiate it down to the smallest possible termination notification period.
- *Wear-and-tear standards*. A lease agreement may contain unreasonable standards for assigning a high rate of wear-and-tear to leased assets when they have been returned to the lessor, resulting in additional fees being charged to the lessee.

In short, many lessors rely upon obfuscation of the lease terms to generate a profit, so it makes sense to delve into every clause in a lease agreement and be willing to bargain hard for changes to the terms. Also, have a well-managed system in place for retaining lease agreements and monitoring when the key dates associated with each lease will arise. Finally, conduct a cost review after each lease agreement has been terminated, to determine the total out-of-pocket cost and implicit interest rate; the result may be the discovery that certain lessors routinely gouge the company, and should not be used again.

In addition to the issues just noted, the lessee also loses access to any favorable changes in the residual value of leased assets, since the lessor usually retains ownership of the assets. Also, the lessee cannot take advantage of the tax benefits of depreciation when a lease is classified as an operating lease; instead, the lessor records the depreciation and takes advantage of the related tax benefits. This latter issue may not be a concern if the lessee has minimal taxable income that could be reduced by a depreciation charge, and does not expect to be able to use a net operating loss carryforward in future years.

The list of concerns with leasing arrangements may appear formidable. However, they also have a number of advantages, as explained in the next section.

Leasing Advantages

The leasing concerns just described should introduce a note of caution into dealings with lessors, since a careful analysis of lease terms may reveal an inordinately high cost. However, there are also a number of advantages to leasing, which include:

- *Asset servicing.* The lessor may have a sophisticated asset servicing capability. Though the cost of this servicing may be high, it can result in fast servicing intervals and therefore extremely high equipment usage levels. In some cases, the presence of a servicing capability may be the main attraction of a leasing deal.
- *Competitive lease rates.* A lessor can offer quite competitive lease rates. This situation arises when a lessor buys assets in such high volumes that it can obtain volume purchase discounts from suppliers, some of which it may pass along to lessees. The lessor may also be able to borrow funds at a lower rate than the lessee, and can share some of the cost differential.
- *Financing accessibility.* A lessor is more likely to enter into a leasing arrangement with a company that is experiencing low profitability than a traditional lender. This is because the leased asset is collateral for the lessor, which can take the asset back if the lessee is unable to continue making timely lease payments. Conversely, a traditional lender might have a considerably more difficult time accessing company assets, and so would be less inclined to lend funds for the purchase of assets.
- *New technology.* A non-monetary advantage of leasing is that a company is continually swapping out old equipment for newer and more technologically advanced equipment. This can present a competitive advantage in those cases where the equipment is being used within a core function, or used to enhance products or services.
- *Off-balance sheet transaction.* Depending on the terms of a leasing arrangement, it may be possible for a lessee to avoid having to state its remaining lease payment liabilities on its balance sheet. By doing so, the balance sheet shows the company as having fewer obligations than is really the case, and so the business appears more solvent. However, it may still be necessary to reveal the annual amount of future lease payments in the accompanying financial statement disclosures.
- *Reserve available debt.* The company can reserve room on its existing line of credit by instead using a lease to buy an asset.
- *Short-term usage.* A leasing arrangement can be an effective alternative for those assets that are expected to have little value by the end of their lease terms, or for which the company expects to install a replacement asset at about the time of the lease termination.

The Make or Buy Decision

The purchasing staff will occasionally be asked whether a product should be produced in-house or manufactured elsewhere. The core issue that should be used to decide the issue is the impact of the product in question on the company's bottleneck (or *constraint*) operation. In essence, if the product is shifted from in-house production to a supplier, what is the financial impact on the constraint? Before we can answer this question, it is necessary to first describe the terms used in constraint analysis, which are:

- *Throughput*. This is the margin left after totally variable costs are subtracted from revenue. This tends to be a large proportion of revenues, since all overhead costs are excluded from the calculation.
- *Totally variable costs*. This is usually just the cost of materials, since it is only those costs that vary when one incremental unit of a product is manufactured. This does not normally include the cost of labor, since employees are not usually paid based on one incremental unit of output. There are a few other possible costs that may be totally variable, such as commissions, subcontractor fees, customs duties, and freight costs.
- *Operating expenses*. This is all company expenses other than totally variable costs. There is no differentiation between overhead costs, administrative costs or financing costs – quite simply, *all* other company expenses are lumped into this category.
- *Investment*. This is the amount invested in assets. The term includes changes in the level of working capital resulting from a management decision.
- *Net profit*. This is throughput, less operating expenses.

When you look at a company from the perspective of constraints, it no longer makes sense to evaluate individual products, because overhead costs do not vary at the individual product level. In reality, most companies spend a great deal of money to maintain a production infrastructure, and that infrastructure is what really generates a profit – the trick is making that infrastructure produce the maximum profit with the best mix of products having the highest possible throughput. Under the constraint analysis model, there are three ways to improve the financial position of the entire production infrastructure. They are:

- *Increase throughput*. This is by either increasing revenues or reducing the amount of totally variable costs.
- *Reduce operating expenses*. This is by reducing some element of overhead expenses.
- *Improve the return on investment*. This is by either improving profits in conjunction with the lowest possible investment, or by reducing profits slightly along with a correspondingly larger decline in investment.

Note that only the increase in throughput is related in any way to decisions made at the product level. The other two improvement methods may be concerned with changes anywhere in the production system.

These concepts are included in the following three formulas, which are used to solve a number of financial analysis scenarios:

$$\text{Revenue} - \text{totally variable expenses} = \text{throughput}$$

$$\text{Throughput} - \text{operating expenses} = \text{net profit}$$

$$\text{Net profit} \div \text{investment} = \text{return on investment}$$

When altering the system of production, one or more of the preceding formulas can be used to decide whether the contemplated alteration will improve the system. There must be a positive answer to one of the following questions, or else no action should be taken:

- Is there an incremental increase in throughput?
- Is there an incremental reduction in operating expenses?
- Is there an incremental increase in the return on investment?

There is an excellent constraint analysis model that was developed by Thomas Corbett, and which is outlined here. The basic thrust of the model is to give priority in the constraint to those products that generate the highest throughput per minute of constraint time. After these products are manufactured, you then give priority to the product having the next highest throughput per minute, and so on. Eventually, the production queue is filled, and the operation can accept no additional work.

The key element in the model is the use of throughput per minute, because the key limiting factor in a constraint is time – hence, maximizing throughput within the shortest possible time frame is paramount. Note that throughput *per minute* is much more important than total throughput *per unit*. The following example illustrates the point.

EXAMPLE

Mole Industries manufactures trench digging equipment. It has two products with different amounts of throughput and processing times at the constrained resource. The key information about these products is:

Product	Total Throughput	Constraint Processing Time	Throughput per Minute
Mole Hole Digger	$400	2 minutes	$200
Mole Driver Deluxe	800	8 minutes	100

Of the two products, the Mole Driver Deluxe creates the most overall throughput, but the Mole Hole Digger creates more throughput per minute of constraint processing time. To determine which one is more valuable to Mole Industries, consider what would happen if the company had an unlimited order quantity of each product, and could run the constrained resource non-stop, all day (which equates to 1,440 minutes). The operating results would be:

Product	Throughput per Minute		Total Processing Time Available		Total Throughput
Mole Hole Digger	$200	×	1,440 minutes	=	$288,000
Mole Driver Deluxe	100	×	1,440 minutes	=	144,000

Clearly, the Mole Hole Digger, with its higher throughput per minute, is much more valuable to Mole Industries than its Mole Driver Deluxe product. Consequently, the company should push sales of the Mole Hole Digger product whenever possible.

The constraint analysis model is essentially a production plan that itemizes the amount of throughput that can be generated, as well as the total amount of operating expenses and investment. In the sample model, we use four different products, each requiring some processing time in the constraint. The columns in the model are as follows:

- *Throughput per minute.* This is the total amount of throughput that a product generates, divided by the amount of processing time at the constrained resource.
- *Constraint usage.* This is the number of minutes of processing time required by a product at the constrained resource. This figure is the sum total of both the setup time for a job and the actual run time for the job.
- *Units scheduled.* This is the number of units scheduled to be processed at the constrained resource.
- *Total constraint time.* This is the total number of minutes of processing time required by a product, multiplied by the number of units to be processed.
- *Total throughput.* This is the throughput per minute multiplied by the number of units processed at the constrained resource.

This grid produces a total amount of throughput to be generated if production proceeds according to plan. Below the grid of planned production, there is a subtotal of the total amount of throughput, from which the total amount of operating expenses are subtracted to arrive at the amount of profit. Finally, the total amount of investment in assets is divided into the profit to calculate the return on investment. Thus, the model provides a complete analysis of all three ways in which the results of a company can be improved – increase throughput, decrease operating expenses, or increase the return on investment. An example of the model follows.

Sample Constraint Analysis Model

Product	Throughput per Minute	Constraint Usage (minutes)	Units Scheduled	Total Constraint Time	Total Throughput
1. Hedgehog Deluxe	$80	14	1,000	14,000	$1,120,000
2. Hedgehog Mini	70	20	500	10,000	700,000
3. Hedgehog Classic	65	40	200	8,000	520,000
4. Hedgehog Digger	42	10	688	6,880	288,960
		Total constraint scheduled time		38,880	
		Total constraint time available*		38,880	
			Total throughput		$2,628,960
			Total operating expenses		2,400,000
			Profit		$228,960
			Profit percentage		8.7%
			Investment		$23,000,000
			Annualized return on investment		11.9%

* Minutes per month = 30 days × 24 hours × 60 minutes × (1 − 0.10 maintenance time)

In the example, the Hedgehog Deluxe product has the largest throughput per minute, and so is scheduled to be the first priority for production. The Hedgehog Digger has the lowest throughput per minute, so it is given last priority in the production schedule. If there is less time available on the constrained resource, the company should reduce the number of the Hedgehog Digger product manufactured in order to maximize overall profits.

In the middle of the model, the "Total constraint scheduled time" row contains the total number of minutes of scheduled production. The row below it, labeled "Total constraint time available," represents the total estimate of time that the constraint should have available for production purposes during the scheduling period. Since the time scheduled and available are identical, this means that the production schedule has completely maximized the availability of the constrained resource.

One calculation anomaly in the model is that the profit percentage is normally calculated as profit divided by revenues. However, since revenues are not included in the model, we instead use profits divided by throughput. Since throughput is less than revenue, we are overstating the profit percentage as compared to the traditional profit percentage calculation.

Use the constraint analysis model in a before-and-after mode, to see what effect a proposed change will have on profitability or the return on investment. If the model improves as a result of a change, then implement the change.

All of the preceding discussion of constraint analysis has been needed in order to make the decision of whether to make or buy a product. The buy decision is always acceptable if the throughput generated by the outsourced products exceeds the price charged to the company by the supplier, *and* the company can replace the throughput per minute that was taken away from the constrained resource. The following example, which uses the basic constraint model as a baseline, illustrates the concept.

EXAMPLE

Mole Industries receives an offer from a supplier to outsource the Hedgehog Classic to it. The downside of the offer is that the supplier's price is higher than the cost at which Mole can produce the Classic internally, so the total monthly throughput attributable to the Classic would decline by $300,000, from $520,000 to $220,000. However, there is a large customer order backlog for the Hedgehog Digger, so Mole could give increased production priority to the Digger instead. The analysis is as follows, with changes to the baseline model noted in bold.

Product	Throughput per Minute	Constraint Usage (minutes)	Units Scheduled	Total Constraint Time	Total Throughput
1. Hedgehog Deluxe	$80	14	1,000	14,000	$1,120,000
2. Hedgehog Mini	70	20	500	10,000	700,000
3. Hedgehog Classic	65	40	200	N/A	**220,000**
4. Hedgehog Digger	42	10	**1,488**	**14,880**	**624,960**
		Total constraint scheduled time		38,880	
		Total constraint time available*		38,880	
			Total throughput		**$2,664,960**
			Total operating expenses		2,400,000
			Profit		**$264,960**
			Profit percentage		**9.9%**
			Investment		$23,000,000
			Annualized return on investment		**13.8%**

* Minutes per month = 30 days × 24 hours × 60 minutes × (1 − 0.10 maintenance time)

Despite a large decline in throughput caused by the outsourcing deal, the company actually earns $36,000 more profit overall, because the Hedgehog Classic uses more of the constraint time per unit (40 minutes) than any other product; this allows the company to fill the available constraint time with 800 more Hedgehog Digger products, which require the smallest amount of constraint time per unit (10 minutes), and which generate sufficient additional throughput to easily offset the throughput decline caused by outsourcing. Mole Industries should accept the supplier's offer to outsource.

For more information about how to identify and deal with constraints, see the author's *Constraint Management* book.

The Outsourcing Decision

It may be possible to avoid a capital purchase entirely by outsourcing the work to which it is related. By doing so, a company may be able to eliminate all assets related to the area (rather than acquiring more assets), while the burden of maintaining a sufficient asset base now shifts to the supplier. The supplier may even buy the company's assets related to the area being outsourced. This situation is a well-established alternative for high technology manufacturing, as well as for information technology services, but is likely not viable outside of these areas.

If outsourcing is a possibility, the cash flows resulting from doing so will be highly favorable for the first few years, as capital expenditures vanish. However, the supplier must also earn a profit and pay for its own infrastructure, so the cost over the long term will probably not vary dramatically from what the company would have experienced if it had kept a functional area in-house. There are three exceptions that can bring about a long-term cost reduction. They are:

- *Excess capacity.* A supplier may have such a large amount of excess capacity already that it does not need to invest further for some time, thereby potentially depressing the costs that it would otherwise pass through to its customers. However, this excess capacity pool will eventually dry up, so it tends to be a short-term anomaly.
- *High volume.* There are some outsourcing situations where the supplier is handling such a massive volume of activity from multiple customers that its costs on a per-unit basis decline below the costs that a company could ever achieve on its own. This situation can yield long-term savings to a company.
- *Low costs.* A supplier may locate its facility and work force in low-cost countries or regions within countries. This can yield significant cost reductions in the short term, but as many suppliers use the same technique, it is driving up costs in all parts of the world. Thus, this cost disparity is useful for a period of time, but is gradually declining as a long-term option.

There are also risks involved in shifting functions to suppliers. First, a supplier may go out of business, leaving the company scrambling to shift work to a new supplier. Second, a supplier may gradually ramp up prices to the point where the company is substantially worse off than if it had kept the function in-house. Third, the company may have so completely purged the outsourced function from its own operations that it is now completely dependent on the supplier, and has no ability to take it back in-house. Fourth, the supplier's service level may decline to the point where it is impairing the ability of the company to operate. Fifth, the supplier may not have sufficient capacity to handle an upturn in transaction volume. And finally, the company may have entered into a multi-year deal, and cannot escape from the contract if the business arrangement does not work out. These are significant issues, and must be weighed as part of the outsourcing decision.

The cautions noted here about outsourcing do not mean that it should be avoided as an option. On the contrary, a rapidly growing company that has minimal access to funds may cheerfully hand off multiple operations to suppliers in order to avoid the up-front costs associated with those operations. This option is also attractive when a business has a poorly-run department, and needs to substantially upgrade its performance level. Outsourcing is less attractive to stable, well-established companies that have better access to capital.

Learning Curve Analysis

When a supplier is producing goods for a company, there is an expectation that the labor component of the supplier's cost of production will gradually decline as its employees become more expert at the manufacturing process. Over time, employees can be expected to learn from ongoing repetitions of their production tasks, resulting in increased efficiencies. There may also be improvements from process changes or the introduction of automation. The same concept applies to services work, since more-experienced employees learn from their previous experience and apply it to their latest projects. This is a gradually-declining rate of improvement, as the supplier's employees find fewer and fewer ways to improve their efficiency over time. This rate of improvement is called a *learning curve*.

The learning curve is measured as the reduction in the cumulative average number of labor hours each time production doubles. For example, if there is a 95% learning rate, this means that the average amount of production labor required to manufacture one unit will decline by 5% each time the production volume doubles. The assumption behind the learning curve concept is that the rate of decline in the cost of labor can be predicted, based on production volumes.

We have just noted a 95% learning rate as an example, but the rate can vary considerably, depending on the situation. If there is a steep learning curve, the learning rate might be 80%, which means that the average amount of production labor will decline by 20% each time the production volume doubles.

When a supplier takes on a contract to produce goods for a company, the supplier may initially take on the work at a relatively small profit, but is relying on the learning curve to reduce its costs over time, resulting in much better profits. The purchasing staff should be aware of this concept when negotiating contracts for unit volumes that are likely to be significant; if it appears that there will be a steep learning curve, it will be reasonable to negotiate for a price per unit that declines over time. Ideally, the purchasing staff wants to share in some portion of the proceeds from the learning curve, while also giving a supplier a reasonable share of the profits over time.

When the purchasing staff incorporates the learning curve into its sourcing plans and contract negotiations, this can lead to a different approach to dealing with suppliers, such as the following:

- Engage in more sole-source contracting, so that more unit volume will be handled by a single supplier. Otherwise, the unit volume will be spread among several suppliers, and none of them will experience much of a learning curve.
- Offer longer-term contracts to suppliers. When suppliers have the security of a lengthy contract, they are more likely to invest in the process analysis and equipment needed to create a steeper learning curve.
- Offer to send the company's industrial engineers to suppliers to assist them in improving their production processes.

The concept does not work everywhere. One must be careful to spot those situations in which the conditions are present to make the learning curve function properly. Otherwise, the purchasing staff might enforce an ongoing price decline on a supplier, and then see the supplier struggle with declining profitability as its margins erode. Consequently, look for the following conditions before factoring the learning curve into a sourcing deal:

- *Employee retention.* The production staff should have a low turnover rate, so that there is an ongoing buildup in employee experience over time.
- *First time.* There is a greater opportunity for the learning curve to function when a supplier will be manufacturing a product for the first time, or doing so using a new process. In this situation, there is a greater opportunity for improvement.
- *High labor content.* The labor component of the cost of a product should be quite high, since this is the part of the product cost that will be impacted by the learning curve.

EXAMPLE

Laid Back Corporation manufactures chairs. It accepts a contract from a major international retail chain to produce a new type of handcrafted wooden executive business chair. The chair proves to be wildly popular, resulting in increasing order volumes from the customer over time. After several years of production, Laid Back's cost accountant collects the following information about the learning curve that the company is experiencing:

Units Produced	Labor Hours Incurred	Labor Hours per Unit	Learning Rate	Learning Curve
50	700	14.0	--	--
100	1,260	12.6	9.8%	90.2%
200	2,300	11.5	8.9%	91.1%
400	4,160	10.4	9.7%	90.3%
800	7,520	9.4	9.2%	90.8%
1,600	13,760	8.6	8.5%	91.5%
3,200	25,280	7.9	8.3%	91.7%

Based on the presented information, Laid Back is experiencing what is roughly a 91% learning curve in its production process.

The company's cost per labor hour is $20, so it was incurring a labor cost of $280 for each unit in the initial 50-unit batch of chairs, and incurred a labor cost of $158 for each unit in the last batch of chairs, which was for 3,200 units. This means that Laid Back has improved its profit per chair by $122 at the 3,200 unit volume level. If the buyer for the retail chain were to negotiate for a lower price at the higher unit volume, the potential price decline to be discussed could be as large as $122, and could be even larger if there is an expectation that the learning curve will still be present at even greater unit volumes.

Quantity Discount Analysis

Suppliers routinely offer discounts for orders placed in larger volumes. These discounts are intended to encourage large order sizes, so that a supplier does not have to incur the incremental costs associated with smaller orders, such as order entry, credit reviews, order picking, and so forth. The trouble is that suppliers do not always do a good job of setting their discounts for larger order volumes, resulting in situations in which a company might actually pay more per incremental unit for a larger order quantity than for a smaller order quantity.

The astute buyer can review pricing discounts for anomalies, and make note of situations in which incremental per-unit prices are not actually being discounted. When this is the case, it is quite possible that suppliers will accede to demands to reduce their discount prices. The following example illustrates how quantity discount analysis works.

EXAMPLE

A buyer for Mulligan Imports is examining the prices being offered by a foreign supplier for golf clubs, and finds the following pricing table:

Units	Price Each
1	$200
5	160
10	150

The pricing is clearly intended to steer buyers away from purchasing a unit count of less than five, since the largest price break occurs at the five-unit level.

Being an analytical type, the Mulligan buyer transfers the supplier's pricing into a spreadsheet that calculates the incremental cost per unit if the order volume is varied from one to ten units, with the following results:

	No Price Break	5-Unit Price Break	10-Unit Price Break
Units per order	1	5	10
Quoted price per unit	$200	$160	$150
Total price (units × quoted price)	$200	$800	$1,500
Pricing variance between orders	$200	$600	$700
Quantity variance between orders	1	4	4
Price per incremental unit	$200	$150	$175

The table reveals that the incremental price per incremental unit has actually increased at the 10-unit pricing level. The Mulligan buyer could reasonably expect to negotiate a price per unit of at least $140 at the 10-unit pricing level. Doing so would result in the following table, where the price per incremental unit no longer increases at the higher order volume:

	No Price Break	5-Unit Price Break	10-Unit Price Break
Units per order	1	5	10
Quoted price per unit	$200	$160	$140
Total price (units × quoted price)	$200	$800	$1,400
Pricing variance between orders	$200	$600	$600
Quantity variance between orders	1	4	4
Price per incremental unit	**$200**	**$150**	**$150**

Early Payment Discounting

When dealing with suppliers, part of the negotiation of a contract may include a discussion of whether a supplier will offer an early payment discount. A supplier may offer these terms if it is cash-strapped, or when it does not have a backup line of credit to absorb any cash shortfalls.

The early payment terms offered by suppliers can have astonishingly high effective interest rates built into them. If so, they can represent a modest source of additional profits for a company, if it regularly takes the discounts and places a large dollar-volume of orders with a supplier. When there is a large amount of order volume, the purchasing staff should certainly request such a discount.

The term structure used for credit terms is to first state the number of days being given to customers from the invoice date in which to take advantage of the early payment credit terms. For example, if a customer is supposed to pay within 10 days without a discount, the terms are "net 10 days," whereas if the customer must pay within 10 days to qualify for a 2% discount, the terms are "2/10." Or, if the customer must pay within 10 days to obtain a 2% discount or can make a normal payment in 30 days, then the terms are stated as "2/10 net 30."

The following table shows some of the more common credit terms, explains what they mean, and also notes the effective interest rate being offered by suppliers with each one.

Credit Terms Table

Credit Terms	Explanation	Effective Interest
Net 10	Pay in 10 days	None
Net 30	Pay in 30 days	None
Net EOM 10*	Pay within 10 days of month-end	None
1/10 net 30	Take a 1% discount if pay in 10 days, otherwise pay in 30 days	18.2%
2/10 net 30	Take a 2% discount if pay in 10 days, otherwise pay in 30 days	36.7%
1/10 net 60	Take a 1% discount if pay in 10 days, otherwise pay in 60 days	7.3%
2/10 net 60	Take a 2% discount if pay in 10 days, otherwise pay in 60 days	14.7%

* EOM is an acronym for "end of month"

In case you are dealing with terms different from those shown in the preceding table, be aware of the formula for calculating the effective interest rate associated with early payment discount terms. The calculation steps are:

1. Calculate the difference between the payment date for those taking the early payment discount and the date when payment is normally due, and divide it into 360 days. For example, under "2/10 net 30" terms, divide 20 days into 360 to arrive at 18. Use this number to annualize the interest rate calculated in the next step.
2. Subtract the discount percentage from 100% and divide the result into the discount percentage. For example, under "2/10 net 30" terms, divide 2% by 98% to arrive at 0.0204. This is the interest rate being offered through the credit terms.
3. Multiply the result of both calculations together to obtain the annualized interest rate. To conclude the example, multiply 18 by 0.0204 to arrive at an effective annualized interest rate of 36.72%.

Thus, the full calculation for the cost of credit is:

$$(\text{Discount \%} \div (1 - \text{Discount \%})) \times (360 \div (\text{Allowed payment days} - \text{Discount days}))$$

Summary

The topics in this chapter allow a company to introduce some quantitative analysis to its dealings with suppliers. The result will likely contribute to a certain amount of improvement in company profitability, if only because of a better knowledge of the costs involved in various decisions. However, more attention to financial analysis should not be used to browbeat suppliers into giving up a larger share of their profits. Instead, be cognizant of the need for suppliers to earn a reasonable profit, so that they will still be willing to work with the company.

Chapter 15
Supply Chain Financing

Introduction

The suppliers that feed materials and services to a company should be well-funded. A financially healthy supplier is more capable of meeting its commitments to the company, and also has more cash to invest in facilities, as well as research and development activities. Such a business is also less likely to suddenly go bankrupt, leaving a hole in the company's supply chain. An organization can contribute to this level of funding by engaging in supply chain financing.

> **Related Podcast Episode:** Episode 143 of the Accounting Best Practices Podcast discusses supply chain financing. It is available at: **accountingtools.com/podcasts** or **iTunes**

Supply Chain Financing

Supply chain financing occurs when a finance company, such as a bank, interposes itself between a company and its suppliers and commits to pay the company's invoices to the suppliers at an accelerated rate in exchange for a discount (which is essentially a factoring arrangement). The following process flow shows the relationship between the parties.

Supply Chain Finance Process Flow

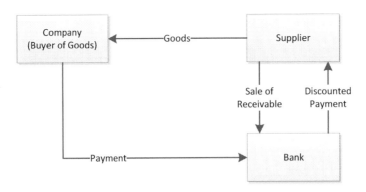

This approach has the following benefits for the entity that is paying its suppliers:

- The company can foster very close links with its core group of suppliers, since this can be a major benefit to them in terms of accelerated cash flow. Because of the ready availability of cash, this may even mean that the company becomes the preferred customer for its supplier base.
- 100% of the invoice value is available for factoring, rather than the discounted amount that is available through a normal factoring arrangement.
- The company no longer has to deal with requests from suppliers for early payment, since they are already being paid as soon as possible.

Supply chain financing has the following benefits for suppliers:

- A cash-strapped supplier can be paid much sooner than normal, in exchange for the finance company's fee.
- The interest rate charged by the finance company should be low, since it is based on the credit standing of the paying company, not the rating of the suppliers (which assumes that the payer has a good rating).

The finance company acting as the intermediary earns interest income on the factoring arrangements that it enters into with the suppliers of the target company. This can represent an excellent source of income over a long period of time, so bankers try to create sole-source supply chain financing arrangements to lock in this income. In addition, the bankers can now develop relations with the entire group of suppliers that it is paying, which may result in an entirely new group of clients for a broad range of banking services.

Supply chain financing is usually begun by large companies that want to improve the cash flow situation for their suppliers. To convince a finance company to be involved in the arrangement requires the expectation of a considerable amount of factoring, which is why this approach is not available to smaller companies.

When first developing a supply chain financing arrangement, it can be difficult to make a reasonable estimate of the amount of financing that a group of suppliers will want. There are a number of factors that could drive the supplier need for cash, including the following:

- *General business environment.* If the economy is robust, suppliers will find that their customers are more likely to pay on time, and so will have less need for accelerated payments. Conversely, if the state of the economy is declining, they may be quite eager to take advantage of supply chain financing in order to assure themselves of a ready source of cash.
- *Existing terms.* If the company has negotiated lengthy payment terms with its suppliers (such as 60 or 90 days to pay), they will be more likely to take advantage of supply chain financing, since this represents a massive acceleration of their cash flow.
- *Interest rate.* If the interest rate being charged by the bank is too high, only the most desperate suppliers will take advantage of the financing.

- *Existing factoring arrangements.* Suppliers may already have long-standing factoring arrangements in place with other lenders, and so may be reluctant to shift their business over to the company's bank. This decision will probably be driven by a comparison of the factoring deals being offered.

There are on-line systems available on which a company can post its approved invoices, and which suppliers can access to select which invoices they want to have paid to them earlier than dictated by the standard payment terms.

Summary

Supply chain financing is an easy way for a larger business to improve the cash flow of its suppliers. However, this option is only available to larger companies, so the suppliers of a smaller company will have to use their own factoring arrangements to achieve the same result. The trouble with independent factoring arrangements is that the cost to suppliers may be higher, and less than the full amount of each invoice may be made available for factoring. If a company wants to help its suppliers out of this situation, it could negotiate with them to reduce the number of days that it will wait before paying them. This does not have to be a unilateral reduction in payment terms; in exchange, the company could negotiate for preferred customer status, which would move it to the front of the queue for order placement, as well as for faster delivery times.

Chapter 16
Purchasing Measurements

Introduction

The amount of cash spent on purchased materials can be the single largest expenditure area of a company, even exceeding the cost of payroll. If so, particular attention should be paid to how well a business is managing these costs. In this chapter, we address how the purchasing department controls costs with purchase orders, procurement cards, and a spend management program, while also noting a variety of ways to track the performance of individual suppliers, and how well the purchasing staff can dispose of excess inventory.

Overview of Purchasing Measurements

Purchasing measurements are designed to control costs. This cannot be done when measurements are made at an aggregate level, since there is not a sufficient amount of actionable information. Instead, virtually every purchasing measurement should be produced at the individual transaction or supplier level. The purchasing staff then uses this information to track down specific instances where costs can be more tightly controlled. However, when creating detailed reports for the following measurements, incorporate a cutoff materiality level, below which no measurements are provided. Doing so focuses the attention of the report recipient on the most actionable information.

There are problems with the traditional measurement of comparing actual purchase prices to a budgeted price, since these measurements can be manipulated. Instead, we have opted for a cost change measurement, which monitors the actual cost of each key purchased item over time and in comparison to a benchmark, such as an inflation index. This approach reveals whether the purchasing staff is able to control the prices paid in relation to market rates.

The traditional method of controlling the cost of purchased goods has been to issue a carefully-researched purchase order to each supplier. However, the cost of generating a purchase order is impractical for low-value purchases, so a useful metric is to track the proportions of purchases made both above and below a designated threshold level with purchase orders. Similarly, the most cost-effective method of purchasing below this threshold level is the procurement card. A card usage percentage can be tracked that reveals the level of acceptance of procurement cards among employees and suppliers.

A well-run purchasing department typically has a spend management system in place, where purchases for certain commodities are concentrated with a small number of suppliers in order to take advantage of volume purchase discounts. This activity can be viewed with a measurement that tracks the proportion of total spend managed.

A variation is to track the proportion of spend already being directed toward preferred suppliers.

The purchasing staff can assist the receiving and production departments by certifying suppliers to bypass the receiving department and send their deliveries directly to the production line. The associated measurement for the proportion of certified suppliers yields general information about the number of qualified suppliers with which the company is dealing, as well as the effort being put into the certification program.

The purchasing manager needs a way to evaluate the performance of suppliers. There are several measurements available for doing so, including the ability of suppliers to fulfill orders in a timely manner, the proportion of received goods that are defective, and whether suppliers tend to bill the company more than was authorized by underlying purchase orders. All of this information can be used to develop report cards for suppliers, which may eventually lead to their replacement.

We also make note of the need to measure transportation charges, specifically those fees associated with premium modes of transport. These costs are usually indicative of problems, either in the production schedule or the supply chain, that require goods to be rushed to the company on short notice.

Finally, we measure the ability of the purchasing staff to disposition inventory that has been identified as not being usable by the company's production processes, or unlikely to be sold as merchandise. This is an area frequently ignored, since it does not directly impact sales, but which can result in inventory obsolescence write-offs if not addressed on a regular basis.

In total, the measurements described in this chapter are designed to fulfill a valuable monitoring function that can yield notable cost reductions, not only in the cost of the purchasing function, but also in the cost of purchased goods.

Cost Change

It can be useful to track the percentage change in key costs over time, especially in comparison to a related inflation index or other evidence of market prices. A cost change that is unfavorable may be still be acceptable, as long as the percentage change is lower than the related benchmark. Conversely, no cost change when related to a declining benchmark could trigger management action, since the cost should have declined in concert with the benchmark.

EXAMPLE

Grissom Granaries operates a number of crop storage facilities along the Mississippi River. The company buys farmer's crops, holds them until the winter months, and then sells the crops at what is usually a higher price. Given the nature of the business, it is critical that Grissom purchase crops at no worse than the market price at all times. The manager of the Hannibal crop storage facility in Missouri is comparing the prices paid by the purchasing staff for metric tons of soybeans to the soybean futures end of day settlement price, which reveals the following information:

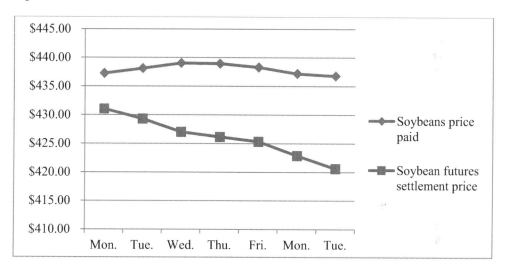

Not only is the purchasing staff not keeping pace with the decline in prices indicated by the futures settlement prices, but the gap is widening. The Hannibal facility manager calls an immediate meeting with the purchasing manager to discuss corrective actions to take.

A possible issue is that cost changes can trail the benchmarks to which they are related, since the purchasing staff may not realize that there is an issue until the benchmark is published. Consequently, managers may need to wait a short time to see if the purchasing staff can make a correction before intruding.

Proportion of Purchase Orders above Threshold

Purchase orders have traditionally been considered a key part of the purchasing process, for they embody a formal authorization to purchase goods. Purchase orders are also used in the three-way matching process by the accounting staff to ensure that supplier invoices have been properly authorized for payment. However, it is quite time-consuming to research and issue purchase orders, which makes them wildly expensive for lower-cost orders. Accordingly, most organizations dispense with purchase orders for smaller orders, electing to use procurement cards instead. Consequently, a measure of when purchase orders should be applied is to set a threshold above which purchase orders should be used, and track the usage level above and below this threshold.

To measure the proportion of purchase orders above the ordering threshold, create a report in the accounts payable system that aggregates all purchases made, sorted by the dollar size of each purchase, and noting which ones had an associated authorizing purchase order. Then aggregate the proportion of authorizing purchase orders above and below the designated threshold at which purchase orders are supposed to be used. The formula is:

$$\frac{\text{Number of authorizing purchase orders issued above threshold}}{\text{Total number of purchases made above threshold}}$$

EXAMPLE

Sharper Designs, maker of ceramic knives for professional chefs, has long had a policy of requiring a purchase order for all purchases made. The result has been a massive purchasing staff that dutifully researches each order, puts larger purchases out to bid, and issues detailed purchase orders. In an effort to save money, the CEO requires the purchasing manager to cut his staff in half. To do so, procurement cards are to be used for all purchases under $5,000. After three months, the purchasing manager measures the results of the program by measuring the issuance of purchase orders both above and below the $5,000 threshold. The results are:

	Above Threshold	Below Threshold
Number of purchase orders issued	640	82
Total number of purchases made	670	5,400
Proportion of purchase orders issued	96%	2%

The measure shows good initial compliance with the new program. The organization is generally taking the purchase order threshold into consideration when the decision is made to use a purchase order or a procurement card.

Procurement Card Usage Percentage

A procurement card is a company-sponsored credit card that can be used to make many types of purchases. The use of procurement cards drastically reduces the amount of time required by the purchasing department to create purchase orders, and so should be strongly encouraged for smaller purchases. To track the company's performance in using procurement cards, divide the total number of these transactions below the procurement card threshold by the total number of purchasing transactions below the card threshold. The card usage threshold typically starts fairly low, at perhaps $250, and then tends to ratchet upward as an organization becomes more accustomed to this form of purchasing.

EXAMPLE

The purchasing manager at Milford Sound has been pleased with the reduced purchasing time spent by her staff since procurement cards were introduced a year ago, but suspects that additional time can be saved. Her particular focus is on shifting 100% of purchases under $500 to these cards. She conducts an analysis of card usage by department, and arrives at the following information:

	Purchases with Procurement Cards	Total Purchases Under $500 Limit	Card Usage Percentage
Accounting	40	43	93%
Engineering	208	212	98%
Maintenance	72	520	14%
Sales and marketing	190	202	94%

The information reveals that the best source of additional time reduction is purchases made by the maintenance department, where the person in charge of the procurement card is clearly not using it very much.

As illustrated in the example, the measure will typically reveal that a specific card user is not employing the card to its full effect. Once corrected, there tend to be only a few residual transactions for which procurement cards are not used.

Proportion of Spend Managed

An active procurement program should aggregate all purchasing information by type of commodity purchased, and gradually work through these commodities, concentrating purchases with a smaller number of suppliers to gain volume discounts. As the spending for each commodity is reviewed and improved upon, the company should create a monitoring infrastructure to verify that the improvements made will continue, thereby ensuring continuing reduced costs. To monitor the amount of this active spend management, the purchasing manager should receive a measurement for the proportion of spend managed. The calculation is to divide the total spend on commodities under active management by the total amount of company spend.

It is entirely possible that some portions of company spend are so minor or difficult to manage that the company will never achieve 100% spend management. At some point below the 100% level, the purchasing manager will likely find that assigning more staff to spend management is not a cost-effective proposition, and will cease further efforts in this area.

EXAMPLE

The purchasing manager of Armadillo Industries initiated a spend management program several months ago, and wants to start tracking his progress toward a higher level of active spend management. The company is in the business of manufacturing body armor, protective shielding, and high-pressure containers (such as submarine hulls). This complex business contains many commodity types, so the manager has been focusing on the top commodities on which the company spends money. His analysis of spend being actively managed so far is as follows:

NAICS Code	Commodity Area	(000s) Spend	Percent of Total Spend	Cumulative Spend Percentage
332111	Iron and steel forging	$90,000	18.0%	18.0%
331523	Nonferrous metal die-casting	12,000	2.4%	20.4%
332114	Custom roll forming	42,000	8.4%	29.2%
332119	Metal stamping	4,500	0.9%	30.1%
332313	Plate work manufacturing	7,800	1.6%	31.7%
332912	Fluid power values	3,900	0.8%	32.5%
332613	Spring manufacturing	1,800	0.4%	**32.9%**

The table reveals clear progress toward a high level of active spend management, with nearly a third of all spend now being closely monitored.

Proportion of Spend with Preferred Suppliers

The use of preferred suppliers is the best way not only to obtain volume purchase discounts, but also to buy from those suppliers proven to have the best product quality, delivery times, and other services and terms considered important to the buyer. There are several ways to measure the amount of total spend being directed toward preferred suppliers. Consider the following alternatives:

- Do so in aggregate, as a single percentage. This is most useful when reporting high-level performance information to management.
- Do so by commodity type. This approach shows where commodities are actively being managed, since close observation of a commodity tends to lead to more supplier concentration.
- Do so by business unit. This approach shows the commitment to purchasing management, and can lead to the revamping of purchasing departments where the use of preferred suppliers is negligible.
- Do so for minority and women-owned business enterprises (MWBEs). If a company sells to the federal or state governments, it may be required to source a certain percentage of its purchases with MWBEs. If so, this report can be used to track the progress toward meeting mandated goals.

EXAMPLE

The vice president of procurement at Electronic Inference Corporation is pushing for the redirection of spend to a small group of preferred suppliers. He elects to aggregate preferred supplier information at the business unit level, which results in the following information:

(000s)	Spend with Preferred Suppliers	Total Spend	Proportion of Spend with Preferred Suppliers
Atomic computing division	$17,890	$21,200	84%
Calculators division	5,230	38,100	14%
Memory chip fabrication division	81,000	96,500	84%
National security computing division	58,280	60,800	96%
Totals	$162,400	$216,600	75%

The vice president finds that, despite an overall excellent 75% spend rate with preferred suppliers, the calculators division is far behind the other business units, which presents a large opportunity for further improvement.

Proportion of Certified Suppliers

In a production environment, a large non-value-added step is the receiving department, where incoming deliveries intended for the production area are first identified, inspected, and logged into the computer system. If there are any hitches in this area, there can be significant delays in the amount of time required for materials to reach the production department. Because of this built-in delay, the production staff will build up an inventory buffer to protect the production process from any shortages in incoming materials. The delay represented by the receiving department can be eliminated by certifying suppliers to deliver their goods directly to the production area. Further benefits are a reduction of staffing in the receiving area, and no need for a protective inventory buffer in front of the production area. Clearly, there is a substantial payoff in maintaining a large proportion of suppliers who have been thoroughly examined and certified to bypass the receiving department.

To calculate the proportion of certified suppliers, first determine the number of suppliers that service the production area (all other suppliers are ignored for the purposes of this calculation). Then aggregate from this subset the total number of suppliers that have been certified within the past 12 months, and divide by the total number of suppliers servicing the production area. The formula is:

$$\frac{\text{Number of production suppliers certified within the last 12 months}}{\text{Total of all production suppliers}}$$

The measurement focuses on recent certifications, on the grounds that the company will likely want to re-certify all suppliers on a regular basis. A variation on the concept is to ignore minor suppliers that rarely send in any deliveries, since it will not be worth the time of the company's certification staff to subject these suppliers to a certification examination.

EXAMPLE

Mole Industries has a convoluted receiving process that adds an extra day to the process of obtaining goods from suppliers. In an effort to eliminate this delay, the purchasing manager and engineering manager jointly undertake a project to certify suppliers to make direct deliveries to the production line for Mole's Ditch Digging machines. There are 43 suppliers involved with this production line. After three months of certification activity, the analysis team has concluded that 18 suppliers can be certified, and that the remaining suppliers have such unreliable processes that they must be replaced. Thus, the company has a 42% certified supplier rate for the designated area, until such time as it can upgrade its supplier base.

Supplier Performance Measurements

The purchasing department is responsible for the performance of suppliers, especially those that supply the company's production department. If a supplier performs poorly, it is up to the purchasing staff to inform the supplier of the problem and to rectify the situation – either by replacing the supplier or upgrading its performance. In this section, we describe three measurements that can be used to grade the performance of suppliers.

Supplier Fulfillment Rate

When a company is operating in a just-in-time production environment, it is absolutely critical that items ordered from suppliers arrive on time. If not, the company is forced to either stop its production lines or build inventory buffers to protect against late supplier deliveries. In this situation, one of the key performance metrics is the supplier fulfillment rate. This is the aggregate amount of order line items that are received on time, divided by the total number of order line items placed. The formula is:

$$\frac{\text{Sum of all order line items received by due date}}{\text{Number of all order line items placed}}$$

It is too simplistic to conduct this measurement at the level of purchase orders placed and fulfilled, since there may be many line items on one purchase order, and only a single line item on another.

When evaluating the results of the measurement, keep in mind whether the purchasing staff has set unrealistic delivery goals for suppliers that are well inside of their stated delivery capabilities. In these cases, the company should not have placed the orders at all, or at least should not use the measurement as the basis for a poor performance evaluation for a supplier that may have actually shipped in accordance with its normal lead times.

EXAMPLE

The production manager of Quest Adventure Gear is planning to shift the company's production of backpacker stoves to a just-in-time process flow. To do so, it is critically important that all suppliers involved with the parts for the stoves deliver their assigned components to Quest by the designated dates and times. The purchasing manager is assigned the task of measuring the performance of three suppliers. The measurement results are noted in the following table:

	Fuel Pumps Ltd.	Titanium Corp.	Windscreens Intl.
Sum of order lines filled	327	490	310
Total order line items	330	520	605
Supplier fulfillment rate	99.1%	94.2%	51.2%

The table reveals that the company has a potentially serious fulfillment problem with Windscreens International, which only appears capable of delivering wind screens for the stoves by the specified date and time for about half of all order line items placed. The purchasing manager decides to look for a replacement supplier.

A variation on the concept is to measure whether a supplier can meet its assigned volume goals when a product is being launched for the first time. This can be a key issue when a business routinely schedules major product releases, and needs to know if any of its suppliers are unable to support the launch schedule.

Supplier Defect Rate

Another element of supplier performance is whether they can deliver goods that are free of defects. The concept of defectiveness means that the delivered goods meet the specifications set by the buyer. Thus, if the buyer sets unusually tight tolerances for a component, and the supplier delivers goods that are considered acceptable for general usage but which do not fit the buyer's tolerance limits, then those goods are considered to be defective. Defective components are an especially pernicious problem in a just-in-time manufacturing environment, for there may be no buffer stock on hand to prevent production from stopping if a part proves to be defective.

To measure the defect rate, divide the total number of rejected components by the total number of components received from a supplier during the measurement period. The formula is:

$$\frac{\text{Total number of rejected units}}{\text{Total number of units received}}$$

Defect rates are one of the more important ways in which to evaluate a supplier, so consider breaking down the measurement in several ways, such as by individual part, by supplier facility, by defect type, and by the trucking firm used to deliver the goods – in short, in any way that can yield insights into the reasons for defects or damage.

One problem with this measurement is that it may not be possible to detect defects in the receiving area; problems may not become apparent until later. In this case, a measurement option is to continue tracing product quality back to suppliers as items move through the production process and on to customers. Ultimately, it may be necessary to tie field failure rates back to suppliers. If the last approach is used as a measurement, a possibility is to create a comparison of field failures to the total installed population of a product. The formula is:

$$\frac{\text{Field failures}}{\text{Total installed population}}$$

Another issue to be aware of is increases or decreases in the defect rate that are caused by changes in the company's threshold tolerance limits. If these limits are relaxed, then the defect rate will improve, and vice versa – and without any change in supplier performance. Thus, it is useful to lock down the tolerance limits over multiple reporting periods, if the supplier defect rate is being measured on a trend line. Otherwise, there will be unusual spikes and declines in the reported defect rate that have nothing to do with the supplier.

EXAMPLE

Billabong Machining Co. manufactures high-tolerance widgets for the military market. These combat-ready widgets must be exactly ¼" thick. In recent months, the receiving department has rejected a substantial number of deliveries from the company's steel plate supplier, because the delivered plates have been as much as 1/8" thinner than specified in the authorizing master purchase order. This has resulted in several late widget deliveries to the military, and a threatened cancellation of the company's sole source contract with the military. Accordingly, Billabong's purchasing manager prepares the following defect rate table, which clearly shows how the problem has increased over the past three months:

	January	February	March
Rejected plate deliveries	5	10	15
Total plate deliveries	55	50	60
Supplier defect rate	9%	20%	25%

The purchasing manager uses this table as the basis for a difficult discussion with the steel plate supplier, to either upgrade its performance or be dropped as a preferred supplier.

Supplier Billed Price Variance

A high-quality supplier will negotiate the price of goods and services with the buyer up-front, and will not attempt to alter this price in subsequent billings under the related purchase order. In this case, the billed price and purchase order price should always match. A more ethically challenged supplier, or one with severe disconnects between its billing and sales departments may issue invoices that bear little relationship to the prices stated in the original purchase order. In the latter case, the buyer may incur such excessive overbillings that the profitability of the business is threatened, or at least seriously eroded. Consequently, management should know which suppliers continually have price variances in their billings.

To calculate the supplier billed price variance, aggregate the amount of excess billings over the amounts stated on purchase orders, divided by the extended prices stated on the purchase orders. The formula is:

$$\frac{\text{Total of excess billings}}{\text{Total of extended prices stated on purchase orders}}$$

This measurement is designed to be calculated for each individual supplier, so it typically takes the form of a report that is sorted in declining order of billed price variance. To save space, the report only lists those variances above a predetermined materiality threshold.

There are cases where a billed price variance is justified. For example, a purchase order may allow the supplier to ship slightly more than the requested amount, in which case the extended price charged by the supplier will be higher than what is noted on the purchase order. This situation usually arises when items are purchased in very large quantities on an ongoing basis, so that slight overages in the units delivered are a standard practice.

EXAMPLE

The purchasing manager of Luminescence Corporation is being paid a bonus if she can restrict the amount the company pays to its LED suppliers for the components used in Luminescence light bulbs. In investigating the company's materials costs, she notes that several suppliers are charging more than the contractual amounts for components. She compiles the following information:

Supplier Name	Extended Price Paid	Purchase Order Price	Billed Price $ Variance	Billed Price % Variance
Dome Ports Ltd.	$52,600	$50,000	$2,600	5.2%
Flange Brothers	40,800	35,000	5,800	16.6%
Glow LED Modules Inc.	21,700	20,000	1,700	8.5%
Totals	$115,100	$105,000	$10,100	9.6%

Based on these results, the purchasing manager meets with the controller and demands tighter three-way matching of supplier invoices, so that these overages will be flagged in the future.

Perfect Order Percentage

The preceding supplier performance measurements can be combined into the perfect order percentage. This is the percentage of orders that suppliers deliver on time, containing the exact quantities ordered, and with no defects. When first measured, the perfect order percentage can be quite low. This can be a significant issue, since any of these problems can be quite expensive to correct; it may call for premium transportation to accelerate late deliveries, administrative hassles to adjust orders, and – worst of all – inconvenienced customers who may cancel their orders.

The perfect order percentage can be tracked by supplier and included in a report card that is issued to each supplier at regular intervals. Hopefully, this should spur both the company and its suppliers to adopt better practices to improve the percentage.

Premium Transportation Charges

When the production schedule is perfectly aligned with purchasing activities, it should be possible for all supplier deliveries to arrive both on-time and via a low-cost mode of transport. However, any changes in the schedule or problems at suppliers may require the use of premium transportation (such as air freight) to ensure that deliveries reach the company on time. The charges associated with premium transportation methods are usually much higher than normal transport fees, and so can cut deeply into profits. To measure the extent of these premium charges, identify these fees as incurred and record them in a separate account in the accounting records. Then compare them to the total amount of transportation charges in the period in which they occurred. The formula is:

$$\frac{\text{Premium transportation charges}}{\text{Total transportation charges}}$$

This measurement should certainly be tracked on a trend line, to see if the premium charges are spiking. If so, it will be necessary to drill down to the issues that caused the premium charges to be incurred in the first place.

Proportion of Targeted Inventory Dispositioned

Despite the best efforts of the purchasing and production planning staffs, some inventory will never be used. There may be no demand for goods or raw materials, or perhaps product redesigns leave some unused components in limbo. Whatever the reason may be, a considerable amount of inventory may be targeted for dispositioning by means other than sale to customers. If so, the purchasing department is typically tasked with the dispositioning effort, where the items are sold off to third parties for the best possible price, or returned to suppliers in exchange for a restocking fee.

It is useful to track the proportion of targeted inventory dispositioned on a monthly basis, since the value of old inventory declines rapidly over time. Ideally, the majority of all targeted items should be sold off within a few months of their initial identification, while these items still retain some value. To measure the dispositioning effort, divide the amount of cash and credits obtained through dispositioning by the aggregate estimated disposition value of all targeted inventory items. The formula is:

$$\frac{\text{Cash receipts from dispositioning} + \text{Supplier credits from dispositioning}}{\text{Total estimated dispositioned value of targeted inventory items}}$$

A potential problem with this measurement is that the actual amounts received from dispositioning activities may vary from what was originally estimated. For example, it may be estimated that a widget can be sold to a third party for $100, while it turns out that the widget must be scrapped. Thus, even if every targeted item is dispositioned within a single reporting period, it is possible that the proportion of the receipts from dispositioned items to their estimated values may not be 100%.

EXAMPLE

Smithy Iron Works has just acquired a small competitor, and intends to earn back a large part of the $5,000,000 purchase price by disposing of excess inventory held by the competitor at the highest possible price. An initial evaluation reveals that it may be possible to eliminate inventory having a disposal value of $1,000,000. After two months of brisk activity, the purchasing manager reports that he and his staff have generated $250,000 in cash from dispositioned inventory, as well as $350,000 in supplier credits. This results in a proportion of targeted inventory dispositioned of 60%.

General Management Measurements

The purchasing department has traditionally been buried under an enormous pile of paperwork, especially when purchasing polices require large numbers of purchases to be put out for competitive bidding, and where there are ongoing negotiations with suppliers over the terms of prospective orders. To streamline purchasing, the general measurements used for the department should change. Consider the following measurements:

- *Total department expense as a percentage of total spend*. This places an increased focus on the cost efficiency of the department.
- *Employee turnover within the department*. Purchasing agents are skilled employees, so a strong effort to retain them should be encouraged.
- *Process training hours per employee*. Advanced purchasing techniques that focus on spend management and a reduction in purchase orders involves a considerable knowledge of the purchasing process. Tracking the hours of training per employee per year places a particular focus on the importance of staff training.

Negative Effects of Measurements

If the wrong performance measurements are installed, they can lead to behavior that does not benefit the organization over the long term. Such measurements are usually installed in reaction to a specific problem, or to enhance short-term results, without considering their long-term implications. Here are several examples:

- *Excessive external cost reduction focus*. In many purchasing departments, the main focus of ongoing activities is to reduce the prices charged by suppliers. The trouble with this approach is that it can be taken to an extreme. When

216

suppliers earn very little from their relationship with a company, they have few funds left to re-invest in the business, are more likely to use lower-quality components, and may assign the company a lower priority in its order queue. Consequently, due thought must be given to making the relationship a valuable one for suppliers – and that means not gouging them on prices.

- *Excessive internal cost reduction focus.* Management may require the purchasing manager to pare the operating costs of the purchasing department, under the mistaken impression that this is a cost center. By cutting back on buyers, a likely outcome is that the total cost to the company will increase, since there are now fewer people to negotiate pricing deals with suppliers, or drop nonperforming suppliers, or to work on developing more cost-effective new products.

- *Excessive focus on premium transport.* The key to success for a business may be a high level of customer service. If so, excessively focusing on driving down the cost of premium transport services can interfere with customer service, which in turn will drive away customers. In this environment, it might be better to put less emphasis on cost overages and more emphasis on the order fulfillment rate for customers.

Summary

Nearly all of the measurements in this chapter are designed to support a streamlined and efficient purchasing department. One measurement that has *not* been included is the classic performance measurement for the department – the purchase price variance. This variance is the difference between the standard price at which a component should be purchased and the actual price. When the purchasing manager wants to produce a positive purchase price variance, the simplest way to do so is to purchase in bulk, so that prices per unit are at their lowest. The trouble with this approach is that it goes against all modern manufacturing principles – to minimize inventory balances on hand, so there is a reduced investment in working capital, less storage space required, less risk of damage to materials, and so forth. Consequently, we strongly recommend eliminating this measurement in favor of a mix (or all) of the measurements stated in this chapter.

It is quite possible that the management team wants to apply other performance measurements to the purchasing group than those noted in this chapter. If so, attempt to limit the measurements to ones that cannot be manipulated. For instance, the baseline against which the department is being measured should be derived from outside the company, rather than one that is listed in a budget or standard. Or, if internal benchmarks are used, at least have them come from other departments, or be automatically calculated or otherwise derived by the computer system, so that the purchasing manager cannot influence them. This tends to result in more believable measurement outcomes.

Chapter 17
Applicable Information Technology

Introduction

There was a time when most of the operations of the purchasing department could be conducted on paper. This is no longer the case, since every other part of the business environment is either assisted or run by information technology. In this chapter, we describe the types of technology being used elsewhere in a business that can impact the purchasing department, as well as technologies that can be of direct use to the department. The result of these systems is a much higher level of integration, both within a company and down the supply chain, plus a higher degree of efficiency.

Enterprise Resource Planning (ERP)

We begin with enterprise resource planning, or ERP. This is an integrated software package that supports all of a company's functional areas. Thus, it can handle the transactional requirements of the accounting, customer service, purchasing, manufacturing, sales, warehousing, and other departments. Many ERP systems also accept data from a company's customers and suppliers for supply chain management purposes, so that the system essentially exceeds the traditional boundaries of a corporation.

The great advantage of an ERP system is that all corporate data is integrated, so that data is only entered into the system once (as opposed to the "silo" approach that is still common in most companies, where information is entered into the separate software packages used by each department). With an integrated ERP system, companies find that their transaction error rates decline, while many tasks that formerly required manual effort are now entirely automated. Also, subject to security issues, employees can access information in other departments that was previously difficult to obtain, or only with the help of special programming by the IT department.

The downside of an ERP system is its extreme complexity. The software requires a great deal of time to set up, as well as to convert a company's existing data into it. Also, because ERP systems can only be configured in a limited number of ways, most companies will find that they must alter their operating procedures to fit the software, rather than altering the software to fit their procedures. These changes call for a large training expenditure, and may result in resistance from those employees accustomed to the old system. These issues call for an implementation budget in the millions of dollars, and several years of intensive effort to complete.

From the perspective of the purchasing department, the presence of an ERP system makes life substantially easier, since there is excellent visibility into purchasing requirements that arise throughout a business. Also, depending on the sophistication of the ERP system, the functionality provided to the purchasing department could be substantial. If not, it may be necessary to acquire supplier relationship management software, which provides more features needed by the department. That software is described next.

Supplier Relationship Management (SRM)

SRM systems provide services specifically designed for the purchasing department, which are not always provided by an ERP system. SRM functionality may include the following:

- *Bid optimization.* This module allows buyers to sort through the mix of bids received for different goods and services, and select the most optimized mix of bids. This feature is especially useful for analyzing bids in highly complex environments, such as situations where there are many bidders for a large number of disparate transportation routes.
- *Contract compliance.* Contract terms are entered into a database, which then monitors purchasing transactions with suppliers to ensure that the terms are followed. For example, the system will warn when a volume purchases threshold has been surpassed that will trigger a volume discount.
- *Cost reporting.* A module accumulates the total estimated cost of ownership related to a purchase, which includes the initial purchase cost, plus inventory holding costs, freight, import fees, and so forth.
- *Purchase order issuances.* The system accumulates information from various sources, such as electronic requisitions, converts it into a purchase order format, and issues electronic orders to suppliers.
- *RFQ processing.* The system automatically configures a request for quote based on the specifications of the purchasing staff, searches a supplier database to determine which suppliers are qualified to receive it, issues the RFQ notification, and monitors supplier responses.
- *Spend analysis.* Organizes purchasing information into different categories of spend activity, to make it easier to determine what is being purchased and from whom. This information can then be used to consolidate purchases, reduce the number of suppliers, and minimize the amount of maverick spending. The savings generated by this one aspect of SRM software can pay for the entire system.
- *Spend compliance.* The system highlights situations in which purchases are not being made within the parameters of established supplier contracts, which hurts volume discounts. The software can also note instances in which billed supplier amounts diverge from contractually-mandated pricing.
- *Supplier performance measurement.* This module pulls in information from other company databases to automatically construct supplier scorecards in such areas as delivery performance, pricing, and quality. The system can either push these results out to suppliers or post the information for suppliers to access.

The ERP suppliers are always expanding the functionality of their software, which is gradually encroaching on SRM software. Eventually, we could find that SRM software is subsumed into the offerings of the major ERP suppliers. At the moment, however, the SRM suppliers provide a valuable add-on to the basic transaction flows managed by ERP systems.

We have already noted the key technologies that impact purchasing – ERP and SRM software. We will now delve into some of the modules contained within an ERP system, to learn about how they impact the purchasing department.

Dependent Demand Reordering Systems

When goods have dependent demand, the need for them is dependent on the stock levels of a different, related inventory item. Thus, if a company sells a widget to a customer, all of the components used to manufacture that widget have dependent demand that is based on the sales of the widget. The demand for these items can be planned with great precision through a computer system called material requirements planning (MRP). This is a module within an ERP system, or it can be a free-standing system.

The goal of an MRP system is to always have sufficient components on hand to support the requirements of a company's production schedule. To do so, an MRP system follows these steps:

1. Create a production schedule that states the quantities of goods to be produced, and the dates on which production is scheduled.
2. Using a bill of materials (i.e., a list of the parts used to manufacture a product), break down the scheduled goods into their component parts, which creates a listing of all the parts needed to support the production schedule.
3. Compare this list of required parts to the on-hand inventory of parts that are not already allocated for other needs.
4. If there are any shortages that must be filled by suppliers, calculate the amount of lead time required to obtain the goods and place orders with the relevant suppliers.

The MRP system is extremely computer-intensive, which means that the information used to construct orders to be placed with suppliers must be accurate. For the system to operate properly, the production department must commit to produce exactly in accordance with the production schedule, while both the bill of material and inventory records must have extraordinarily high accuracy levels. Otherwise, the system will generate nonsensical orders to suppliers (or no orders at all), possibly resulting in the inability to produce goods and/or excessive raw material inventory quantities.

Conversely, if the information used as input to an MRP system is accurate, the result can be quite low raw material inventory balances on hand, since only enough is kept on-site to deal with planned production. Also, the ability of a business to manufacture on a timely basis is heightened, since all component parts are available on time.

A different type of dependent demand reordering system is provided by a just-in-time (JIT) system. A JIT system is designed around the concept of only producing goods if there is a customer order. If there is no order, there is no production. This is a general target that is not always achieved; in reality, estimates of expected customer orders may also be used.

A JIT system uses very short production runs. Since the goal is to immediately produce to the requirements of a single order, it may be necessary to manufacture just a single product in a production run. From an inventory perspective, this means that a small amount of component parts may be needed at any time for immediate production purposes. Accordingly, a notification is sent to suppliers whenever a product is to be manufactured, which calls for an immediate delivery from a supplier, preferably straight to the production area, and only for the amount immediately needed. The notification sent to a supplier is usually an electronic one, to eliminate transit times.

A JIT system is not a specific type of computer package, but rather a philosophy intended to strip excess inventory out of the production process (among other goals) by compressing the time required to produce goods, as well as to produce only in accordance with actual customer orders.

Warehouse Management System

As the name implies, a warehouse management system (WMS) is a computerized system that essentially runs the warehouse. It can be a module within an ERP system, or it can be a free-standing system. It is a core ingredient of a large-scale warehouse that must handle thousands of transactions on a regular basis. The main features of a typical WMS are as follows:

- Track the locations of all in-house and in-bound inventory items in real time.
- Instruct the warehouse staff where to putaway and pick goods within the warehouse's racking system. This includes replenishment activities that move goods from reserve storage to the main picking areas. The instructions should minimize the amount of travel time when no goods are being moved.
- Organize the flow of goods used in cross-docking (where goods flow in one door and out another).
- Monitor the flow of picked goods into packed customer orders, and organize their shipment through the correct shipping dock.
- Optimize the locations of inventory items based on their usage patterns and other factors.
- Track the productivity of those employees engaged in the higher-volume warehouse activities.

As just noted, a WMS may have the functionality to cross-dock inventory. If so, the system takes note of supplier deliveries that have just arrived, and matches them with customer orders. There are two types of cross-dock matching that a WMS could make. These are:

- *Planned matching.* The system matches receipts with existing customer orders. The WMS then directs that the goods be sent to a specific shipping dock, where an outbound truck is awaiting the goods.
- *Opportunistic matching.* The system matches receipts with expected customer orders. The WMS then directs that the goods be staged near a specific shipping dock, in the expectation that a near-term customer order will be received and then shipped from that location. This approach works well for seasonal items for which there is a high level of demand, or if a high level of demand is being triggered by a specific marketing promotion.

Another WMS feature is to offer yard management. A yard management module tracks the contents of every trailer stored in the yard. The WMS uses this information to schedule when a trailer needs to be moved to a receiving dock for offloading. Since trailers are essentially an additional set of warehouse bin locations, tracking them should be considered an essential element of a WMS.

The system must communicate with employees via wireless terminals, so that transactions can be handled "on the fly," as employees move through the warehouse. There are many ways to communicate information to employees, including a standard computer screen, a heads-up display, by synthesized voice, and pick-to-light systems.

The ideal WMS is one that operates in the background, handling the bulk of all warehouse transactions via wireless terminals so smoothly that warehouse performance is vastly improved.

Tip: A WMS is so specialized and industry-specific that the standard warehouse module provided by an ERP supplier is probably not adequate. Instead, consider using a more specialized best-of-breed system, and integrating it into the company's other computer systems.

The existence of a WMS system is critical to the purchasing department, since it monitors where inventory is located within a company. If there is a question about whether additional goods should be purchased, the WMS can be used as a research tool to discover whether the goods already exist on-site.

Distribution Requirements Planning

A company may employ a central warehouse that feeds goods to regional warehouses, which in turn send goods as needed to customers, retail stores, and distributors. This multi-layered system may result in the efficient distribution of goods, but does not give the central warehouse any visibility into the actual demand for goods in the field. If the company owns all of the various tiers in the distribution chain, or can convince them to use it, a good solution to this problem is a distribution requirements planning (DRP) system. A DRP system can be a module of an ERP system, or it can be a free-standing system.

Under a DRP system, those distribution points closest to the end user enter their demand forecasts. The system then compares these forecasts to the inventory balances already on-hand at the regional warehouses to determine how much additional stock is needed, factors in lead times, and arrives at the amount of inventory that must be shipped from the central warehouse in order to satisfy the demands of the entire distribution system. A DRP system is also used to adjust the timing of deliveries, so that on-hand balances are kept to reasonable levels at all points in the distribution chain. The system is also used to aggregate deliveries so that transportation costs can be minimized with the use of full truck loads.

The main problem with a DRP is that the resulting information is completely dependent upon the reliability of the forecast information entered into it. If someone supposedly close to the end user creates a seriously incorrect forecast, it can have a major negative effect on overall inventory levels. Consequently, it makes sense to compare the forecasts being entered into the system by adjacent regions, to see if there are any anomalies that should be examined in more detail.

Purchasing employees may find that they use the DRP system as a research tool, to determine which forecasts are driving the demand that ripples back through the supply chain. When an unusually large demand spike appears, a possible source of the spike lies in the DRP database.

We have now touched upon the major functional areas within an ERP system that can impact the purchasing department. In the following sections, we address more specific information technology tools and features that can impact the department, listed in alphabetical order.

Advance Shipping Notices

An advance shipping notice (ASN) is an electronic message sent from the seller to the buyer, stating which items have just been shipped to the buyer, when the goods left the seller, when they are expected to arrive at the buyer's facility, and even the specific locations of goods within the trailer. This message is extremely useful, because the receiving staff can preposition unloading equipment and a crew at the designated receiving door. If any of the items listed on the ASN are needed immediately, they are assigned a forklift operator for immediate movement elsewhere in the facility. All other items in the load are pre-assigned a storage location by the warehouse management system, which directs the unloading crew to the noted locations. Thus, ASNs are useful for streamlining the receiving workload by giving advance warning of deliveries.

The ASN is not just a workflow management tool. Since it provides early notice of which goods will arrive and when, this reduces the uncertainty of the materials management staff in estimating the amount of safety stock that should be kept on hand. Since there is certain knowledge of incoming deliveries, it is now possible to selectively reduce the safety stock investment. In addition, if an ASN indicates that certain goods will not be delivered on time, the purchasing staff can then work on expediting a delivery from an alternative source. In short, expanding the use of ASNs among all company suppliers can reduce a company's investment in inventory and assist with the timely inflow of goods.

Backflushing

Backflushing is the concept of waiting until the manufacture of a product has been completed, and then recording all of the related issuances of inventory from stock that were required to create the product. This approach has the advantage of avoiding all manual assignments of costs to products during the various production stages, thereby eliminating a large number of transactions and the associated labor. It also eliminates the need to manually record production picks, which is an area in which errors are particularly difficult to eradicate.

Backflushing is entirely automated, with a computer handling all transactions. The backflushing formula is:

Number of units produced × Unit count listed in the bill of materials for each component

= Pick total

Backflushing is a theoretically elegant solution to the complexities of assigning costs to products and relieving inventory, but it is difficult to implement. Backflushing is subject to the following problems:

- *Accurate production count.* The number of finished goods produced is the multiplier in the back flush equation, so an incorrect count will relieve an incorrect amount of components and raw materials from stock.
- *Accurate bill of materials.* The bill of materials contains a complete itemization of the components and raw materials used to construct a product. If the items in the bill are inaccurate, the back flush equation will relieve an incorrect amount of components and raw materials from stock.
- *Accurate scrap reporting.* There will inevitably be unusual amounts of scrap or rework in a production process that are not anticipated in a bill of materials. If these items are not separately deleted from inventory, they will remain in the inventory records, since the back flush equation does not account for them.
- *Rapid production.* Backflushing does not remove items from inventory until after a product has been completed, so the inventory records will remain incomplete until such time as the backflushing occurs. Thus, a very rapid production cycle time is the best way to keep this interval as short as possible. Under a backflushing system, there is no recorded amount of work-in-process inventory.

Backflushing is not suitable for long production processes, since it takes too long for the inventory records to be reduced after the eventual completion of products. It is also not suitable for the production of customized products, since this would require the creation of a unique bill of materials for each item produced.

As just noted, backflushing is not easy to use, but introduces a great deal of record keeping simplicity if it *can* be used. The purchasing staff should definitely be aware of its usage, since errors in the inventory records can quite possibly be caused by a systems failure that must be corrected promptly. Otherwise, a number of purchase orders may be prepared in error.

Electronic Catalogs

A company can set up an on-line electronic catalog, for use by employees when ordering standard items. Based on the history of goods ordered, the purchasing staff assembles a listing of the most commonly-ordered items, along with key information that can be used to compare the attributes of similar items. If an employee wants to place an order, the system first checks to see if there is a sufficient amount of available funding, and whether a supervisory approval is required. If the conditions are acceptable, the system automatically places an order with a pre-approved supplier.

When an electronic catalog is set up, the purchasing staff pre-selects the suppliers whose products will be featured in the catalog, and negotiates pricing in advance. All other day-to-day tasks are handled automatically by the system, with no staff intervention. However, it will be necessary to periodically examine the quantities being ordered through the electronic catalog and outside of it, to see if some items should be drop from or added to the catalog. Also, depending on the resulting purchase volumes, it may be necessary to renegotiate volume pricing with the participating suppliers.

Electronic Requisitions

A somewhat less effective version of the electronic catalog is the electronic requisition, in which employees enter the same information used on a normal purchase requisition into an on-line form. The request can be electronically routed to a supervisor for approval before being forwarded to the purchasing department. The purchasing staff must still manually review the resulting request; the time savings comes from (in some cases) pressing a button to automatically convert the information in the electronic requisition into a purchase order.

An electronic catalog is a better solution than an electronic requisition, since the catalog approach completely sidesteps the need for any involvement by the purchasing department.

Electronic Tools

There are a number of purchasing-specific tools that can be used to organize certain purchasing activities. These tools are frequently provided on-line, so that no software needs to be loaded onto computers within the company. Instead, providers typically charge a monthly fee per user. Samples of these tools are:

- *Supplier surveys.* When the department wants to conduct a supplier selection process, it can create an on-line survey form for prospective suppliers to complete, and post an on-line link to the survey form. Suppliers then enter their answers into the on-line form, which can be accessed at any time.
- *Electronic billing.* A number of sites allow a company to set up a link into their accounts payable systems, so that suppliers can enter their invoices to the company on-line and receive an on-line confirmation that their invoices have been received. In some cases, the systems provide further visibility, allowing suppliers to check the approval status of their invoices and when they will be paid.
- *Preventive maintenance scheduling.* A preventive maintenance program is quite useful for keeping equipment operational at all times, thereby improving capacity levels. Proper preventive maintenance requires that specific maintenance activities be completed at regularly scheduled intervals, which frequently require the prior purchase of maintenance parts. The preventive maintenance system should issue notifications to the purchasing department, noting the need for parts purchases well before the parts are needed.
- *Reverse auctions.* Online systems allow a company to set up a reverse auction, where suppliers can bid the price of a prospective purchase downward in order to obtain the purchase contract. Either bid prices or the relative rankings of the bidders are visible to the bidding suppliers. Multiple bids can be made in order to drop under the bid prices posted by competitors. These auctions are most heavily used for commoditized items where the central focus is on obtaining the lowest possible price.

Inventory Data Collection Methods

The method chosen to collect information about inventory transactions can have a profound impact on the accuracy of inventory records, which in turn impacts the accuracy of the requisitions that the purchasing staff receives. In the following table, we note the issues and benefits associated with the most common inventory data collection methods.

Inventory Data Collection Methods

Data Collection Method	Description, Issues and Benefits
Paper-based	Description: All transactions are recorded on paper and forwarded to a warehouse clerk for entry in a manual ledger. Advantage: Can be maintained under primitive conditions and high-stress environments where computer systems are not available or usable. Disadvantages: Subject to data entry error at the point of origin as well as by the warehouse clerk. Notification documents may also be lost or seriously delayed before they reach the clerk. These delays can interfere with inventory counting. This approach is likely to cause significant errors in the requisitions sent to purchasing.
Bar code scanning	Description: Bar codes are assigned to all bin locations and inventory items. The bar codes for other commonly-used information, such as employee identification numbers, quantities, and activity descriptions can be included on bar code scan boards that employees carry with them. The warehouse staff scans bar codes to initiate a transaction, and then uploads the information to the computer system. No manual entries are required. Advantages: Eliminates data entry errors, reduces the time of the warehouse staff in recording transactions, and eliminates the data entry work of the warehouse clerk. This approach is highly favored by the purchasing staff, since inventory record accuracy can be quite high. Disadvantages: Scanners are moderately expensive and can be broken. There is a risk of data loss if the memory component of a scanner is broken before scanned transactions can be uploaded. Does not work if there is no direct line of sight access to a label. Labels are subject to tearing, which can make them unreadable. If a label is encoded incorrectly, this will result in the recordation of incorrect information for as long as the label is used.
Radio frequency terminals	Description: This is a portable scanning unit that also accepts instructions by wireless communication from the warehouse management system. Scanned transactions are uploaded in real time. Advantages: An excellent technique for maintaining a mobile workforce in the warehouse that sends back and receives transactional information from anywhere in the facility. Results in high record accuracy, so this investment is a good one from the perspective of the purchasing department. Disadvantages: Terminals are expensive and can be broken. Transmissions do not always work in hostile environments where there are stray radio signals.

Data Collection Method	Description, Issues and Benefits
Radio frequency identification	Description: Transponder tags are attached to inventory items, which emit an encoded set of information to a receiver when inventory items pass a receiving station. These tags are usually passive, which means they only transmit information when impacted by a transmission signal. Active tags contain their own power source, and so can transmit at any time. Advantages: Can automatically receive information from passing inventory, so that inventory movements are tracked in real time without operator intervention. Can operate even if there is no direct line of sight communication with the receiver. Receivers can accept high volumes of information within a short period of time, and can collect information from tags located relatively far away. Disadvantages: Relies upon the ability of transponder tags to properly transmit information and of receiving units to receive the information, which does not always happen. The result is incomplete transactions from data dropout. Tags are not individually expensive, but so many are needed to track all inventory items that the total tag cost can be prohibitive; the cost currently limits their use to unit-loads. The risk of data dropout means that inventory record accuracy may not be perfect, which impacts the requisitions received by the purchasing department.
Voice	Description: The warehouse management system (WMS) sends wireless instructions to an employee, who is wearing a headset and microphone attached to a small portable computer. The computer converts the instructions to voice commands. The employee can respond with a specific set of words that the WMS can understand. Advantages: Useful in environments where hands-free communication is necessary, such as cold storage. Increases record keeping accuracy and employee productivity, while eliminating rekeying errors. Has a lower error rate than bar code scanning. A minimal training period is required. Disadvantages: Can be difficult to communicate with the WMS if there are stray signals in the warehouse environment. Not usable if the WMS must capture long strings of random numbers.
Pick to light	Description: A picking person receives a tray that contains a bar coded order number. After the order number is scanned, a display panel mounted above each storage bin flashes a light, indicating that a pick should be made; a display shows the number of units to pick, and a button is pressed when the pick is complete. The tray containing all picked items then moves to the next picking zone, where the order bar code is scanned again and all items to be picked from that area are lit up. The system can also be used to make on-the-spot cycle counting adjustments.

Data Collection Method	Description, Issues and Benefits
	Advantages: Can be retrofitted onto existing rack space. Works well for high-speed picking operations, and eliminates any need for the manual entry of transactions. There is also no need for a pick list. Requires minimal training. The resulting inventory record accuracy is high, which favors the purchasing department's activities.
	Disadvantages: Requires a linkage to the WMS, which controls the operation in real time. Can be expensive when large numbers of bins must be outfitted with display panels. The cost tends to limit its use to higher-volume picking operations.

From the perspective of the purchasing department, all of the preceding data collection methods are an improvement over the use of paper-based systems, so the main point is to argue in favor of *any* of the other options. The bar code scanning alternative has proven to be highly accurate and reliable, and when combined with radio frequency terminals results in real-time updates to the inventory records. This combination is recommended when the circumstances allow for its use.

The Customized Systems Conundrum

The purchasing manager may be tempted to authorize the creation of entirely new or heavily customized purchasing software. The advantage of doing so is that the system can then mesh into the exact types of information that the department uses, as well as its forms and process flows. The result can be a high level of operational efficiency.

Despite the advantages of customized information technology, this path is usually not recommended, for the following reasons:

- A customized system requires a great deal of maintenance, possibly by an on-site programmer. The maintenance cost increases if the purchasing staff routinely requests changes to the system.
- If the system has custom interfaces into the off-the-shelf software used by other departments or suppliers, these interfaces may crash when the off-the-shelf software undergoes routine upgrades.
- Training has to be adjusted to match the customized software, and altered when the system is changed.

Instead, it is usually much more cost-effective to acquire off-the-shelf purchasing software from a reputable supplier. It may be necessary to alter the department's processes to match the requirements of the system. However, the overall cost of the system is lower, maintenance is handled by the supplier, and training is offered in a prepackaged format by the supplier.

Further, it is worth considering the services of those software suppliers who run the software on their own websites. Employees then log into these sites to access the software. The advantages of this approach are a monthly fee (rather than a large up-front charge) and seamless software upgrades that are handled by the supplier. This approach also requires no on-site IT expert to maintain systems, and the software can be accessed from anywhere where there is Internet access.

If the decision is made to use off-the-shelf software, a good way to leverage this decision is to obtain an integrated software solution that combines many purchasing applications within one package. This means that the purchasing staff has access to a single database of information that is applicable across multiple purchasing tools. In addition, there will be a set of software-based controls that can be implemented in all functional areas of the department.

The key downside of using off-the-shelf software is its limited configurability. A more advanced system will allow for some changes, which are made by altering the configuration flags in the software settings. However, there will be few of these optional settings in lower-priced systems, so a company usually has to alter its manual processes to match the requirements of the software.

Impact of information Technology on Purchasing

The main impact of information technology is on the clerical aspects of the purchasing function. They take away the need to calculate detailed purchasing requirements, examine purchase requisitions, and create purchase orders, which used to comprise a large proportion of the total staff time. Instead, the work load shifts to more value-added activities, such as long-range planning, supplier negotiations, risk mitigation, supplier evaluations, and spend management activities.

This shift in emphasis also means that there is a notable change in the department budget. The expenditure for clerical staff declines precipitously, to be replaced by an increase in funding for more-experienced staff that can address the increased emphasis on strategic and tactical issues.

Summary

The use of information technology is a key differentiating factor for the world-class purchasing department. When properly applied, it can eliminate many of the clerical aspects of the purchasing function, allowing employees to work on more value-added activities. However, this does not mean that the purchasing manager should invest a vast amount in technology. Instead, it is possible to minimize the upfront investment by using the monthly fee structures offered by many on-line software providers. This approach also leaves systems maintenance in the hands of the software providers, rather than encumbering the purchasing manager with esoteric technology issues about which he or she has no knowledge.

Glossary

A

Advance shipping notice. An electronic message from a seller to a buyer, noting delivery information.

B

Backflushing. The recordation of inventory issuances based on production information.

Bid package. A set of bidding documents issued by a company to prospective bidders who want to participate in a competitive bidding situation.

Blanket purchase order. A document that commits a buyer to a number of purchases from a supplier over an extended period of time.

C

Change order. An adjustment to the pricing or other arrangements stated in a purchase order.

Commodity. A product that is so standardized that there is no differentiation among the offerings of different suppliers.

Common carrier. A general carrier of goods that charges based on a standard pricing schedule.

Concession. Something given away in order to reach an agreement.

Constraint. A bottleneck that caps the amount of output that can be generated.

Contract carrier. A freight hauler that services a company's specific needs in exchange for a negotiated price.

Cycle counting. The process of counting small amounts of the total inventory on an ongoing basis.

D

Dependent demand. Goods whose demand is dependent on the stock levels of a different inventory item.

Discounted cash flows. The concept that cash received today is more valuable than cash received in the future.

Distribution requirements planning (DRP). Software used to support the needs of a multi-layered warehousing system.

E

E-Procurement. An electronic process flow for the purchasing function, so that no paper documents are needed.

Early payment discount. A discount allowed to customers if they pay an invoice within a certain period of time.

Enterprise resource planning (ERP). A comprehensive software package that integrates information from all functional areas.

F

FOB destination. Freight terms under which the buyer takes official delivery at its receiving dock.

FOB shipping point. Freight terms under which the buyer takes official delivery at the supplier's shipping dock.

H

Hedging. A risk reduction technique whereby an entity uses a derivative or similar instrument to offset future changes in the fair value or cash flows of an asset or liability.

I

Intermodal transport. The routing of goods using multiple types of transport.

K

Kaizen costing. The process of continual cost reduction that occurs after a product design has been completed and is now in production.

L

Learning curve. The concept that production labor declines as unit volumes increase.

Lease. An arrangement where the lessor agrees to allow the lessee to use an asset for a stated period of time in exchange for a series of payments.

M

Material requirements planning. A computerized method for calculating the amount of materials needed, based on a production plan, inventory on hand, and bills of material.

Maverick spending. Unauthorized spending by employees, usually to unauthorized suppliers.

MRO. An acronym for Maintenance, Repair, and Operations.

N

NAICS. An acronym for the North American Industry Classification System, which classifies a wide range of industries by a unique code, and which is commonly used for spend analysis.

Negotiations. The process of having two parties formally discuss their differences, with the objective of forming a mutually beneficial agreement.

P

Perpetual inventory system. A method for tracking inventory balances that involves constant updates for all withdrawals from and additions to inventory.

Price analysis. The comparison of prices offered by different suppliers.

Procurement card. A credit card used by employees to purchase goods and services on behalf of the business that pays for the card.

Purchase order. An authorization from a buyer, for a supplier to deliver specified goods or services at the price, quality level, delivery date, and other terms specified in the document.

Purchase requisition. A form on which an employee requests that specific goods or services be ordered from a third party.

Q

Quality. The creation and delivery of a product that meets the expectations of a customer.

R

Reverse auction. An on-line auction in which suppliers bid down the prices of listed items to determine which supplier will be selected.

Reverse price analysis. The estimation of the costs incurred by a supplier to construct a product.

S

Safety stock. Excess inventory that acts as a buffer between forecasted and actual demand levels.

Six sigma. A set of techniques used to improve quality by eliminating defects.

Spend management. The aggregation of purchasing information to determine the commodity classifications in which a company is expending funds, and using the information to concentrate purchases with a preferred group of suppliers.

Statement of work. A document that describes the types of services to be provided by a supplier.

Supplier. An entity that provides goods or services.

Supplier relationship management (SRM). Software containing features designed specifically to support the activities of the purchasing function.

Supply chain. The network of entities providing an organization with goods and services.

T

Target costing. A system under which a business plans in advance for the product price points, product costs, and margins that it wants to achieve.

Throughput. Revenues minus all variable expenses; used in bottleneck analysis.

Total cost analysis. A product cost analysis that includes the costs of ownership.

W

Warehouse management system (WMS). Software containing features designed specifically to support the activities of the warehouse function.

Index

Made in United States
Orlando, FL
23 June 2023

34462378R00137